ISO 9000
Pocket Guide

David Hoyle

BUTTERWORTH
HEINEMANN

OXFORD   AUCKLAND   BOSTON   JOHANNESBURG   MELBOURNE   NEW DELHI

Butterworth-Heinemann
Linacre House, Jordan Hill, Oxford OX2 8DP
225 Wildwood Avenue, Woburn, MA 01801-2041
A division of Reed Educational and Professional Publishing Ltd

R A member of the Reed Elsevier plc group

First published 1998
Reprinted 2000

© David Hoyle 1998

British Library Cataloguing in Publication Data
A catalogue record for this book is available from the British Library

Library of Congress Cataloguing in Publication Data
A catalogue record for this book is available from the Library of Congress

ISBN 0 7506 4025 1

Typeset by Butford Technical Publishing, Bodenham, Hereford
Printed and bound in Great Britain by
Martins the Printers Ltd., Berwick-upon-Tweed

FOR EVERY TITLE THAT WE PUBLISH, BUTTERWORTH-HEINEMANN
WILL PAY FOR BTCV TO PLANT AND CARE FOR A TREE.

Printed on acid free paper

Contents

Foreword

When dealing with ISO 9000 there are hordes of books available, not to mention the 19 standards in the ISO 9000 family. It has been my experience that to find enough information to write a policy, a procedure or a letter, or resolve a problem, conduct an audit, answer or ask a question associated with ISO 9000, one needs several books open at the same time. When I contracted with Butterworth-Heinemann to produce my first book on ISO 9000 it was to be this pocket guide, but at that time I didn't know what to put in and what to leave out. Implementing the strategy I had adopted for the *ISO 9000 Quality Systems Handbook* took me well beyond pocket book size. It is not easy to condense such information into a small package first time around. Three books later, I found that I had assimilated sufficient information of the type needed by quality practitioners to be able to condense it into one pocket guide.

From the *ISO 9000 Quality Systems Handbook* I have taken the questionnaires, many lists from Part 2, the task lists, do's and dont's, together with key messages covering every one of the 57 clauses in ISO 9001. From the *ISO 9000 Quality System Assessment Handbook* I have taken the list of 322 requirements, dispersed to the relevant clauses together with the inconsistencies in Chapter 8 of the same book. I have included all of the auditor questions that were available on a separate disk and packaged this information clause by clause. From my *Quality System Development Handbook* I have taken many of the task lists to create several chapters taking the reader through the complete quality system development process and on to system improvement.

I have included many new features not covered by the other three books: the consequences of not doing what the standard requires; key messages to get across the quality concepts; true and false perceptions about ISO 9000; and many new flowcharts and diagrams. The layout of Part 2 on *Satisfying ISO 9000 requirements* is uniform for each clause.

Many arguments, options and solutions have been left out due to size restrictions. Also it has not been possible to include all the flow diagrams as many require the broader format; therefore this pocket guide is not meant to replace the other books but to complement them – a sort of portable encyclopaedia.

Small enough for the pocket or the briefcase, I hope this little book becomes a good companion on your journey towards world class quality.

David Hoyle

Monmouth
August 1998

Other books by the same author:

ISO 9000 Quality Systems Handbook   ISBN 0-7506-2130-3

QS-9000 Quality Systems Handbook   ISBN 0-7506-9861-6

ISO 9000 Quality System Assessment Handbook   ISBN 0-7506-2563-5

ISO 9000 Quality System Development Handbook   ISBN 0-7506-2562-7

Part 1

Introduction to ISO 9000

Contents

1   Quality concepts

Quality, its meaning and its management, control, assurance and improvement are addressed in this chapter, not in a narrative style but as a series of short messages, which may help change perceptions about quality.

Quality

- In supplying products or services there are three fundamental parameters which determine their saleability: price, quality and delivery.

- Customers require products and services of a given quality to be delivered by or be available by a given time and to be of a price which reflects value for money.

- *Price* is a function of cost, profit margin and market forces.

- *Delivery* is a function of the organization's efficiency and effectiveness and the availability of external resources.

- Quality is determined by the extent to which a product or service successfully serves the purposes of the user during usage (not just at the point of sale).

- Price and delivery are both transient features whereas the impact of quality is sustained long after the pleasure or the pain of price and delivery has subsided.

- An organization will survive only if it creates and retains satisfied customers.

- Satisfied customers arise from offering for sale products or services that respond to customer needs and expectations.

- Quality is a degree of excellence.

- Quality is conformance with requirements.

- Quality is the totality of characteristics of an entity that bear on its ability to satisfy stated and implied needs.

- Quality is fitness for use.

- Quality is freedom from defects.

- Quality is freedom from imperfections or contamination.

- Quality is doing the right things right first time.

- Quality is never having to apologise to customers for mistakes.

- Quality is never having to repeat again what was done imperfectly the first time.

- Quality is delighting customers.

- Quality is not expensive.

- Quality is not separate to reliability, maintainability, safety or design; these are quality characteristics, just as size, weight, speed and capacity are quality characteristics.

- Quality is not the name of a department.

- Quality is not perfection.

- Talk of quality without specifying the subject is fruitless – one has to have an answer to the question 'The quality of what?' before the discussion can continue.

- Specified requirements are an imperfect definition of customer needs because needs can be difficult to express clearly with precision in any language.

- A product may be unfit for use when conforming to specification or fit for use when not conforming to specification because of the imprecision of written specifications.

- If a company sets its own standards and these do not meet customer's needs, its claim that it produces quality products is bogus.

- If the standards are well in excess of what the customer needs, the price tag may well be too high for what customers are prepared to pay.

- Customers decide whether the quality of the products and services supplied is satisfactory.

- Comparisons of quality between entities of different grades, classes, categories or types are invalid as they have been designed for a different use or purpose.

- Comparisons of quality between entities are valid only for entities of the same grade.

- Price is not a feature or characteristic of the product but a feature of the service offered.

- When certain products and services are rare, the price tends to be high; when plentiful, the price is low (regardless of their quality).

- Price can be changed by the pressure of competition without affecting product quality.

- Price is negotiable for the same quality of product.

- Quality is not negotiable – the product either meets or does not meet customer needs.

- Quality costs are the costs incurred because failure is possible.

- Any feature or characteristic of a product or service which is needed to satisfy customer needs, or achieve fitness for use, is a quality characteristic.

- It is the quality characteristics which need to be specified and their achievement controlled, assured, improved, managed and demonstrated.

Quality management

- Quality is achieved by managing three parameters: the quality of design, the quality of conformance and the quality of use.

- *Quality of design* is the extent to which the design reflects a product or service that satisfies customer needs. All the necessary characteristics need to be designed into the product or service at the outset.

- *Quality of conformance* is the extent to which the product or service conforms to the design standard. The design has to be faithfully reproduced in the product or service.

- *Quality of use* is the extent by which the user is able to secure continuity of use from the product or service. Products need to have an acceptable cost of ownership and be safe, reliable, maintainable and easy to use.

- Quality exists in three dimensions: the business quality dimension, the product quality dimension and the organization quality dimension.

- The *business quality* dimension is the extent to which the business services the needs of society.

- The *product quality* dimension is the extent to which the products and services provided meet the needs of specific customers.

- The *organization quality* dimension is the extent to which the organization maximizes its efficiency and effectiveness, achieving minimum waste, efficient management and effective human relations.

- Organizations comprise many functions and all must be essential for the organization to function efficiently and effectively.

- Products may not sell – not because their quality is poor but because the quality of the business or the organization that produces them does not meet the needs of society.

- The degree of success of any quality initiative depends upon the level of attention it receives. There are three primary organization levels: the enterprise level, the business level and the operations level. There are barriers between each level.

- At the *enterprise level*, the executive management responds to the voice of ownership and is primarily concerned with profit, return on capital employed, market share etc.

- At the *business level*, the managers are concerned with products and services and hence respond to the voice of the customer.

- At the *operations level* the middle managers, supervisors, operators etc. focus on processes that produce products and services and hence respond to the voice of the processes carried out within their own function.

- Quality should be a strategic issue that involves the owners as it delivers fiscal performance.

- Low quality will cause fiscal performance to decline.

- Several methods have evolved to *achieve, sustain and improve quality*; they are quality control, quality improvement and quality assurance which, collectively, are known as quality management.

- The basic goal of quality management is the elimination of potential, suspect and actual failure. These failures may be a failure to meet customer requirements, a failure of products, a failure of processes, a failure of systems, a failure of organizations, a failure of business and a failure to get the appropriate level of attention.

- If we could design products, services, processes, organizations and business that could not fail we would have achieved the ultimate goal. However, man has limited foresight and has to balance unequal forces, some within his control, others natural and out of his control, and some brought about by the society in which we live.

- Failure might be inevitable but most can be predicted, eliminated, avoided or compensated for by the application of management principles.

- Quality does not appear by chance or, if it does, it may not be repeated. One has to design quality into the products and services.

- Inspection measures quality in a way that allows us to make decisions on whether to release a piece of work.

- In the service industries, the quality of the service depends upon both the technical and non-technical aspects of the service.

- Customers in the service industries who are given the wrong advice would remain dissatisfied even if their papers were in order or even if they were given courteous and prompt attention.

- A faulty product delivered on time, within budget and with a smile remains a faulty product.

- Quality management is both a technical subject and a behavioural subject.

- Behaviour is formed by the core values to which an organization subscribes.

- Quality management requires the presence of a quality culture in the organization.

- Culture is the result of an organization's vision and values – what it aspires to become and where it places its priorities.

- Values form the foundation stone of the organization and unless these are shared by everyone in the organization, performance will not be of a level to sustain survival.

- People work best when management shows it cares about them.

- Neglect the people and you eventually impact product quality.

Quality control

- Quality control is a process for maintaining standards and not for creating them.

- Quality control is a process for regulating performance.

- Quality control is a process which ensures that only those products or services which emerge from the process meet the standards.

- Quality control is a process to control results before, during or after the results are created.

- Quality control is not inspection – a product remains the same after inspection as it did before, so no amount of inspection will change the quality of the product.

- Quality control can be applied to control the quality of any entity – it is not limited to the production domain.

- Quality control processes can be applied in design, in procurement, in servicing, in marketing, in human resources: in fact, in any part of the organization. All it takes is to find the answer to the question: 'What is the process, the quality of which requires control?'

- Quality control is a process for setting standards, measuring performance, detecting whether quality has been achieved, and taking action to correct any deficiencies and prevent their recurrence.

- The reviews and evaluations before the product is produced are as much a part of quality control as the inspections and test that occur after the product is made.

- Some failures cannot be allowed to occur and so must be prevented from happening through rigorous planning and design.

- Other failures are too expensive to prevent beforehand and must be detected and eliminated before release of product.

- Quality control is not a function but a process.

Quality is controlled by the following steps:

1   Determine what parameter is to be controlled.

2   Establish its criticality and whether you need to control before, during or after results are produced.

3   Establish a specification for the parameter to be controlled which provides limits of acceptability and units of measure.

4   Produce plans for control which specify the means by which the characteristics will be achieved and variation detected and removed.

5   Organize resources to implement the plans for quality control.

6   Install a sensor at an appropriate point in the process to sense variance from specification.

7   Collect and transmit data to a place for analysis.

8   Verify the results and diagnose the cause of variance.

9   Propose remedies and decide on the action needed to restore the status quo.

10 Take the agreed action and check that the variance has been corrected.

Quality improvement

- Quality improvement is anything which causes a beneficial change in quality performance.

- Quality improvement is about finding better ways of meeting customer needs.

- Quality improvement comes about by better control or by innovation.

- Quality improvement (for better control) is about improving the rate at which agreed standards are achieved.

- Quality improvement (for better control) is a process for reducing the spread of variation so that all products meet agreed standards.

- Quality improvement (innovation), is about raising standards and setting a new level of performance.

- Quality improvement (innovation) is a process for designing new products, processes and systems.

- Quality improvement (innovation) is about finding ways to provide products with features that give greater satisfaction.

- Quality improvement (innovation) is about finding less-costly solutions to meeting customer needs.

Quality improvement can be accomplished by the following steps:

1 Determine the objective to be achieved.

2 Determine the policies needed for improvement.

3 Discover whether accomplishment of the objective is feasible.

4 Produce plans for the improvement which specify the means by which the objective will be achieved.

5 Organize the resources to implement the plan.

6 Carry out research, analysis and design to define a possible solution and credible alternatives.

7 Model and develop the best solution and carry out tests to prove it fulfils the objective.

8 Identify and overcome any resistance to the change in standards.

9 Implement the change: that is, new products into production and new services into operation.

10 Put in place the controls to hold the new level of performance.

Quality assurance

- Quality assurance is all those planned and systematic actions necessary to provide adequate confidence that an entity will fulfil requirements for quality.

- Quality assurance is needed by both customers and managers as they cannot oversee operations for themselves.

- Customers and managers need to know *what is to be supplied* before they order it.

- Customers and managers need to know *how you intend to supply* it before they order it.

- Customers and managers need to know whether *your intentions will satisfy their needs* before they order it.

- Customers and managers need to know that *you do what you say you will do* before they order it.

- Customers and managers need to know that the *entities meet their requirements* before they accept delivery.

- Assurance is provided through knowledge and knowledge is secured through objective evidence.

- Quality assurance activities do not control quality.

- Quality assurance is not a means to prevent problems – that is the purpose of quality control and quality improvement.

- Quality assurance activities establish the extent to which quality will be, is being, or has been controlled.

- Quality assurance is not a function but a process.

- Quality assurance is not ISO 9000 – ISO 9000 is a quality system requirement which, if implemented, may provide an assurance of quality.

Assurance of quality can be gained by the following steps:

1 Acquire the documents which declare the organization's plans for achieving quality.

2 Produce a plan which defines how an assurance of quality will be obtained (that is, a quality assurance plan).

3 Organize the resources to implement the plans for quality assurance.

4 Establish whether the organization's proposed product or service possesses characteristics which will satisfy customer needs.

5 Assess operations, products and services of the organization and determine where and what the quality risks are.

6 Establish whether the organization's plans make adequate provision for the control, elimination or reduction of the identified risks.

7 Determine the extent to which the organization's plans are being implemented and risks contained.

8 Establish whether the product or service being supplied has the prescribed characteristics.

Quality goals

To control, assure and improve quality you need to focus on certain goals. There follow some key actions from which specific goals may be derived:

- Establish your customer needs.

- Design products and services with features that reflect customer needs.

- Build products and services so as to reproduce faithfully the design which meets the customer's needs.

- Verify before delivery that your products and services possess the features required to meet the customer's needs.

- Prevent supplying products and services that possess features that dissatisfy customers.

- Discover and eliminate undesirable features in products and services, even if they possess the requisite features.

- Find less expensive solutions to customer needs because products and services which satisfy these needs may be too expensive.

- Make your operations more efficient and effective so as to reduce costs because products and services that satisfy customer needs may cost more to produce than the customer is prepared to pay.

- Discover what will delight your customer and provide it. (Regardless of satisfying customer needs your competitor may have provided products with features that give greater satisfaction!)

- Establish and maintain a management system that enables you to achieve these goals reliably, repeatedly and economically.

2 Benefits of ISO 9000

ISO 9000, its purpose, origin, benefits and requirements are outlined in this chapter as a series of short messages.

What is ISO 9000?

- The purpose of the ISO 9000 family of standards is to provide a means of ensuring that suppliers provide products and services which satisfy specified requirements.

- ISO 9000 aims to prevent nonconformities throughout the chain of supply to customers.

- Specified requirements may be specific customer requirements, where suppliers are contracted to supply certain products and services, or the requirements of a particular market, as determined by the supplier.

- ISO 9000 is a family of 19 International Standards for Quality Systems.

- The ISO 9000 family consists of the ISO 9000 series, certain standards in the ISO 10000 series and ISO 8402.

- The ISO 9000 series comprises two basic types of standard: those addressing quality assurance and those addressing quality management.

- ISO 9001, ISO 9002 and ISO 9003 are the quality assurance standards and are designed for contractual and assessment purposes.

- The quality management standard is ISO 9004 (together with all its parts) and is designed to provide guidance for companies developing and implementing quality systems.

- The ISO 9000 family of standards specify requirements and recommendations for the design and assessment of quality systems.

- These requirements and recommendations apply to the organizations which supply products or services and, hence, affect the manner in which the products and services are designed, manufactured, installed, delivered etc.

- ISO 9000 is not a product standard.

- ISO 9000 does not contain any requirements with which a product or service can comply.

- Products can't be inspected against ISO 9000.

- ISO 9000 does not require you to document what you do and do what you document – it requires you to establish, document and maintain a quality system.

- ISO 9000 does not require you to document everything – it requires the range and detail of documented procedures to be dependent upon the complexity of the work, the methods used and the skills and training needed.

- ISO 9000 does not require you to achieve error-free operations.

- ISO 9001 is used when the customer requirements are stated principally in performance terms.

- ISO 9002 is used when the customer requires a product or service of existing design.

- ISO 9003 is used when assurance of quality can be obtained principally by end product inspection.

- ISO 9000-1 is a guide to the complete series of standards.

- ISO 9000-2 is a guide to the application of ISO 9001, ISO 9002 and ISO 9003.

- ISO 9000-3 is a software supplement to ISO 9000-2.

- ISO 9004 and its various parts do not follow the same structure as the quality assurance standards.

- ISO 8402 is a requirement of the quality assurance standards and defines the terms used in the ISO 9000 family of standards.

Origin

- 1959 – The first national standard, Mil Std 9858A, on quality programmes issued by the American Department of Defense.

- 1968 – NATO published their Allied Quality Assurance Publications (AQAP) based on Mil Q 9858.

- 1970 – The UK Ministry of Defence brought out Def Stan 05-08 which was based on the AQAPs.

- 1972 – The British Standards Institution brought out BS 4891, 'A guide to Quality Assurance'.

- 1973 – The UK Ministry of Defence published their quality control system requirements for industry in Def Stan 05-21, 05-24 and 05-29.

- 1974 – The British Standards Institution brought out BS 5179 as a guide to quality assurance.

- 1979 – The British Standards Institution published BS 5750 as the commercial equivalent to the UK's Defence Standards.

- 1984 – BS 5750 was put to ISO for development as an international standard.

- 1987 – ISO 9001, ISO 9002, ISO 9003 and ISO 9004 issued.

- 1994 – Phase One revision of the ISO 9000 series.

- 1999 – Phase Two revision of the ISO 9000 family.

Benefits of quality systems

- If you are capable of supplying nonconforming products or services you need a quality system to prevent you from doing so.

- If the right tasks are carried out right first time there will be no waste, costs will be at a minimum and profit at a maximum.

- Fire-fighting is reduced and managers are free from constant intervention in the operations of the business.

- Means are provided for enabling the right tasks to be identified and specified in a way that will yield the right results.

- Means are provided for documenting a company's experience in a structured manner that will provide a basis for education and training of staff and the systematic improvement of performance.

- Means are provided for identifying and resolving problems and preventing their recurrence.

- Means are provided for enabling people to perform tasks right first time.

- Objective evidence is provided that can be used to demonstrate the quality of products and services and to demonstrate that operations are under control.

- Assurance is provided to assessors, customer representatives and, should the situation arise, the lawyers in a product liability claim.

- Data is provided which can be used to determine the performance of operating processes, products and services and to improve business performance and customer satisfaction.

ISO 9000 requirements

ISO 9000 requires:

- The commitment of top management for the quality system to function effectively

- The commitment of middle management to deploy approved policies and objectives

- The commitment of the workforce to abide by the approved policies

- Changes in behaviour and often changes in the culture (values and beliefs than underpin behaviour)

- That policies and practices be designed to ensure continual customer satisfaction

- That policies and practices are effectively implemented: that is, achieve their purpose

Applying the standard

- There are two ways of applying the ISO 9000 family of standards – management-motivated and stakeholder-motivated.

- The *stakeholder-motivated approach* is dominated by the quest for certification.

- The *management-motivated approach* is focused on designing an effective management system that will cause conformity and prevent nonconformity.

- The stakeholder-motivated approach aims for compliance with ISO 9001, ISO 9002 or ISO 9003.

- The management-motivated approach aims for compliance with ISO 9004, followed by the selection of an appropriate quality assurance standard (ISO 9001, ISO 9002 or ISO 9003).

- Compliance with ISO 9001 demonstrates that you have the capability to design certain products.

- Compliance with ISO 9002 demonstrates you have the capability to manufacture, install or service certain products, or deliver certain services.

- Compliance with ISO 9003 demonstrates you have the capability to supply products, or perform services, that can be verified by final inspection and/or test.

- If you are not required to demonstrate to your customers that you have a design capability (even though you may carry out design) ISO 9001 does not apply.

- If you design products for customers you cannot register your system to ISO 9002.

- If you design products for your own use, such as tools, test equipment, machinery or software, you do not need to apply ISO 9001.

Registration

- Companies which have been assessed and meet the requirements of ISO 9000 are registered in a directory of companies of assessed capability.

- Companies that are registered to ISO 9000 receive a certificate of registration from the accredited certification body or registrar.

- All ISO 9000 certifications are limited by the scope of registration.

- All ISO 9000 registered organizations do not have the same capability – it depends on the scope of registration.

- The scope of registration is not the same as the scope of the quality system.

- You may include functions and processes in the quality system that are not addressed by ISO 9000 or which do not affect product or service quality.

- The scope describes the products and services for which the quality system is certified and identifies the locations from which these products and services are supplied.

- Following registration, if you change the range of products or services, or the locations specified in the scope, the system will require re-assessment as the scope of registration has changed.

- If you change the policies and practices or the organization structure, and the products, services and locations remain the same, you have not changed the scope of registration. These changes will be assessed on a subsequent surveillance visit by the third-party auditors.

- In assessing the quality system, assessors are looking to see that the system is capable of ensuring that the products and services specified in the 'scope' meet specified requirements.

The benefits of registration

- To be registered to ISO 9000, organizations must submit their quality system to an assessment by an accredited certification body or registrar.

- It is not illegal to use an unaccredited certification body but unaccredited certificates have far less credibility in the market place and may not be accepted by your customers.

- The assessment is intended to determine whether the quality system has the capability of enabling the organization to meet its customer's particular requirements.

- Registered organizations are permitted to advertise that the company has been registered to ISO 9000 and this will help your marketing profile and exposure.

- Registered organizations will be able to tender for contracts that are only let to ISO 9000 registered organizations.

- Registration demonstrates to potential customers that the organization is serious about quality and this will help create and retain customers.

- Registered organizations have to submit to frequent surveillance by independent auditors to verify that the registered system is being maintained and improved. This is a distinct advantage over other quality initiatives that have no periodic surveillance.

- ISO 9000 certificates are recognized world-wide.

- Multiple assessments of your management systems by customers should reduce.

- The use of registered suppliers reduces the amount of on-site surveillance by your staff and the amount of incoming inspection.

The assessment

- The assessment is intended to determine whether you possess the capability to meet your customer requirements.

- The results are obtained by sampling.

- The assessment should seek compliance with all requirements of the standard on a sample of activities, personnel, locations, documents and products/services.

- The assessor tests the sample for conformance and ensures that sufficient samples are taken to show conformance against each requirement of the standard.

- The granting of a certificate does not mean that you have no noncompliances – it means that no significant ones were found in the sample taken.

Anatomy of ISO 9001

- There are 8 conditional procedures.

- There are 10 mandatory procedures.

- There are 20 types of quality records.

- There are 20 elements.

- There are 59 clauses.

- There are 138 'shall' statements (137 in ANSI/ASQC Q9001-1994).

- There are 184 'shall' statements if lists are included.

- There are 322 requirements.

- An *element* is a sub-section of a quality assurance standard (e.g. 4.1, 4.2, 4.3 etc.)

- A *clause* is a paragraph under a heading. Therefore 4.1.2 is not a clause; 4.1.2.1 is a clause. 4.17 is a clause *and* an element because there are no subheadings in 4.17.

- Where there is a 'shall' there is at least one requirement but often more than one.

- Everywhere there is an 'and' or a 'comma' there is an additional requirement.

The basic requirements of ISO 9001

Here are the 322 requirements summarized in 24 simple statements:

1   Establish, document and maintain a system for ensuring that products and services meet customer requirements.

2   Define and document the organization's policy and objectives for quality.

3   Define and document the organization's commitment for quality.

4   Define and document the responsibility and authority of personnel.

5   Appoint a representative of management with authority to ensure a quality system is established, implemented and maintained.

6   Conduct periodic reviews of the quality system to ensure it is effective.

7   Employ documented procedures that ensure that the company has the capability of meeting contracts before acceptance.

8 Employ documented procedures that ensure product and service design is planned, organized and controlled.

9 Employ documented procedures that prevent the use of invalid documents and data.

10 Employ documented procedures that control purchasing activities.

11 Employ documented procedures that control product provided by the customer.

12 Employ documented procedures that provide products with unique identity.

13 Employ documented procedures that control result-producing processes.

14 Employ documented procedures that ensure products and services received, produced and supplied by the organization are verified as conforming to specified requirements before their release.

15 Employ documented procedures that control, calibrate and maintain verification devices.

16 Employ documented procedures that prevent uninspected product being mistaken for inspected product and conforming product being mistaken for nonconforming product.

17 Employ documented procedures that prevent use of nonconforming product.

18 Employ documented procedures that prevent the occurrence and recurrence of nonconformities.

19 Employ documented procedures that prevent damage or deterioration to product.

20 Employ documented procedures that ensure maintenance of records of products, processes and system effectiveness.

21 Employ documented procedures that ensure audits are performed to verify that the quality system is effective.

22 Employ documented procedures that ensure personnel are qualified to carry out the work assigned to them.

23 Employ documented procedures that ensure servicing operations meet the customers requirements.

24 Employ documented procedures that control the selection and application of statistical techniques.

The intent of ISO 9000

Organizations should offer products and services that:

- Meet a well-defined need, use or purpose.

- Satisfy customer expectations.

- Comply with applicable standards and specifications.

- Comply with requirements of society.

- Are provided economically.

To be able to offer such products and services, organizations should:

- Bring all operations under control that affect the quality of their products and services.

- Employ systems that prevent nonconformity.

- Establish an environment with shared values, attitudes and beliefs that focus on customer satisfaction.

- Improve the quality of their own operations so as to meet continually all stated and implied needs of customers and other stakeholders.

- Achieve, maintain and seek to improve continually the quality of its products in relationship to the requirements for quality.

- Provide confidence to its internal management and other employees that the requirements for quality are being fulfilled and maintained, and that quality improvement is taking place.

- Provide confidence to the customers and other stakeholders that the requirements for quality are being, or will be, achieved in the delivered product.

3 Perceptions about ISO 9000

In this chapter we look at some popular myths about ISO 9000 taken from conversations and literature on the subject over the last few years – asking whether they are true of false.

Popular myths

For companies demonstrating compliance with ISO 9000 standards, the results will be the delivery of products and services in a repeatable and consistent manner.
True, but not a complete message because it implies that companies can satisfy ISO 9000 by the delivery of rubbish.

Fundamentally, ISO 9000 can be summarized as: 'Say what you do, do what you say and prove it.'
Untrue because ISO 9000 requires the suppliers establish, maintain and document a quality system and demonstrate that it is suitable and effective. What you do has to meet the requirements of the standard and not everything you do has to be documented.

ISO 9001 does not deal with the whole of a company's quality system.
True because ISO 9001 only specifies the minimum requirements for assuring customers of the quality of products and services supplied. It takes no account of internal efficiencies.

In actuality, what is produced (the end product or service) is immaterial to the registration process. The ISO 9000 registration is in effect a confirmation of the processes only.
Untrue. To gain ISO 9000 registration companies must demonstrate that they have the capability to supply products and services that meet their customer's requirements. It confirms that the processes are capable of supplying specific products and services. For example, a company would not gain registration if it did not posses the staff, materials, equipment (that is,

the resources) to produce the products it claims to produce – clause 4.1.2.2 requires adequate resources.

ISO 9000 establishes the need for a third-party audit.

Untrue. There is no requirement in ISO 9001, ISO 9002 or ISO 9003 for third-party registration. ISO 10011 provides for quality system audits and does not stipulate that they be third-party audits.

ISO 9000 merely requires that each employee document what it is they do.

Untrue. There is no requirement for this. What is required is that the supplier documents a quality system that ensures product meets specified requirements and in doing so prepares specific procedures.

As opposed to many other quality programs, ISO 9000 is a bottom-up approach.

Untrue. ISO 9000 is a top-down approach. First the company must define its quality policy and quality objectives then establish a system as a means of implementing them.

One of the mainstays of the ISO 9000 process is the act of documenting the functions' processes.

Untrue. A system has to be established and, in ISO 8402, a system comprises the organization structure, procedures, processes and resources for implementing quality management. Processes cross functional boundaries as this is how work is done in a company. Therefore, documenting functions only defines what each function does. It does not create a system.

The internal audit process should reflect the comparison of 'Do what you say and prove it'.

Untrue. According to ISO 8402, audits have to verify that activities comply with planned arrangements and also verify that the system is effective in enabling the organization to achieve its stated quality objectives. Verifying that people do what they say and have evidence to prove it is only the first step – the auditor has to verify that what they do is compliant with ISO 9000.

Basically, the external auditors are attempting to verify that what you have stated is, in fact, what you are doing.

Untrue. The external auditors should be looking for objective evidence that the system is effective – not only that you are doing what you say you will do. You may say you do things that are simply not practical, simply noncompliant with the standard or not consistent with your quality policy and objectives.

Basically, you must be ISO 9000 registered to do business.

Untrue. Many unregistered companies provide excellent products and services and will continue in business due to their impressive reputation. It is only in the minority of cases that customers demand ISO 9000 registration as a condition of placing orders.

ISO registration represents the end result of a quality documenting and control process which has been implemented, followed and verified by an auditor.

Untrue. ISO 9000 registration represents the end result of demonstrating that you have the capability to meet your customer requirements.

In ISO 9000 there is practically no emphasis on customer satisfaction.

Untrue. In section 1 of ISO 9001 it is clearly stated that the aim of the standard is to achieve customer satisfaction by prevention of nonconformity during all stages. In ISO 9004-2 an ongoing assessment and measurement of customer satisfaction is recommended.

ISO 9000 emphasizes documentation over true quality methods

Untrue. Documentation is secondary in ISO 9000. The policies and practices that have to be defined are those that will ensure customer requirements are met. Documenting policies and practices that will not result in quality products and services will result in an ineffective quality system and, hence, should result in a failure to gain registration.

There is no value differentiation in ISO 9000 because results are not evaluated.

Untrue. The results, that is, the level of customer satisfaction is evaluated through the customer complaint procedures and subsequent corrective actions. A company that cannot show it is preventing the recurrence of problems will fail registration. Results should be evaluated in the audit process because the degree to which quality objectives are being achieved has to be demonstrated.

The company defines the scope and purpose of the assessment and whether to go for ISO 9001 or ISO 9002.

Untrue. The scope and purpose of the assessment is dictated by the processes required to supply products and services to customers. If the company has to design such products and services in order to meet its customer requirements then ISO 9001 applies. If a company supplies product or service of an existing design then ISO 9002 applies. A company cannot exclude processes simply because it chooses to. A process that is in the supply chain from customer order to delivery cannot be excluded. All the processes that are required to implement the quality policy and meet the quality objectives must be included in the scope.

ISO 9000 is about conformance and TQM is about commitment.

Untrue. ISO 9000 requires a commitment to quality and that the organization conforms to its established policies and procedures.

There is no requirement for continuous improvement in ISO 9000 whereas continuous improvement is at the heart of TQM.

Untrue. Whilst the phrase 'continuous improvement' is not mentioned in ISO 9001, the requirements for internal audits, management review, corrective and preventive action clearly result in continuous improvement. The ISO 9000 family also includes ISO 9004-1 and ISO 9004-2 which address quality improvement and ISO 9004-4 is dedicated to quality improvement. If a company is meeting the intent of ISO 9000 then it will be continually improving quality. It follows therefore that an auditor would be looking for records showing a continuous improvement in quality by a reduction in identified nonconformities in products, services, processes and the quality system. If there is no evidence of reduction then, clearly, the corrective action procedures are not working effectively.

A nonconformity is a failure to meet specified requirements and these specified requirements are your quality procedures.

Untrue. The specified requirements are not your quality procedures. It is true that a nonconformity is a failure to meet specified requirements but the specified requirements are those of your customer which have either been specified in a contract or order with your customer, or have been determined by you from an analysis of your customer needs and expectations.

4 Quality system principles

Philosophy of quality systems

- A quality system is defined as: *The organizational structure, procedures, processes and resources needed to implement quality management.*

- Quality management is defined as: *All activities of the overall management function that determine the quality policy, objectives and responsibilities, and implement them by means such as quality planning, quality control, quality assurance and quality improvement within the quality system.*

- We invent systems to direct resources in order to achieve certain objectives; to deliver a certain result.

- Having stated our quality policy and our objectives, we need a 'system' to ensure the policy is implemented and the objectives achieved.

- All managerial activity is directed either at achieving new levels of performance or holding the resulting gains[1].

- Quality management is no different. There is therefore quality improvement (for achieving new levels of performance) and quality control (holding the resulting gains).

- Hence the quality system must enable the organization to improve quality and control quality.

- To rely on a task achieving the same result, no matter who does it, requires a strategy that causes the right things to be done.

- In managing quality we have to know what causes success and what causes failure.

- Quality systems are systems that cause conformity and prevent nonconformity.

- A system isn't a collection of procedures but the interconnection of processes.

From the preface of the first edition of Managerial Breakthrough by J.M. Juran (1964).

- In organizations with unstructured management systems, memoranda and directives form the basis of written communication.

- The unstructured systems do not guarantee that customers will be supplied with services that consistently meet their expectations.

- Unstructured systems are susceptible to unpredictable variation since the processes that cause the results can be driven by personal motives which may be at variance with the goals of the organization.

Customer expectations

- Quality results from knowing your customer needs and expectations and faithfully meeting them consistently within an organization that promotes leadership and continual improvement as its core values.

- In managing quality we need to know what is meant by quality and, to get an answer, to that question we look to our customers.

- We need to establish who and where our customers are.

- We need to establish our customer needs and expectations.

- We need to establish what customer needs and expectations are currently unsatisfied.

- It is from the customer needs and expectations that the quality policy and quality objectives are derived.

Failure

- The basic goal of quality management is the elimination of potential, suspect and actual failure.

- Quality does not appear by chance or, if it does, it may not be repeated.

- Plans need to define the right things to be done without relying on chance.

- A system which appears to prevent nonconformity may not cause conformity as some activities may occur by chance.

- People may be doing things that only they know how to do so that, when they no longer apply their informal methods, the process fails.

- Hence, the problem with informal methods is that one never knows how important they are until they cease to be applied.

- It is untrue that if people follow procedures they will deliver quality products and services.

- Unless the procedures are designed to work together to deliver quality so that product or information passes through controlled processes, quality, if achieved at all, will be achieved by chance and not by design.

- Without a structured system the fixes are never permanent and the problems eventually recur.

Prevention

- In the design of products and processes, we can build in features that prevent failure and where this is not possible, due to other constraints, we can install failure alarms or fail-safe devices.

- We can do the same with our quality system: build in features that prevent failure and, where this is not possible, install early warning devices.

- In managing quality we have to know what causes success and what causes failure. We cannot operate blindly.

- We do not need to look over the shoulder of every operator.

- We can control quality by preventing failure before the event, by preventing failure during the event or by correcting failure after the event and before our quality standards are breached.

- There is the possibility of external forces outside our direct control being present and changing a previously checked parameter and so we have to watch very closely and constantly check systems.

Processes

- All work is a process.

- Work is not done by passing instructions from managers to staff, vertically upwards and downwards in the organization.

- Work is carried out horizontally with responsibility passing upwards and authority passing downwards.

- We need to know how we conduct our business from the identification of customer needs and expectations up to the delivery of the product or service and beyond (through after-sales services).

- If we don't know how our operations work we will never understand what causes success or failure.

- It is not a matter of knowing what every function does in the organization, but how these functions work together to deliver the product or service.

- We need to know all the activities in the chain that lead to, and subsequently cause, customer satisfaction.

Documentation

Verbal messages

- Without documented requirements, policies and practices people learn by example and from their mistakes.

- Without documented practices, best practice can only be passed on to others through personal experience.

- People retain different parts of verbal messages thus making verbal communication unreliable.

- People don't listen to everything they hear or observe everything they see.

- Knowledge in the head of the individual may not be able to be recalled on demand or may not be willingly offered to others.

- Verbal communication cannot reach everyone who needs to know when they need to know it.

- Unwritten requirements, policies and practices allow dispute, contradiction and ignorance.

Documented messages

- Documentation provides proof of requirements, policies and practices, and results and, hence, provides a common source for reference.

- Documentation can reach those too distant to hear verbal messages, or observe events.

- Documentation removes the need to repeat verbal instructions.

- Documentation makes communication more reliable.

- Documentation provides customers and managers with the means to convey their requirements remote from their point of use.

Document integrity

- Documentation has to be used and maintained to serve the organization effectively.

- Documentation in use needs to be current, accurate, approved and authorized for use.

- Documentation needs to be secure from inadvertent change or unauthorized change.

- Documentation needs to be promptly accessible and easy to use to avoid regression to verbal communication.

Behaviour

- A quality system includes people, their interrelationships and their behaviour.

- The behavioural system is part of the quality system.

- One can define some very practical policies and procedures but if the culture is not conducive to encouraging staff to use them, the desired output will not materialize.

- Quality results not only from using the right tools, the right processes etc. but also approaching the task with the right attitude.

- A person may be given everything needed to do an excellent job but, lacking motivation, will invariably fail to meet the organization's expectations.

- Without shared values, no quality system will fulfil its purpose.

5 ISO 9001 self-assessment questionnaire

This questionnaire of 50 questions addresses all the key requirements of ISO 9001 and will help you determine the margin between where you are now and where you need to be to achieve ISO 9000 registration. If your business is the provision of services rather than products then replace the word 'product' with 'service' in the following questions.

Element	Question	Yes	No
4.1	Have the quality policy, quality objectives and commitment to quality been defined and documented by executive management?		
4.1	Is the quality policy understood, implemented and maintained at all levels in the organization?		
4.1	Is the responsibility, authority and interrelationship of all personnel who manage, perform and verify work affecting quality, defined and documented?		
4.1	Have adequate resources been provided for management, performance of work and verification activities?		
4.1	Have the personnel assigned to management, operational and verification activities been properly trained?		
4.1	Has a representative of management been appointed to ensure that the requirements of ISO9000 are implemented and maintained?		
4.1	Do executive management establish the continuing suitability and effectiveness of the quality system through periodic reviews?		
4.2	Are the means used to ensure that product conforms to specified requirements documented in the form of a quality manual and quality system procedures?		
4.2	Have the means by which the requirements for quality will be met for specific products, projects or contracts been defined and documented?		
4.3	Are tenders, contracts and subsequent amendments reviewed in accordance with documented procedures prior to submission or acceptance as appropriate?		

Element	Question	Yes	No
4.3	Do the reviews ensure that the customer requirements are adequately defined and that the company has the capability to meet them prior to submitting a tender or the acceptance of a contract?		
4.4	Is product design controlled in accordance with documented procedures?		
4.4	Do the design controls ensure that design inputs and outputs are documented, that design and development activities are planned, that design reviews are conducted, that product design is verified and validated to ensure it meets the design input and user requirements and that results of reviews and verifications are recorded?		
4.5	Are all internal and external documents that relate to the requirements of ISO 9001 controlled in accordance with documented procedures?		
4.5	Are all documents and data and changes thereto reviewed and approved by authorized personnel prior to issue?		
4.5	Are any obsolete or invalid documents in use?		
4.6	Is product purchased in accordance with documented procedures?		
4.6	Are subcontractors selected on the basis of their ability to meet subcontract requirements		
4.6	Are records of acceptable subcontractors maintained?		
4.6	Do purchasing documents clearly describe the product ordered and, where applicable, the on-site verification arrangements?		
4.7	Is customer supplied product verified, stored and maintained in accordance with documented procedures?		
4.7	Is lost, damaged or unsuitable customer supplied product recorded and reported to the customer?		
4.8	Is product identified in accordance with documented procedures when the identity is not inherently obvious?		
4.9	Are the production, installation and servicing processes that directly affect quality identified and planned?		

Element	Question	Yes	No
4.9	Is production, installation and servicing carried out in accordance with documented procedures?		
4.9	Do the production, installation and servicing controls include the use of suitable equipment and working environment, compliance with reference standards, monitoring of process parameters, approval of processes and equipment, criteria for workmanship and equipment maintenance?		
4.10	Are incoming products, semi-finished products and finished products inspected and tested in accordance with documented procedures?		
4.10	Are the required inspection and tests and the records to be established detailed in documented procedures or quality plans?		
4.10	Do the inspections and test verify that incoming products, semi-finished products and finished products conform with specified requirements before use, processing or dispatch?		
4.10	Are records maintained which provide evidence that product has been inspected and tested and meets the specified requirements?		
4.11	Are the devices used to demonstrate conformance of product with specified requirements controlled, calibrated and maintained in accordance with documented procedures?		
4.11	Is measuring equipment selected on the basis of the accuracy and precision required and do all measurements have a known relationship to national standards?		
4.12	Is product identified in a way which indicates its conformance or nonconformance with regard to inspections and tests performed?		
4.13	Are documented procedures employed to prevent the inadvertent use or installation of nonconforming products?		
4.13	Are reworked or repaired products subject to re-inspection in accordance with documented procedures prior to release?		

Element	Question	Yes	No
4.14	Are customer complaints and reports of product non-conformities handled in accordance with documented procedures?		
4.14	Are documented procedures employed to determine the cause of nonconformities in products, processes and the quality system and to prevent their recurrence?		
4.14	Are documented procedures employed to detect and eliminate potential causes of nonconformance and prevent their occurrence?		
4.15	Is the handling, storage, packaging, preservation and delivery of product carried out in accordance with documented procedures?		
4.15	Do the measures taken prevent damage or deterioration of product in handling, storage and delivery?		
4.16	Are quality records collected, indexed, accessed, filed, stored, maintained and dispositioned in accordance with documented procedures?		
4.16	Is the retention time for quality records established and recorded?		
4.16	Are quality records maintained which demonstrate conformance to specified requirements and the effectiveness of the quality system?		
4.17	Are internal quality audits planned and implemented in accordance with documented procedures?		
4.17	Do the internal audits verify whether quality activities and related results comply with planned arrangements?		
4.18	Are training needs identified in accordance with documented procedures?		
4.18	Are the personnel performing specific assigned tasks qualified on the basis of appropriate education, training and/or experience?		
4.19	Is product servicing performed and reported in accordance with documented procedures?		
4.20	Are mechanisms in place to identify the need for statistical techniques required for verifying the acceptability of process capability and product characteristics?		
4.20	Is the application of statistical techniques controlled in accordance with documented procedures?		

6   Quality management standards

Ref	Origin	Application	Title
AIAG-APQP 1994	USA	Automotive	Advanced product quality planning and control plan
AIAG-FMEA 1995	USA	Automotive	Failure mode and effects analysis
AIAG-MSA 1995	USA	Automotive	Measurement systems analysis
AIAG-PPAP 1995	USA	Automotive	Production part approval process
AIAG-QS-9000 1995	USA	Automotive	Quality system requirements
AIAG-QSA 1994	USA	Automotive	Quality system assessment
AIAG-SPC 1991	USA	Automotive	Fundamental statistical process control
ANSI/API Spec Q1-1992	USA	General	Quality Programs
ANSI/ASQC A1-1987	USA	General	Definitions, symbols, formulas and tables for control charts
ANSI/ASQC A2-1987	USA	General	Terms, symbols and definitions for acceptance sampling
ANSI/ASQC B1 -1996	USA	General	Guide for Quality Control Charts
ANSI/ASQC B2 -1996	USA	General	Control Charts Method of Analyzing Data
ANSI/ASQC B3-1996	USA	General	Control Charts Method of Controlling Quality during Production
ANSI/ASQC C1-1996	USA	General	Specification of general requirement for a quality program
ANSI/ASQC D1160 -1995	USA	General	Formal Design Review

Ref	Origin	Application	Title
ANSI/ASQC E1 1996	USA	Power	Quality program guidelines for project phase of non-nuclear power generation facilities
ANSI/ASQC E2-1995	USA	General	Guide to inspection planning
ANSI/ASQC M1-1996	USA	General	Calibration systems
ANSI/ASQC Q2 1990	USA	General	Quality Management and Quality System Elements for Laboratories – Guidelines
ANSI/ASQC Q3-1988	USA	General	Sampling Procedures and Tables for Inspection of Isolated Lots by Attributes
ANSI/ASQC S1-1995	USA	General	An Attribute Skip-Lot Sampling Program
ANSI/ASQC S2-1995	USA	General	Introduction to Attribute Sampling
ANSI/ASQC Z1.4-1993	USA	General	Sampling Procedures and Tables for Inspection by Attributes
ANSI/ASQC Z1.9-1993	USA	General	Sampling Procedures and Tables for Inspection by Variables for Percent Nonconforming
ANSI/EIA 670-1997	USA	Electronics	Quality Systems Assessment
AQAP-1 1984	USA	Defence	NATO Requirements for an Industrial Quality Control System
AQAP-13 1981	USA	Defence	NATO Software Quality Control Requirements for Industry
AQAP-150 ED 1 AMD 0 1993	USA	Defence	NATO Quality Assurance Requirements for Software Development
AQAP-6 1976	USA	Defence	NATO Measurement and Calibration System Requirements for Industry

Ref	Origin	Application	Title
AVSQ 94	Italy	Automotive	Valutazione del Sistema Qualità nelle aziende del settore automobilistico.
BS 3811-1993	UK	General	Glossary of maintenance management terms in terotechnology
BS 4778 Part 2 1991	UK	General	Quality concepts and related definitions
BS 4778 Part 3.1 1991	UK	General	Availability, reliability and maintainability terms – Guide to concepts and related definitions
BS 4778 Part 3.2 1991	UK	General	Availability, reliability and maintainability terms – Glossary of International Terms
BS 5729 Part 5 1993	UK	General	Guide to stock control – Storekeeping
BS 5760 Part 0 1993	UK	General	Introductory guide to reliability
BS 5760 Part 1 1996	UK	General	Dependability programme elements and tasks
BS 5760 Part 14	UK	General	Guide to formal design reviews
BS 5760 Part 2 1994	UK	General	Guide to the assessment of reliability
BS 5760 Part 23 1997	UK	General	Guide to life cycle costing
BS 5760 Part 3 1993	UK	General	Guide to reliability practices: examples
BS 5760 Part 5 1991	UK	General	Guide to failure modes effects and criticality analysis (FMEA and FMECA)
BS 5760 Part 7 1991	UK	General	Guide to fault tree analysis
BS 5882 1996	UK	Nuclear	Specification for a total quality assurance programme for nuclear installations

Ref	Origin	Application	Title
BS 6079 1996	UK	General	Guide to Project Management
BS 6143-Part 1 1992	UK	General	Guide to the economics of quality – Process cost model
BS 6143-Part 2 1990	UK	General	Guide to the economics of quality – Prevention, appraisal and failure model
BS 7000 Part 1 1989	UK	General	Design management systems – Guide to managing product design
BS 7000 Part 10 1995	UK	General	Design management systems – Glossary of terms used in design management
BS 7000 Part 3 1994	UK	Service	Design management systems – Guide to managing service design
BS 7000 Part 4 1996	UK	Construction	Design management systems – Guide to managing design in construction
BS 7165 1991	UK	Software	Recommendations for achievement of quality in software
BS 7373-1991	UK	General	Guide to the preparation of specifications
BS 7750 1994	UK	Environment	Specification for environmental management systems
BS 7799 1995	UK	Security	Code of practice for information security management
BS 7850 Part 1 -1992	UK	General	Total quality management – Guide to management principles
BS 8444 Part 3 1996	UK	General	Guide to risk management – Guide to risk analysis of technological systems
BS 8800 1996	UK	Safety	Guide to occupational health and safety management systems

Ref	Origin	Application	Title
CAN3-N286.0-82	Canada	Nuclear	Exigences Relatives Au Programme D'Assurance De La Qualite Des Centrales Nucleaires Fiche No 1
CAN3-N286.1-84	Canada	Nuclear	Procurement Quality Assurance for Nuclear Power Plants General Instruction No 1 R(01-jan-1994)
CAN3-N286.2-86	Canada	Nuclear	Design Quality Assurance for Nuclear Power Plants General Instruction No 1 R(01-jan-1994)
CAN3-N286.3-83	Canada	Nuclear	Construction Quality Assurance for Nuclear Power Plants General Instruction No 1 R(01-jan-1994)
CAN3-Z299.1-85	Canada	General	Programme D'assurance De La Qualite – Categorie 1 Fiche No 1 R(01-jan-1991)
CAN3-Z299.2-85	Canada	General	Programme D'assurance De La Qualite – Categorie 2 Fiche No 1 R(01-jan-1991)
CAN3-Z299.3-85	Canada	General	Programme D'assurance De La Qualite – Categorie 3 Fiche No 1 R(01-jan-1991)
CAN3-Z299.4-85	Canada	General	Programme D'assurance De La Qualite – Categorie 4 Fiche No 1 R(01-jan-1991)
CEN PREN 724 1992	Europe	Medical	Quality Systems for Medical Devices
CENELEC PREN 50 103 1992	Europe	Medical	Quality Systems for Medical Devices
Def Stan 00-40 Part 1 Issue 3 1994	UK	Defence	Management responsibilities and requirements for programmes and plans
Def Stan 00-41 Issue 3 1993	UK	Defence	MoD Practices and procedures for reliability and maintainability

Ref	Origin	Application	Title
Def Stan 00-52	UK	Defence	General requirements for test specifications and test schedules
Def Stan 00-54	UK	Defence	Technical Publications for Defence Material
Def Stan 00-56 Part 1 Issue 2 1996	UK	Defence	Safety management requirements for Defence Systems
Def Stan 00-60 Part 0 Issue 1 1996	UK	Defence	Integrated logistics support – Application of integrated logistic support (ILS)
Def Stan 05-57 Issue 3 1993	UK	Defence	Configuration Management Requirements for Defence Equipment
Def Stan 05-58 Issue 2 1986	UK	Defence	Sampling procedures and tables for inspection by attributes of isolated lots
Def Stan 05-61 Part 1 Issue 2 Amd 1 1996	UK	Defence	Concessions and production permits
Def Stan 05-61 Part 3 Issue 1 Amd 1 1996	UK	Defence	Quality assurance of sub-contract work
Def Stan 05-91 Issue 2 1995	UK	Defence	Quality system requirements for design development, production, installation and servicing (Adoption of ISO 9001 1994 with supplementary requirements)
Def Stan 05-94 Issue 2 1995	UK	Defence	Guidance on quality system requirements for the implementation of Def Stan 05-91, 05-92 and 05-93
Def Stan 05-95 Issue 3 1995	UK	Defence	Quality system requirements for the design, development, supply and maintenance of software
Def Stan 05-97 Issue 1 1995	UK	Defence	Requirements for deliverable quality plans
EAC/G3	UK	General	Guidelines on the application of EN 45012

Ref	Origin	Application	Title
Electronic Engineering Association	UK	Software	Guide to Software Quality Audit
EN 45002 1989	Europe	General	General criteria for the assessment of testing laboratories
EN 45003 1995	Europe	General	General criteria for laboratory accreditation bodies
EN 45004 1995	Europe	General	General criteria for the operation of various types of bodies performing inspection
EN 45011 1989	Europe	General	General criteria for certification bodies operating products certification
EN 45012 1995	Europe	General	General criteria for certification bodies operating quality system certification
EN 45013 1989	Europe	General	General criteria for certification bodies operating certification of personnel
EN 45014 1989	Europe	General	General criteria for suppliers' declaration of conformity
IEEE 730.1-1995	USA	Software	Guide for Software Quality Assurance Planning
IEEE 1298: 1992	USA	Software	Software Quality Management System Part 1: Requirements
IEEE 730-1989	USA	Software	Software Quality Assurance Plans
ISO 2859	International	General	Sampling procedures for inspection by attributes
ISO 3951	International	General	Sampling procedures for inspection by variables
ISO 8402-1986	International	General	Quality vocabulary
ISO Guide 40	International	General	General requirements for the acceptance of certification bodies

Ref	Origin	Application	Title
ISO Guide 48	International	General	Guidelines for third-party assessment and registration of a supplier's quality system
ISO/IEC Guide 25 1990	International	General	General requirements for the competence of calibration and testing laboratories
MIL-STD-498	USA	Defence	Software development and documentation
MIL-STD-973	USA	Defence	Configuration management (CM)
SBAC TS 157 Issue 3 1997	UK	Aerospace	Technical Specification – Objects, scope and application (Aerospace industry interpretation of the ISO 9000 series)
SBAC TS 163 Issue 3 1997	UK	Aerospace	Authentication of aerospace experience of auditors of quality systems
VDA 6 Part 1 1996	Germany	Automotive	European Quality Management System for Automotive Suppliers

Part 2

Quality system management

Contents

1 Preparing for project launch

Project overview

- The development of a quality system should be treated as a project and not as a job for someone when time can be found, because the time needed will never be found.

- A project has a start and an end. Quality system operations, maintenance and improvement never cease.

- Projects are executed in phases with each phase representing a parcel of work that is required to drive the project towards completion and with the end of a phase being a milestone en route.

- **Phase 1** is the *Exploration Phase* in which the managers are convinced that a formal quality system is necessary.

- **Phase 2** is the *Project Feasibility Phase* in which studies are undertaken in order to establish current performance, the prevailing culture and the appropriate strategy for securing success.

- **Phase 3** is the *Project Planning Phase* in which a plan of action is produced for implementing the strategy and the resources organized so that the effort is directed along a course that will lead to a successful conclusion.

- **Phase 4** is the *System Design Phase* in which the business processes are defined, the documentation needs and areas requiring change identified.

- **Phase 5** is the *Documentation Development Phase* in which new and existing practices are documented.

- **Phase 6** is the *System Implementation Phase* in which resistance to change is overcome, a plan of implementation is produced, training undertaken and documented practices released for use.

- **Phase 7** is the *System Evaluation Phase* in which the effectiveness of the system is evaluated internally and in which external assessments are conducted and the system is certified against an international standard.

- **Phase 8** is the *System Maintenance Proving Phase* in which the maintenance elements are proven to cause practices to remain in line with policy and records to be kept updated.

- **Phase 9** is the *System Improvement Proving Phase* in which the improvement elements are proven to cause improvements in performance, reduction in variation and better ways of doing things.

- Projects that skip the Exploration Phase will be dogged by a lack of commitment.

- Projects that skip the Feasibility Phase will be dogged by a constantly changing strategy and cultural traits that persistently cause poor communication, disruption and delays.

- Projects that skip the System Design Phase will produce a system of documentation not a documented quality system.

- Projects that skip the Maintenance and Improvement Proving Phases will inevitable fail the next assessment.

What type of organization are we?

Here are some questions to determine the type of organization you have become and which may prove the need for a formal quality system:

- Are many employees unaware of the company's vision, values and mission?

- Are we incapable of meeting all our obligations all of the time?

- Are we capable of supplying nonconforming products or services?

- Do we rely on verbal requests to get work done?

- Do we hold on to our authority rather than delegate it to those at the scene of the action?

- Do we often repeat the mistakes of the past?

- Do we often have to repeat work because we misunderstood the requirements?

- Do we expect our staff to know what to do without being informed?

- Do we change our practices when we re-organize?

- Do we consider our suppliers as vital to our success?

- Do we expect our staff to learn to do their job without formal training?

- Do we assign staff to jobs based on their availability rather than their capability?

- Do we rely on managers telling staff how they want jobs carried out?

- Do we often put the blame for our problems onto others rather than onto our own managerial competence?

- Do we give priority to fixing problems rather than to preventing their recurrence?

- Do the deeds of the managers differ from what they say?

- Do improvement initiatives fail to sustain the gains after a project is finished?

- Would we have difficulty proving that we have done everything that we told our customers we would do?

- Are we unable to quantify our true performance with respect to our key processes?

- Are there any employees who are in doubt of the management's expectations?

Pre-launch task list

- Identify the reasons why you want a quality system.

- Identify why you wish to certify your quality system.

- Obtain copies of the relevant international standards.

- Prepare a case for the quality system to present to your executive.

- Obtain agreement to determine project feasibility before proceeding further.

- Identify the critical success factors.

- Collect data to indicate current performance against critical success factors.

- Carry out a preliminary review against ISO 9004 to determine a baseline.

- Perform a cultural analysis to identify the values, beliefs and norms that permeate the organization.

- Carry out a SWOT on the results and judge the feasibility of project success.

- Prepare a budget for the project, obtaining estimated fees from consultants and registrars.

- Commission executive awareness sessions to gain commitment.

- Gain agreement on the terminology to be used.

- Test the climate for change and decide whether or not to proceed.

- Determine what you want the consultant to do and invite quotations.

- Select and appoint the Project Manager.

- Select the consultant.

- Determine the project objectives.

- Determine quality system purpose and scope.

- Get buy-in at the right managerial level.

Pre-launch questionnaire

- Why do you want a formal quality system?

- What do you expect from a formal quality system?

- Why do you intend to seek registration of your quality system?

- Who made the decision to create a formal quality system?

- What are the project objectives?

- What is the quality system intended to cover?

- What functions of the organization will be excluded from the system and why?

- What is your current level of performance relative to your critical success factors?

- What factors will drive the project towards success?

- What factors may act as barriers to a successful project?

- What changes in the organization or in technology have been planned to be made during the duration of the project?

- How will you limit the adverse effect of these barriers to success and changes in the organization?

- What resources have been allocated to the project?

- How much time have the executive managers allocated to the project?

- What action has been taken to gain the commitment of the executive managers?

- Is the executive fully aware of its role in the project?

- Are you clear on the division of work between the consultant and the company?

- Is there a signed contract with your consultant?

2 Managing the project

The priorities

- The *first priority* is to obtain commitment by the management to provide the resources.

- The *second priority* is the creation of an agreed system model of the business.

- The *third priority* is the identification of process owners, after which design work can commence – but not without a plan.

- Design always comes before documentation.

- You can't document procedures until you have defined what documents you need.

- You can't define the documents you need until you have defined the processes.

- You can't define the processes until you have modelled the business.

- You would be unwise to do any of these tasks until your staff have received appropriate training.

- Before you start to produce the documentation, you need to put in place the documentation control procedures.

- Before you create the document control procedures you need to design the documentation tools as part of the Quality Information System (QIS).

- Before you assign tasks to people you need a plan, a means of allocating work (such that everyone knows what they are required to do) and a means of determining progress.

- Before giving out the work instructions you need to set up the problem-reporting part of the QIS to capture concerns and queries and provide a common source of information. As sure as eggs are eggs, people will not do the right things right first time!

Management task list

- Meet with selected consultant and agree project strategy.

- Deliver executive briefing if not carried out previously.

- Get commitment to the project from executive management.

- Set up a steering group of executive managers and provide them with role descriptions.

- Design the project organization structure.

- Appoint project team members and provide them with role descriptions.

- Arrange facilities such as office space, training rooms, computers etc.

- Determine project milestones and produce the project plan.

- Select or produce data requirements for project deliverables.

- Establish a problem reporting database to capture concerns.

- Establish an Action Item Tracking system to progress actions from meetings.

- Convene first steering group meeting to agree the project plan.

- Determine how decisions will be made/changed and communicated.

- Commission project team training.

- Initiate communication media.

- Set up documentation tools.

- Co-ordinate system design activities.

- Capture existing documentation.

- Convene monthly steering group meetings.

- Convene weekly project reviews with project team.

- Monitor progress on data for system design review.

- Conduct system design review when system design is complete and documentation needs are identified.

- Deliver documentation training.

- Monitor progress on data for critical design review.

- Conduct Critical Design Review when documentation has been produced and is ready for implementation.

- Deliver staff awareness briefings.

- Request quotations from suitable certification bodies.

- Select certification body.

- Determine internal audit strategy and select internal auditors.

- Commission auditor training.

- Monitor progress on data for final design review.

- Conduct Final Design Review when implementation has been proven to be effective and ready for external assessment.

- Commission pre-assessment and resolve nonconformities.

- Commission third-party assessment and resolve nonconformities.

- Establish the organization to manage the system after the assessment.

Management questionnaire

- Have you got the commitment of the executive management for the project?

- Do all the executive managers know what they have to do?

- Has agreement been reached on the resources needed?

- Have the key milestones been agreed?

- Has the project plan been agreed by the executive management?

- What induction have the executive managers received?

- Have all existing documents been registered?

- Have dates been set for steering group meetings?

- Have the process owners been nominated and trained?

- Does everyone on the project team know what is expected of them?

- Do you know what the consultant will provide to the company?

- Do you know what tasks the company have to do?

- Have you identified any inhibitors and ensured they are not on your team?

- Have you agreed how, and when, communication with the staff will be handled?

- Have you requested quotations from at least three certification bodies?

- Have you interviewed the prospective auditors or sent them a questionnaire?

- Are you continuing to conduct progress meetings and design reviews?

- Are steering group meetings being held on schedule?

- Are problems/solutions passed to the executive being promptly resolved?

- Will you make the target date?

3 System design

System design overview

- Quality systems have to ensure that products and services meet specified requirements and, to do this, the system has to cause outputs of the required quality and prevent outputs of poor quality.

- To cause anything to happen, there has to be a chain reaction which, in this case, extends from the customer requirements through all the processes that convert these requirements into products and services and out to the satisfied customer.

- To ensure this chain reaction produces consistent results that meet business goals, the system has to be carefully designed.

- What makes a collection of components into a system is the way they are connected and energized.

- Quality systems are not designed by assembling together a set of existing documented practices to see what you can make from them.

- Systems are designed by determining what processes are required to receive customer and supplier inputs, add value, and deliver the desired outputs and how they need to be connected together to achieve the required objectives

System design task list

- Produce a system requirement specification defining the purpose, scope, conditions, constraints and composition of the system.

- Create a context diagram showing the business interfaces and quality system interfaces.

- Create a system model showing the key processes that drive the business.

- Define the purpose and scope of each key process.

- Appoint process owners for each key business process.

- Produce a Function Deployment Matrix that shows who executes which process.

- Set up Process Development Teams to take the process design through to completion.

- Chart the business processes.

- Chart the work processes that comprise the business processes.

- Chart the tasks that comprise the work processes.

- Deploy the requirements of ISO 9000 to the process models.

- Perform risk analysis against the critical success factors.

- Add controls to meet relevant requirements and to reduce, or eliminate, adverse impact on critical success factors.

- Produce a Requirement Deployment Matrix that shows where requirements are implemented by processes or tasks.

- Add provisions to the process charts to collect the data needed to measure process performance.

- Identify types of documents needed to transmit input requirements, perform work and supply process outputs.

- Perform document reduction to identify the minimum number of separate documents required.

- Create a document register.

- Match existing documents against identified needs and update document register.

- Define the development requirements for the listed documents.

Practical document identification

You can search the relevant standards for references to documents, respond to the requirements of the standards, or chart the processes and identify where documents are needed. Here is a practical method that starts with the processes charts:

1 Chart processes down to task level.

2 If the tasks cross functional boundaries then you have identified the need for a control procedure.

3 Produce the control procedure following the tasks identified on the chart.

4 For the first task on the chart, determine what form the input takes. If the input is in the form of *information* you will have identified a derived document from the interfacing process.

5 Determine what activities are required to carry out the task. If there are many sequential activities, you have identified an operating procedure.

6 If the task is one that will generate information, determine what form the derived documents will take. This will identify plans, specifications, reports or derivations of the same.

7 If the task is an acceptance decision for which criteria needs to be specified, you will have identified the need for a standard.

8 If the task is a moving-type task you may have identified a requirement for labels and notices.

9 If the task is one where personal or equipment safety is at risk, you may have identified a requirement for standards, guides and notices.

10 If the task is a decision for which there may be many possible options and for which some consistency is required, you will have identified the need for a guide.

11 If in the execution of the task, *reference material* is to be consulted then you have identified the need for a reference document.

12 Determine whether it is necessary to maintain a record of the results of the decision, or action, to feed other processes. Should such a record be needed you will have identified a controlled record.

13 For the final task in the flowchart, determine what form the output takes and if it is *information* determine the type of derived document it is.

14 If the output of the process is product, then you will have identified a requirement for labels and routing instructions.

The requirement for the document derives from the description of the policy, task or activity which causes it to be generated. Here are some examples:

- *The plan shall be prepared in accordance with procedure OP23.*

- *The results shall be recorded on form BF45.*

- *The product shall be inspected using standard ST04.*

- *In deciding which course of action to take, consideration shall be given to the guidance provided in guide GD14.*

- *An acceptance label (BL09) shall be attached to those products that have passed the specified tests.*

- *When installing replacement blades in the machine, the safety precautions defined in DN06 shall be observed.*

Documentation identification is therefore a progressive process. You chart the process, identify a document or two. You chart another process, identify a few more documents, write a procedure and identify many more. You produce the documents you identified and identify many more documents, and so on, until all have been identified and produced.

System design questionnaire

- Have you decided what form of system you require – paper-based or electronic?

- Have you identified all external business and system interfaces?

- Have you identified the core business processes?

- Have you charted the business processes and associated work processes?

- Have you defined the business and work processes and set the boundary conditions?

- Do all the inputs and outputs on the work process charts link with the corresponding interfaces on the associated business process chart?

- Do the charts match your process descriptions?

- Have you taken account of optional routes for product and information to follow as it passes through the process?

- Have you given names to the processes that reflect the function of the process rather than the organization which executes it?

- Have you identified the documentation or product which passes between tasks on your flowcharts?

- Have you checked that all functions have been represented on your Function Deployment Matrix?

- Have you identified the corresponding tasks on the flowcharts which will implement the requirements in your Requirement Deployment Matrix?

- Have you added all the necessary controls and responded to the relevant requirements identified in the matrix?

- Have you completed your risk analysis and put in place the necessary controls to minimize the risks as product or information passes through the processes?

- Have you identified the principle control procedures required and charted the corresponding flowcharts?

- Have the flowcharts been agreed by the process owners and the development teams?

4   Documentation development

Types of document

- There are several types of document used in work processes, each having a specific purpose.

- There are only three categories of information that need to be conveyed: requirements, plans and results. The *requirements* are what you have to achieve, the *plans* are the provisions made to achieve the requirements and the *results* are what you actually achieved.

- These documents attract different names dependent on the level in the system from which they originated and whether they are generated internally or externally to the quality system.

The documents used to convey such information can be divided into four classes: policies, practices, derived documents and reference documents.

Policies
Policies are the documents that define your intentions for meeting the obligations placed upon you. These can be subdivided into *corporate policies, business policies and operational policies*.

Practices
Practices are statements that define the what, when, where, how, who and why of your operations. These can be subdivided into the following types:

- *Control procedures* are documents that control work on a product or information as it passes through a process. They are generally multifunctional.

- *Operating procedures* are documents that prescribe how specific tasks are to be performed.

- *Standards* are documents that define acceptance criteria for judging the quality of an activity, a document, a product or a service. They change infrequently and can be applied to ranges of activities, products etc. There are international, national, industry and company standards.

- *Guides* are non-mandatory documents that are an aid to decision making and to conduct activities.

- *Blank forms* are used to collect and transmit information for approval or for addition or other information.

- *Labels* are documents that identify product status and are often disposed of when the status changes.

- *Notices* are documents that alert staff to regulations that must be followed, to precautions that must be taken, to dangers that exist.

- *Job descriptions* are documents that define the responsibility, authority and accountability of personnel.

Derived documents
Derived documents are documents that are produced from implementing the policies and practices. The names of these documents vary significantly, depending on the industry. There are two types of derived documents – prescriptive and descriptive. The *prescriptive* documents contain requirements and the *descriptive* documents contain results and intentions. Some common derived documents are: *action plans, product specifications, work instructions, business proposals, conformity certificates, activity reports* and *controlled records*.

Reference documents
Reference documents are documents that contain data that is to be used in conjunction with the policies and practices and could be derived documents or external documents. Examples are: *contractual agreements, purchase orders, work orders, national standards, drawings, and specifications.*

Benefits of documented procedures

Properly documented procedures provide several benefits; they:

- Encourage the people involved to think a problem through.

- Convert solved problems into recorded knowledge so as to avoid having to solve them repeatedly.

- Maximize company performance rather than departmental performance.

- Cause people to act in a uniform way and so make processes predictable.

- Provide freedom for management and staff to maximize their contribution to the business.

- Free the business from reliance on particular people for its effectiveness.

- Provide legitimacy and authority for the deeds needed.

- Make responsibility clear and create the conditions of self-control.

- Provide co-ordination for inter-departmental action.

- Enable the effects of potential process changes to be assessed.

- Minimize variance and eliminate bottlenecks.

- Improve communication and provide consistency and predictability in carrying out repetitive tasks.

- Provide training and reference material for new and existing staff.

- Provide evidence to those concerned of your intentions.

- Provide auditable criteria for execution against authorized practices.

- Provide a basis for studying existing work practices and identifying opportunities for improvement.

- Demonstrate after an incident the precautions that were taken or should have been taken to prevent, or minimize, its occurrence.

Effective procedures

An effective procedure would contain some, or all, of the following elements:

- A flowchart of the process that depicts the sequence of actions and decisions, inputs, outputs and interfaces with other procedures.

- Paragraphs describing the actions and decisions required, indicating the role responsible by matching the flowchart in the sequence in which they occur.

- The minimum information and equipment needed to perform each activity or make each decision.

- The criteria for decisions as a list of aspects to be considered or a statement of requirement which the decision should satisfy.

- The criteria for choosing optional routes and the sequence of steps to be taken.

- The entry conditions for starting the process in terms of the minimum inputs and approvals to be satisfied before the procedure may commence.

- The exit conditions for ending the process or task in terms of the minimum outputs and approvals to be satisfied for successful completion of the process.

- The source of information or product needed in terms of from which process, which procedure, which person (role) or organization it comes.

- The routing instructions for information or product emerging from the procedure.

- Any precautions needed to prevent incident, accident, error, problems etc.

- Any rules that have to be followed in order to ensure that the task is carried out in a uniform manner and satisfies statutory obligations.

- Controls needed to verify the quality of any products with feedback loops.

- Controls needed to verify that the process, or task, achieves its purpose and to verify that critical activities and decisions occur when required.

- Any forms to be completed together with form-filling instructions and responsibilities, the numbering system to be used and the registers to be maintained.

- Cross references to other documents in which essential supplementary information can be found.

Hints and tips on style

- Quality system documents do have some legal significance – they disclose your policies and practices, not your dreams and ambitions.

- If you have found the best way of carrying out a task you will want the task to be carried out that way and will not allow the documentation to offer too much flexibility.

- Policies and procedures need to *cause* things to happen. They are not history books, statements of what we once did.

- If you write in an inappropriate style for a particular document, you may not *cause to happen* what you had intended.

- Using the word 'shall' indicates a provision that is binding.

- Using the word 'should' indicates a provision that is advisory.

- Using the word 'must' indicates a provision that is compulsory.

- Using the word 'will' indicates a provision of intent and not necessarily an obligation.

- Using the word 'may' indicates that a provision is optional.

- The instructional style contains statements that use none of the auxiliary verbs and contain instructions; for example: 'Send out the agenda for the design reviews two weeks before the review meeting date.' In this way procedures can be a series of instructions, or steps, as might be found in a self-assembly kit of furniture.

- The descriptive style uses statements that also use none of the auxiliary verbs and are statements of fact; for example: 'Design reviews are held at defined stages during product development'. This does not *cause* things to be done, unlike the 'shall' and 'are to be' statements.

- Use 'shall' statements for policies, control procedures and standards.

- Use 'should' statements for guides.

- Use 'must' statements for compulsory issues.

- Use 'will' statements for proposals.

- Use 'may' statements only for conditional issues.

- Use descriptive statements for expositions.

- Use instructional statements for operating procedures.

What and what not to document

- Document those practices where judgement is not required or necessary.

- Document those practices where their accomplishment is not intuitive.

- Document those practices where the method used is critical to the result achieved.

- Document best practice because you cannot expect staff to know what best practice is unless you tell them.

- Document practices where too much choice can be bad for efficiency.

- Document practices where it would be unreasonable, unsafe or unreliable to expect staff to commit the knowledge required to memory.

- Don't attempt to tell people how to read, write or do arithmetic.

- The procedures need only detail that which would not be covered by education and training.

- In order to provide training of consistent quality, it too should be documented in the form of training manuals, training aids and facilities.

- Don't attempt to tell people how to conduct their trade or profession, how to write, how to design, how to type, how to answer the telephone, how to paint, lay bricks, etc. unless a uniform approach is essential to the results you wish to achieve.

- The way to achieve consistency in all things is to provide examples of good and bad, right and wrong, so that staff are aware of the standards they have to attain.

- You may use such books to bridge gaps in education and training but these are not your procedures.

Documentation standards

- The title should convey the subject and its scope in a few choice words.

- All documents should have Purpose, Scope and Applicability sections.

- Purpose statements should commence: *The purpose of the (subject) is to ... so that (specified requirement) ...*

- Scope statements should commence: *This procedure covers the ...*

- Applicability statements should commence: *This document applies to ...*

- Procedural statements should be in the form: *On receipt of A from B, C shall be carried out by D in accordance with E in order to F* – thus indicating WHEN, WHERE, WHAT, WHO, HOW and WHY.

- The date denoted on a document should indicate one of the following: the date of creation, date of release, date of approval, date of print or date it becomes effective.

- Documents should have a simple unique identification code for reference purposes.

- Document status should identify whether a document is Draft, Approved or Obsolete.

- Logos are unnecessary on quality system documents.

- Approval signatures are not required on every page, neither are they necessary on the front page providing there is an effective means of determining approval status.

- Except for electronic versions, each page should carry the page number and number of pages to help determine if any are missing.

- Obsolete or unmaintained documents do not need to be marked with any special labels if there is an effective means of identifying current and maintained documents.

- Except for electronic versions document codes should be applied to all pages.

- Except for electronic versions, all pages should carry a date.

- All documents should have a revision record.

- Use roles in place of job titles, department titles and names.

- Use generic place names for locations that can be carried with the process wherever it is carried out.

- Don't put room numbers, geographic locations etc. in documents. If you need to add such data then place it in a reference document so that only one document has to be changed.

- Limit dates in documents (other than document release dates) to those that define objectives, plans or schedules.

- Spell out abbreviations in full the first time they are used.

- Every document should have a parent document that requires its use up to the Corporate Policy.

Documentation task list

1   Prepare the document development plan.

2   Determine the documentation method.

3   Prepare a specification defining the features you require of the documentation tools.

4   Set up the documentation tools (word processors, database etc.)

5   Provide user instructions for the document database.

6   Test the tools to verify they meet your specification before production use.

7   Determine the documentation standards.

8   Develop and issue a glossary of terms.

9   Produce the document development procedure.

10   Produce the document change procedure.

11   Nominate the authors.

12   Set up a review panel for documents.

13   Determine approval authorities.

14   Issue the document requirements.

15   Issue the document development procedures.

16   Create the control procedures.

17 Create the policy manual.

18 Review and approve the policy manual.

19 Review and approve the control procedures.

20 Issue the document change procedure.

21 Develop the supporting documents.

22 Review and approve the support documents.

23 Update the development plan.

Documentation questionnaire

1 Have you decided on a paper system or an electronic system?

2 Have you tested the tools to verify they provide all the features you require?

3 Have you provided access control to the database?

4 Have you decided how the documents will look on screen and on paper?

5 Have you defined the numbering system?

6 Have you decided how document approval will be indicated?

7 Have you decided on the document dating convention?

8 Have you chosen the document revision convention?

9 Have you decided how you will indicate revisions in draft documents?

10 Have you chosen a style for the documents and communicated it to the authors?

11 Have you decided what to do about existing stocks of paper forms?

12 Have you decided what to do about existing documents produced using different software packages?

13 Do you know which documents you need to produce?

14 Have the authors, reviewers and approvers been nominated?

15 Do the authors know how to operate the tools?

16 Have you chosen the location for the quality system documents?

17 Have you decided what to do about electronic versions of documents located on remote servers or computers?

18 Have you decided what to do about the control of derived documents?

19 Have you defined the external documents and what to do about their control?

20 Have you provided a document in which special terms can be defined?

21 Have you defined what a 'policy' is and provided guidance on their preparation?

22 Have you defined what a 'procedure' is and provided guidance on their preparation?

23 Which version is to be the master, the paper version or the electronic version?

24 Will the forms be included in the procedure or be separate documents?

25 Have you decided how you will provide immunity to organizational change?

26 Have you decided which procedures are to be common to all sites?

27 Are all control procedures traceable to policies?

28 Are the policies compatible with the control procedures?

29 Are all supporting documents traceable to the control procedures?

30 Are all forms traceable to the procedures that requires their use?

31 Have you decided what will constitute your quality manual?

5 System implementation

System implementation tasks

1 Prepare implementation plan.

2 Implement by process, not function.

3 Identify resistance to change.

4 Plan progressive documentation release.

5 Acquire necessary resources to implement.

6 Conduct dry run.

7 Maintain action list.

8 Ensure understanding.

9 Monitor execution.

10 Resolve problems.

11 Continue awareness and training sessions.

12 Check effect at the functional interfaces.

13 Start in areas of least resistance.

14 Set up computers/equipment.

15 Withdraw obsolete documents and data.

16 Organize paper and electronic data.

17 Commence conversion where necessary.

18 Ensure ownership rests with users.

19 Commence audit program.

20 Audit frequently.

21 Analyse results.

22 Gather feedback from users.

23 Determine process and system effectiveness.

24 Take remedial and corrective action.

25 Set audit frequency for post qualification.

26 Update training records.

27 Update document status records.

28 Give encouragement.

29 Move on to next process.

System implementation questionnaire

1 Have you identified which functions will be affected by the changes?

2 Have you briefed the managers about the changes?

3 Have you trained staff in the use of the databases?

4 Have you notified staff what to expect from the internal audits?

5 Have you created prototype databases on which to prove any changes found during implementation?

6 Have you communicated with all affected sites?

7 Have you got the commitment of the managers?

8 Have you identified what changes will be made to existing practices and communicated this to the relevant staff?

9 Have you trained the auditors and analysed their results before extending the audit programme?

10 Have you installed the problem management database or reporting procedures?

11 Have you initiated document control?

12 Does everyone affected know what to do?

13 Are you monitoring progress against plan?

14 Are you raising concerns with management and getting prompt action?

15 Have you identified the areas of resistance and are you dealing with them before they jeopardize your programme?

16 Have you removed the obsolete documents from offices and file servers?

17 Have you decided how you will measure system effectiveness and put the data collection channels in place?

6 System evaluation

System evaluation tasks

1 Develop the audit management tools, procedures and forms.

2 Decide on your audit strategy.

3 Prepare the audit schedule.

4 Train the auditors.

5 Make management aware of what audits aim to achieve and how information will be gathered and used.

6 Assign auditors.

7 Plan, conduct and report individual audits.

8 Track remedial and corrective actions.

9 Analyse the results, determine root cause and plot trends.

10 Compile compliance tables showing the coverage of the audit programme and where the significant problems lie.

11 Form Corrective Action Teams to resolve problems.

12 Check that sensors are in place to monitor performance in key processes.

13 Determine and agree performance indicators with process owners.

14 Collect performance data to determine if quality objectives have been met.

15 Consolidate data to produce reports indicating the effectiveness of the system.

16 Provide reports for the system review.

17 Organize system reviews and agree the composition of the System Review Board.

18 Obtain management commitment to the system reviews.

19 Conduct system reviews and meet with management to agree results.

20 Record the results of the review and follow up on any corrective actions.

21 Arrange external audit.

22 Agree external audit schedule.

23 Take ownership of baseline quality manual for auditors to sign.

24 Co-ordinate on-site audit.

25 Deal with nonconformities as they arise.

26 Enter external audit results into database.

27 Organize follow-up audits.

System evaluation questionnaire

1 Have you decided how you are going to determine the effectiveness of the quality system?

2 Are the tools in place for scheduling and reporting audits?

3 Have the auditors been trained in auditing and in the use of the tools?

4 Have you decided on the classification of audit findings?

5 Have you decided whether auditors will audit products and processes as well as systems?

6 Have you decided whether you will audit managerial decisions?

7 Has management been appraised of what to expect from the auditors?

8 Have managers been trained in the use of the corrective action tools?

9 Have you decided how many audits are needed to meet your audit objective?

10 Have you a sufficient number of trained auditors for the task?

11 After each audit do you know what was audited, what was checked and what the results were?

12 Are all audit results logged in the database?

13 Have the managers been given time limits to propose remedial and corrective actions?

14 Are the managers meeting their commitments?

15 Have you decided how you will measure the effectiveness of auditing?

16 Have you decided how you will present the results of audits to management?

17 Are you adjusting the audit frequency based on previous audit results?

18 Have you surveyed management reaction to audits and adjusted the strategy accordingly?

19 Are you retraining your auditors in response to negative feedback from managers?

20 Is there an escalation process in place to deal with problems which remain outstanding?

21 Have the performance indicators being used been agreed with the managers before reporting performance at the system review?

22 Have you decided who is to participate in the system review?

23 If the CEO cannot chair the meeting, have you established who will deputize?

24 Have you recorded the results of the system review of the quality system?

25 Have you recorded the agreements reached on current performance?

26 Have you decided whether the system will remain suitable after any planned changes are implemented in the organization?

27 Have you decided whether the system is effective and whether changes are required?

7 System maintenance

System maintenance tasks

1 Allow the system to work.

2 Demonstrate commitment.

3 Test understanding regularly.

4 Gather data from using the system.

5 Use it to make decisions.

6 Either work the system or get the system changed.

7 Eradicate bad habits.

8 Revise documentation as needed.

9 Maintain the audit programme and management reviews.

10 Submit to surveillance visits.

11 Take corrective actions to prevent recurrence of problems.

12 Set up a System Change Board to handle all system changes.

13 Maintain the records.

14 Maintain the policies and procedures.

15 Don't allow deviations.

16 Document and implement – don't implement then document.

17 Eliminate informal practices.

18 Record and resolve problems.

19 Change practices under controlled conditions.

20 Monitor business changes and technology changes.

21 Monitor staff changes, organization changes and resource changes.

System maintenance questionnaire

1 Have you decided how and who will monitor the system performance?

2 Have you chosen the monitoring tools and trained the personnel in their application?

3 Have you installed the sensors to detect variance in performance?

4 Have you arranged for the collection and analysis of data?

5 Have you installed a problem management tool?

6 Is root-cause analysis being carried out on detected problems?

7 Is the root-cause analysis effective in identifying the true source of the problems?

8 Are corrective action teams organized for cross-functional problems?

9 Are corrective plans prepared for preventing the recurrence of problems?

10 Are corrective plans endorsed by management?

11 Has the impact of change on other processes been evaluated and appropriate action taken?

12 Are the reasons for abandoning any corrective action plans justified?

13 Is there an escalation process in place to bring in specialist and management support if needed?

14 Have champions been appointed to lead the improvement effort?

15 Are corrective action plans being expedited?

16 Have provisions been made and executed for verifying the effectiveness of agreed corrective actions?

17 Is the documentation always changed ahead of the practices?

18 Are staff trained in the use of new practices?

19 Are you supplied with information about the business, organization, staff changes and technology changes so that you can take action to maintain the system?

8 System improvement

System improvement tasks

1 Set new objectives and targets.

2 Develop annual improvement programmes.

3 Look for potential problems and take preventive action.

4 Seek suggestions for improvement.

5 Simplify and optimize.

6 Reduce complexity.

7 Reduce the number of suppliers.

8 Reduce variation, waste, time and error.

9 Reduce job classifications.

10 Reduce inspection.

11 Reduce negative attitudes.

12 Increase utilization and training.

13 Increase discipline and adherence to policy.

14 Increase tidiness and cleanliness.

15 Increase availability and retrievability.

16 Increase motivation.

17 Stabilize controls, methods and materials.

18 Stabilize supplier performance.

19 Stabilize processes.

20 Stabilize the environment.

21 Keep commitments and records.

22 Keep measuring performance and analysing results.

23 Keep auditing and questioning.

24 Keep reducing, increasing and stabilizing.

25 Keep maintaining, improving and innovating.

System improvement questionnaire

1 Have you decided on your quality improvement strategy?

2 Do you have a policy for continual improvement?

3 Has every manager committed resources to the pursuit of continual improvement?

4 Are the tools in place to capture potential improvements in the quality system?

5 Have you provided training in the use of the improvement tools?

6 Is everyone aware of these tools and how to use them?

7 Are procedures in place to guide the improvement process?

8 Have you decided how improvement opportunities will be reported and to whom they will be reported?

9 Have you decided how you will organize improvement teams?

10 Do the improvement plans have management backing?

11 Are the reasons for abandoning any implementation plans justified?

12 Are the agreed improvement plans being implemented as agreed?

13 Are the plans effective in preventing the occurrence of problems?

14 Is progress on the implementation of the plans monitored and reported to the systems review?

15 Is there an escalation process in place to bring in specialist and top-management support, if needed?

16 Are you researching literature and using contacts to discover ways of enhancing your quality improvement programmes?

Part 3

Satisfying ISO 9000 requirements

Contents

1 Quality policy

Requirements of ISO 9001 clause 4.1.1

Suppliers are required to:

1 Define and document policy for quality.

2 Define and document objectives for quality.

3 Define and document commitment to quality.

4 Cause the policy to be relevant to organizational goals.

5 Cause the policy to be relevant to needs of customers.

6 Cause the policy to be understood at all levels.

7 Implement the quality policy at all levels.

8 Maintain the quality policy at all levels.

Purpose of requirements

The purpose of defining the quality policy is to direct everyone in the organization in a particular direction regarding quality and give them a sound basis for the actions and decisions they execute. The quality system implements the quality policy and, therefore, the quality policy establishes the requirements which govern the scope and applicability of the quality system.

Guidance on interpretation

Applicability

The requirements apply to the organization's top management. No tailoring is needed for specific industries.

Quality policy

Any statement made by management, at any level, which is designed to constrain the actions and decisions of those it affects is a policy. ISO 8402 defines quality policy as the overall quality intentions and direction of an organization with regard to quality, as formally expressed by top management. Many quality policy statements declare:

- The intention to satisfy customer requirements.

- The position regarding the treatment of customers, employees, suppliers.

- The intentions regarding investment in training, new technology, continuous improvement and best practice.

- The intentions regarding the law, national and international standards, industry practices, human safety, reliability, natural resource conservation, and the environment.

- The intentions regarding the use of a documented quality system and its certification to national standards.

- The scope of the policy and the quality system if applying to all operations of the business.

- Management commitment to the policy.

Quality objectives

Quality objectives are those results which the organization needs to achieve in order to improve its ability to meet current and future customer needs and expectations. Examples are improved reliability, improved response time, zero defects, ISO 9000 certification, 100% delivery on time etc. Quality objectives often include:

- Objectives for business performance addressing markets, the environment and society

- Objectives for product or service performance addressing customer needs and competition

- Objectives for process performance addressing the capability, efficiency and effectiveness of the process, its use of resources and its controllability

- Objectives for organization performance addressing the capability, efficiency and effectiveness of the organization, its responsiveness to change, the environment in which people work etc.

- Objectives for worker performance addressing the skills, knowledge, ability, motivation and development of workers

Executive responsibility

Executive responsibility is responsibility vested in those personnel who are accountable for the whole organization's performance – often referred to as top management. These are the people who make policy decisions affecting the whole organization and may include the person with the title Quality Manager, but will not and should not be exclusive to this position.

Commitment

Commitment is an obligation a person or organization undertakes to fulfil (that is, doing what you say will do). The road to commitment is a seven-stage process, as shown in the following table.

Stage	Level	Meaning
0	Zero	I don't know anything about it.
1	Awareness	I know what it is and why I should do it.
2	Understanding	I know what I have to do and what I need to do it.
3	Investment	I have the resources to do it and I am ready to deploy them.
4	Intent	This is what I am going to do and how I am going to do it.
5	Action	I have completed the first few actions and it has been successful.
6	Commitment	I am now prepared do everything I said I would do.

Consequences of failure

If there was no formal quality policy, each person would by default set an unwritten policy that governs behaviour. This would result in inconsistency in decisions and actions that affect quality, and no clear direction for staff to follow. With no quality policy, other priorities (such as price and delivery) would take precedence and cause a decline in standards.

Inconsistency of requirements

- It is unclear whether the quality policy should include objectives for quality or whether the quality objectives can be defined and documented separately from the quality policy. To resolve this remember that policies remain in force until changed, whereas objectives remain in force until achieved.

- There is no specific requirement for the quality objectives to be relevant to the supplier's organizational goals and expectations or needs of customers but it would be illogical for the objectives not to be as relevant to these goals.

- Quality policy has to be understood, implemented and maintained but not the quality objectives if they do not form part of the quality policy statement. Organizations that ignore quality objectives are showing a lack of commitment to quality.

- Documented procedures are not required for establishing and maintaining the quality policy and quality objectives. The process by which the policy and objectives are formed and maintained should be defined to show that it is a controlled process.

Tasks for developers

1   Define, agree and publish your corporate quality policy.

2   Define, agree and publish operational policies for meeting each of the requirements of the standard and publish them in a policy manual.

3   Define your quality objectives, then document and publish them in an Annual Quality Programme.

4   Initiate seminars and meetings to gain understanding of the policies and objectives.

5   Audit commitment and understanding of the policies and objectives periodically.

6   Reference policies to the procedures which implement them.

7 Introduce a procedure for changing and deviating from the agreed policies.

8 Conduct periodic reviews of your policies and objectives.

9 Ensure the managers know their objectives and have plans to meet them.

10 Ensure your staff know where to find the quality policies.

11 Don't issue edicts or directives which violate the declared policies.

12 Don't write procedures which violate published policies.

13 Don't publish policies that your managers cannot or will not abide by.

Questions to stimulate policies

1 In what documents do you define your policy for and commitment to quality?

2 In what documents do you define your objectives for quality?

3 How do you ensure that the quality policy is relevant to your organizational goals and the expectations and needs of your customers?

4 How do you ensure that your policy for quality is understood at all levels in the organization?

5 How do you ensure that your policy for quality is implemented at all levels in the organization?

6 How do you ensure that your policy for quality is maintained at all levels in the organization?

Questions for auditors

1 Who are your customers?

2 What specific products and services do you provide?

3 What method is used to determine current customer needs and expectations?

4   How do you establish the future needs and expectations of customers?

5   Who carries out the data collection and analysis?

6   What are the expectations of your customers?

7   How often is your perception of customer expectations reviewed?

8   What are your organization's goals?

9   Who defined the organizational goals?

10 How often are the organizational goals reviewed?

11 Who defined the quality policy?

12 How was the quality policy developed?

13 In what document is the quality policy defined?

14 What feedback do you receive that informs you that the policy is not being met?

15 What are the organization's quality objectives?

16 How did you formulate the quality objectives?

17 In what document are the quality objectives defined?

18 What feedback do you receive that informs you whether the objectives are being met?

19 In what document is the commitment to quality defined?

20 What have you told your staff about this audit?

21 How do you establish that your staff are carrying out their work as directed?

22 Who is responsible for conveying the quality policy and quality objectives to the staff and dealing with its interpretation?

2 Responsibility and authority

Requirements of ISO 9001 clause 4.1.2.1

Suppliers are required to:

1 Define and document the responsibility and authority of managers, workers and verification staff.

2 Define and document the responsibility and authority of staff who prevent the occurrence of nonconformities.

3 Define and document the responsibility and authority of staff who identify and record problems relating to products, processes and the quality system.

4 Define and document the responsibility and authority of staff who provide solutions to problems.

5 Define and document the responsibility and authority of staff who verify the implementation of solutions.

6 Define and document the responsibility and authority of personnel who control the processing, delivery or installation of nonconforming product.

Purpose of requirements

The purpose of defining responsibility and authority of personnel is to ensure that staff are in no doubt as to the results they are expected to achieve, the decisions they have a right to take and to whom they are accountable for their actions and decisions.

Guidance on interpretation

Applicability

The requirements apply to all the organization's managers responsible for activities affecting the quality of the products and services provided to external customers. No tailoring is needed for specific industries.

Responsibility

Responsibility is in simple terms an area in which one is entitled to act on one's own accord. It is the obligation that subordinates have to their superiors for performing the duties of the assigned jobs. If you caused something to happen then you must be responsible for the result, just as you would if you caused an accident – so, to determine a person's responsibility, ask: 'What can you cause to happen?'

Authority

Authority is, in simple terms, the right to take actions and make decisions. Authority in the management context constitutes a form of influence and a right to take action, to direct and co-ordinate the actions of others, and to use discretion in the position an individual occupies. The delegation of authority permits decisions to be made more rapidly by those who are in more direct contact with the prevailing situation.

Interrelationships

Interrelation means to place in mutual relationship, so what is needed is a definition of the relationships between staff with quality responsibilities. Staff need to know from whom they will receive their instructions, to whom they are accountable, to whom they should go to seek information to resolve difficulties, and to whom information or product should be submitted when complete.

Documenting responsibility and authority

There are four principal ways in which responsibilities and authority can be documented:

1   In an organization structure diagram or organigram

2   In job descriptions or role descriptions

3   In terms of reference

4   In procedures

Consequences of failure

If the responsibilities and authority of staff are not defined, staff will assume responsibility and authority for those activities and decisions which give them personal and financial benefits. They will neglect those activities and decisions that are unpalatable or which have no personal or financial benefit. There will be a power struggle as staff fight for the right to make certain decisions or carry out certain tasks. There will be no structure which causes the right actions and decisions to be carried out and, hence, no confidence that the requirements for quality will be achieved by design. Results will be achieved by chance.

Inconsistency of requirements

- Documented procedures are not required for the assignment, review and evaluation of responsibility and authority. If there are conflicting responsibilities or authority, duplication or gaps then the absence of any rules indicates that a potential cause of nonconformity exists for which preventive action is required under clause 4.14.3.

- Responsibilities are not required to be *clearly* defined and documented. If this situation arises then the argument above can be used to secure corrective action.

Tasks for developers

1   Create, agree and publish rules for the assignment of responsibilities and delegation of authority.

2   Produce, agree and publish organization charts.

3 Produce, agree and issue to those concerned descriptions for each defined position or role.

4 Produce, agree and publish flow diagrams of the processes which contribute to the achievement of quality and identify the interfaces and responsibilities.

5 Ensure everyone knows their responsibilities and what decisions they are permitted/not permitted to take.

6 Ensure signatures are legible and traceable to those with the necessary authority.

7 Ensure that job descriptions and procedures are compatible.

8 Ensure everyone knows the source of their requirements.

9 Ensure that everyone knows what to do if they can't meet the requirements imposed upon them.

10 Ensure there is no conflict between the responsibilities and authority of different managers.

11 Ensure staff know who has the right to stop the process.

12 Don't issue edicts or directives which violate the declared policies.

13 Don't sign documents unless you have the necessary authority to do so.

Questions to stimulate policies

1 In which document do you define the responsibility and authority of all personnel who manage, perform and verify work affecting quality?

2 In which documents do you define the interrelation of all personnel who manage, perform and verify work affecting quality?

3 How do you ensure that, when needed, personnel have the organizational freedom to: identify quality problems, provide solutions, initiate action to prevent their recurrence and verify the implementation of solutions?

4 How do you ensure that those responsible for results have the organizational freedom necessary to control processing and delivery or installation of product?

Questions for auditors

1 Who defines the responsibility and authority of the managers?

2 In what documents are their responsibilities and authority defined?

3 How do you ensure there is no overlap or gaps in responsibility and authority?

4 How do you ensure that your staff understand their responsibilities and authority?

5 To whom are you accountable for your actions and decisions?

6 Whose work do you manage or supervise?

7 What is the relationship between this division and other divisions in the group?

8 Upon what products and services from these other divisions do you depend to meet your customer requirements?

9 How are the activities of the company structured?

10 Which of these departments interface directly with your customers and suppliers?

11 In what documents are these internal and external relationships defined?

3 Resources

Requirements of ISO 9001 clause 4.1.2.2

Suppliers are required to:

1 Identify resource requirements.

2 Provide adequate resources.

3 Assign trained personnel to management activities.

4 Assign trained personnel to performance of work.

5 Assign trained personnel to verification activities.

Purpose of requirements

The purpose of identifying resource requirements is to ensure that the organization is equipped with the capability needed to honour its intentions and its commitments.

Guidance on interpretation

Applicability

The requirements apply to the organization's management. No tailoring is needed for specific industries.

Scope

The term *resource* is often used to imply only human resources, when there are in fact other types of resources. Resources include manpower, time to do the job, machines, materials, finance, plant, facilities – in fact, any means available to the supplier for implementing the quality system.

Solutions

The way many companies identify resource requirements is to solicit resource budgets from each department covering a 1 to 5 year period. For specific contracts, products, projects etc. estimates are often prepared so that the necessary resources can be secured before a task is accepted.

Assigning trained personnel

Only trained personnel should be assigned to work affecting quality. The controls to be exercised over training are covered by clause 4.18 of the standard. You are free to determine the training necessary for such personnel but it should be commensurate with the level of responsibility, the complexity of the task and the experience and qualifications of the person.

Consequences of failure

If you do not identify your resource requirements before commencing work, there is a possibility that you will not be able to complete the work due to a lack of time, equipment, materials etc. or the unavailability of personnel. It could also be that the work will not meet the requirements since the assigned personnel may not possess the necessary skills and knowledge to do the job.

Inconsistency of requirements

- Clause 4.2.1 requires the system to be documented; therefore, whatever the method used to identify resources, the resources that have been identified have to be documented.

- The standard requires the assignment of trained personnel but not qualified personnel, as specified in clause 4.4.2 for design and development, or educated and experienced personnel, as specified in clause 4.18. Personnel need to be competent rather than trained and a test of competence is the ability to perform the job effectively over a long period of time.

- Documented procedures are not required for ensuring that adequate resources are identified and documented. However, clause 4.2.1 does require the system to be documented; therefore, the system for identifying and providing resources should be documented in the system.

- Records of the resources provided do not have to be maintained. Alas, there is no way an auditor can require such records to be produced unless ISO 9001 is a contract requirement.

Tasks for developers

1 Produce and agree resource budgets for management, productive work and verification activities.

2 Assign trained personnel to all tasks.

3 Ensure you have sufficient resources, including time, to carry through your plans.

4 Don't allocate funds for managing the quality system without providing a means of collecting the costs or time spent.

Questions to stimulate policies

1 How do you identify resource requirements?

2 How do you ensure that adequate resources are provided?

3 How do you ensure that trained personnel are assigned for management, performance of work and verification activities (including internal quality audits)?

Questions for auditors

1 How do you identify the resources needed to meet your company's commitments?

2 How often are these resources reviewed?

3 How are you alerted to shortages and surpluses in resources?

4 What is the process for the acquisition of additional resources?

5 What is the process for depleting surplus resources?

4   Management representative

Requirements of ISO 9001 clause 4.1.2.3

Suppliers are required to:

1   Appoint a member of the supplier's own management.

2   Delegate authority for ensuring that the quality system is established and implemented.

3   Delegate authority for ensuring that the quality system is maintained.

4   Delegate authority for reporting on the performance of the quality system.

Purpose of requirements

The purpose of appointing a management representative is to have a person who represents management with employees, with the certification body, the customer and suppliers on matters of quality. The role ensures that a coherent quality system is developed, implemented and evaluated with the delegated authority of the organization's executive management. It also puts a leader in charge of improvement efforts and someone to carry the wishes of management (i.e. the policies) to the workforce so that the workforce makes decisions that take into account the wishes of management.

Guidance on interpretation

Applicability

The requirements apply to the organization's top management. No tailoring is needed for specific industries.

Waterford Institute of Technology

Issue Receipt

Customer name: Lowry, Kathie

Title: ISO 9000 pocket guide / David Hoyle.
ID: a4002262626

Due: 10-03-15

Total items: 1
24-02-2015
Checked out: 1
Overdue: 0
Hold requests: 0
Ready for pickup: 0

Thank you for using the self service system. You
can renew items and check you due date
online at
http://library1.lyit.ie

Job title

The term *management representative* is an invention of ISO 9000. Other than in the title to clause 4.1.3, there is no other mention of a position with this name. It was also not the intention of ISO 9000 to force position titles upon companies. The management representative is a role and not a position. Hence the person performing this role can have whatever title the company chooses. The person carries the wishes of management (i.e. the policies) to the workforce so that the workforce makes decisions that take into account the wishes of management. This person also represents management with customers, suppliers and certification bodies on matters of quality.

Member of own management

The emphasis has been put on management appointing a member of its own management, indicating that the person should have a managerial appointment in the organization. This implies that the role cannot be filled by a contractor or external consultant.

Reporting level

The position needs to report at a level that will avoid conflicting responsibilities and enable the incumbent to exert some authority over every other manager, otherwise they are an adviser and cannot ensure that the quality system requirements are established, implemented and maintained.

Authority of management representative

The authority for establishing the system may be delegated to a *Project Manager* and that for maintaining the system may be delegated to a *Quality System Manager* and if necessary the authority for improving the system could be delegated to a *Quality Improvement Manager*. Each of these managers should report to the management representative.

To meet this requirement the management representative needs the right to:

- Manage the design, development, implementation and evaluation of the quality system, including the necessary resources (the *management role*).

- Determine whether proposed policies and practices meet the requirements of the standard, are suitable for meeting the business needs, are being properly implemented and cause noncompliances to be corrected (the *regulatory role*).

- Determine the effectiveness of the quality system (the *analysis role*).

- Report on the quality performance of the organization (the *scorekeeper role*).

- Identify and manage programmes for improvement in the quality system (the *innovative role*).

- Liaise with external bodies on quality matters (the *ambassador role*).

Consequences of failure

Without a champion for the quality system there would be no co-ordination, no unity and no focus for quality efforts. There would be not one but many systems, each competing and, thus, wasting resources. Customers, suppliers and third parties would have multiple points of contact, each perhaps sending out conflicting messages.

Inconsistency of requirements

- The management representative is not required to have executive responsibility. If the MR does not have authority for resourcing, then it needs to be demonstrated how he/she ensures (that is, causes) the system to be implemented and maintained.

- If the MR works through persuasion and, in cases of conflict, refers to the CEO, then clearly the MR does not have the required authority.

Tasks for developers

1 Appoint a management representative to manage the quality system and define, agree and publish the responsibilities and authority.

2 Ensure there is no conflict between the responsibilities and authority of the MR and other managers.

3 Give your management representative the teeth to get things done.

Questions to stimulate policies

1   Whom have you appointed to ensure that the requirements of ISO 9000 are implemented and maintained?

2   In what document is the management representative's authority and responsibility defined?

3   How do you ensure that the management representative remains a member of your own management?

4   How do you ensure that the management representative reports on quality system performance to the management review?

Questions for auditors

1   Who are the managers with executive responsibility?

2   Who appointed the management representative?

3   What is the tenure of this appointment?

4   What qualifications and experience are required of this person?

5   What training has this person received since taking up the appointment?

6   What responsibility and authority has been delegated to this person?

7   At what level does this person report in the organization?

8   What resources have been assigned for this person to carry out the role?

9   What authority has this person to require other managers to respond to requests for action?

10 How are concerns resolved between this manager and the executive management?

11 What authority has this person to obtain data on the performance of the quality system?

12 What data is used to report on the performance of the quality system?

5   Management review

Requirements of ISO 9001 clause 4.1.3

Suppliers are required to:

1   Review the quality system at defined intervals.

2   Establish that the quality system continues to be suitable and effective in satisfying ISO 9001.

3   Establish that the quality system continues to be suitable and effective in satisfying the stated policy and objectives.

4   Record the results of management reviews.

Purpose of requirements

The purpose of management review is for executive management to establish whether the quality system as a whole remains suitable and effective for its intended purpose and, if not, to direct it be changed.

Guidance on interpretation

Applicability

The requirements apply to the organization's top management. No tailoring is needed for specific industries.

Function of management review

The requirement is strictly referring to a review of the quality system, not a review of management. The management review is not a meeting, although there may be a meeting to discuss the results of the review and decide on any actions necessary. Management review is an activity aimed at assessing information on the performance of the quality system.

The management review should do several things:

- Establish whether the system is being used properly.

- Establish whether the audit programme is being effective.

- Establish whether customer needs are being satisfied.

- Establish whether the defined quality objectives are being met.

- Establish whether there is conflict between the stated quality policy, the quality objectives and the organizational goals, and the expectations and needs of your customers.

- Establish whether the quality philosophy is being honoured.

- Establish whether the system requires any change to match changing business needs.

- Establish whether the system provides useful data to manage the business.

The key questions to be answered are: 'Is the system effective?' and 'Is it suitable to continue without change?' At every meeting of the review team these questions should be answered and the response recorded.

Consequences of failure

Management need to understand that the system is their tool for driving the organization towards its quality objectives and ensuring their policies are implemented. If executive management fail to review the quality system periodically, there is a distinct possibility that the system would either fall into disuse or develop in a direction away from the declared quality policy and objectives. It is only the executive managers that have a vision of the business and have their hands on the steering wheel – why they, and they alone, should establish that they quality system remains fit for its purpose.

Inconsistency of requirements

- The title is not wholly consistent with the requirements of this clause, as the review required is only of the quality system and not of any other aspect of management.

- The quality system may be reviewed by the management representative, providing he/she has executive responsibility and there are no other executive managers. Where there are other executives, a single manager review would be a nonconformity.

- The intervals of management review have to be defined but not documented. As the quality system is required to be documented in clause 4.2.1, the defined intervals have to be documented in the system.

- There is a requirement to review the quality system at defined intervals but not its documented procedures (clause 4.2.2b) or the other documents used in the quality system (clause 4.2.1). As the quality system consists of procedures, responsibilities, resources, processes and organization structures, a review of the system includes a review of all of these.

- The minutes of the management review meeting contain the results of the meeting, not the results of the quality system review. The content of management review records is not specified in the standard. A quality record should provide objective evidence of the fulfilment of the requirements for quality. The activity is a review of the quality system; therefore, the record should contain objective evidence of the suitability and effectiveness of the system.

Tasks for developers

1   Collect and analyse data on quality performance.

2   Conduct periodic reviews of the quality system using the collected data.

3   Carry out corrective actions to improve the effectiveness of the quality system.

4   Maintain records of the management reviews.

5   Keep the management reviews separate from other meetings.

6   Don't grant concessions without giving time limits and valid reasons.

7   Don't let your management reviews degenerate into a talking shop.

8   Don't let the action list from the management review become a wish list!

Questions to stimulate policies

1 How does your management ensure the continuing suitability and effectiveness of the quality system in satisfying the requirements of ISO 9001 and the company's stated quality policy and objectives?

2 Who is defined as management with executive responsibility?

3 What records are maintained to demonstrate the quality system is effective?

Questions for auditors

Review methods

1 What methods do you employ to determine customer satisfaction?

2 What method is employed to establish the effectiveness of the quality system?

3 What criteria are used to determine that the system is suitable and effective?

4 Who carries out the review of the quality system?

5 How often is the management review carried out?

6 Under what circumstances would the review frequency be altered?

7 What recent changes have occurred in the business, the processes or the organization?

8 What data is used in order to carry out the review?

9 What method do you employ to ensure that the complete quality system is reviewed?

10 Who participates in the review?

11 Who analyses the data used in the review?

12 Who leads the review and decides on the action to be taken?

Review records

1 What records are kept of the reviews?

2 Who maintains these records?

3 What conclusions have been reached in previous reviews?

4 What records are there of actions taken to improve system effectiveness?

6　Quality system development

Requirements of ISO 9001 clause 4.2.1

The supplier is required to:

1　Establish a quality system.

2　Document a quality system.

3　Maintain a documented quality system.

4　Prepare a quality manual covering the requirements of the standard.

5　Include or make reference in the quality manual to the procedures used in the quality system.

6　Outline the structure of the documentation used in the quality system in the quality manual.

Purpose of requirements

The purpose of establishing a quality system is to provide a management tool to implement the quality policy and ensure that all products and services supplied to customers satisfy their needs and expectations. The purpose of these requirements is to prevent an unstructured and incoherent approach to satisfying the requirements of the standard.

Guidance on interpretation

Applicability

The requirements apply to the organization's management. No tailoring is needed for specific industries.

Establishing the system

To establish a quality system means to set up on a permanent basis – that it is part of the organization's management system – the way it conducts its business.

Outlining the structure of the system

The outline of the system may be presented by a diagram or by text.

Handling non-applicable requirements

It is required that the quality manual cover the requirements of the standard. However, not all requirements may apply to your business so how should you proceed? There are several ways of handling requirements that are not applicable:

- Include a cross-reference matrix.

- Refer to the non-applicable requirements within the introductory sections of the manual.

- Refer to non-applicable requirements in the relevant sections of the policy manual.

- Omit any reference to those requirements which are not applicable.

- Prepare a separate document which provides a response to each of the requirements.

Covering the requirements of ISO 9001

The requirements of the standard can be addressed either in the sequence they are presented in the standard or through policies that govern the business processes (the preferred method).

Consequences of failure

Without establishing a formal quality system, the achievement of the organization's objectives and implementation of its policies becomes a matter of chance and is dependent on the influence of certain people in the organization. Fail to maintain the system and results will revert to relying on chance; bad habits and irregular practices will emerge and dominate the organization. Without a manual that describes the system, personnel will not understand how work is carried out, what the relationship is between the various units of the organization and the various processes that serve to create and maintain satisfied customers.

Inconsistency of requirements

- The quality system has to provide a means of ensuring that product conforms to specified requirements and not a means for implementing the supplier's quality policy and objectives. This is an oversight as, logically, the system should be the means of implementing the policy and achieving the objectives of the organization.

- The quality manual has to cover the requirements of the standard but is not required to respond to all requirements of the standard or the supplier's quality policy. Covering a requirement depends upon what a requirement is: an element, a clause or a 'shall' statement or part of such a statement. Where the manual does not cover the requirements to this extent, it should cross reference the documents that do respond to these statements.

- The quality manual has to outline the structure of the documentation used in the quality system but is not required to describe or specify the documentation structure. An outline, by definition, should include all types of documents (including quality records) that constitute the quality system documentation, otherwise the outline is incomplete.

- There is no requirement that changes to the quality system have to be documented, reviewed and approved *prior* to implementation. System changes are not the same as documentation changes. The former changes the configuration of the system, whereas the latter only changes documentation. Auditors should therefore establish how the *system* is maintained, not only how documentation is maintained.

Tasks for developers

These are addressed in Part 2.

Questions to stimulate policies

1   What is the purpose of the quality system and where is it defined?

2   What is the scope of the quality system and where is it defined?

3   What documents constitute the quality manual?

4   In which document is the outline structure of the quality system defined?

5   What document covers the requirements of the standard?

6   What document includes or makes reference to the quality system procedures?

7   In which document is the outline structure of the documentation used in the quality system described?

8   How is the quality system maintained?

Questions for auditors

System development

1   What is the scope of this quality system?

2   Which sites are covered by this quality system?

3   What documents constitute your quality system?

4   What type of documents are not governed by this system?

5   How do you distinguish between documents that are governed by the system and those that are not?

6   Who is responsible for developing the system?

7   To what extent have the executive managers been involved in the development of the system?

Quality manual

1   In what document do you define your response to the requirements of ISO 9000?

2   Which requirements of ISO 9000 are not applicable to your operations?

3 Where are these exceptions defined?

4 Which document contains a complete list of the procedures which implement ISO 9000 requirements?

5 What is the relationship between all these documents?

6 In what document are the terms you use defined?

7 To what extent have you taken account of ISO 8402 and ISO 9000 in deriving these terms?

8 How have you conveyed understanding of the terminology to the personnel who implement the system?

9 To what extent do staff need to refer to the quality manual?

10 Which policies in the quality manual are not directly implemented through your documented procedures?

11 What instruction have staff received to familiarize them with the quality manual?

12 How do you prevent a change to the system causing a deviation from ISO 9000 requirements?

System maintenance

1 Who is responsible for maintaining the system documentation?

2 How do you become aware of a need to change the system?

3 How do you prevent the practices from being changed ahead of the documented policies and procedures?

4 What provisions have been made to permit deviations from the approved policies and procedures?

5 How do you ensure that amendments are embodied promptly?

6 What measures do you take to keep your practices up to date with industry norms and changes in the organization?

7 How are staff made aware of changes to the system?

8 What action is taken on the system when staff levels and organization structures change?

7 Quality system procedures

Requirements of ISO 9001 clause 4.2.2

The supplier is required to:

1 Prepare documented procedures consistent with the requirements of the standard.

2 Prepare documented procedures consistent with the requirements of the quality policy.

3 Effectively implement the quality system and its documented procedures.

4 Ensure that the range and detail of procedures is dependent upon the complexity of work, methods used and the skills and training needed.

Purpose of requirements

The purpose of quality system procedures is to implement policy and regulate processes which are essential to the business.

Guidance on interpretation

Applicability

The requirements apply to the organization's management. No tailoring is needed for specific industries.

Meaning of procedures

Although the standard refers to documented procedures the intent is towards documented practices that include procedures, standards, guides and references: in fact, the documentation of all measures that are needed to ensure that the output of a process meets the input requirements.

Consistency with requirements

Procedures consistent with the standard means that wherever the standard requires documented procedures, procedures covering the topics addressed by the requirement have to be produced, implemented and maintained. Where there is no requirement for a documented procedure you can choose to document your response to the requirements of the standard in procedures, standards, guides, references or policies because *the system has to be documented*.

Consistency with policy

Procedures consistent with the quality policy means that your procedures have to meet the intentions declared in your quality policy. If you have declared that you will satisfy customer requirements on time and within budget, your procedures need to enable you to do that.

Effectively implement procedures

This means that you have to apply the procedures when they are intended to be applied and to follow the instructions that are stated. It also means that your actions in following the procedures should meet the objectives of the procedure.

Numbers of procedures

Your procedures do not have to correspond to the headings in the standard. You may document your response to a requirement for documented procedures in one document or in several documents. You may respond to one or more requirements for documented procedures in the standard by combining procedures in one document or dividing the subject into several procedures.

Consequences of failure

Without documented practices:

- Everyone has their own interpretation of best practice: there is no uniformity – every job will be executed differently.

- People have to make mistakes before learning the best way to do something.

- The burden of communicating everything verbally gets unworkable.

- Methods cannot be relayed reliably from one person to another or through a chain of command. There is no guarantee that a message will reach its destination uncorrupted.

- Methods will be susceptible to unpredictable variation since the processes that cause the results may be driven by personal motives which may be at variance with the goals of the organization.

- The prevention of error is achieved by chance rather than by design.

- Performance will be adversely affected when key people are absent or when new people join the organization.

- People compensate for the inadequacies by working long hours and doing things themselves rather than depending on others whose job it really is.

- Problems are fixed by focusing on symptoms rather than root causes.

- Fixes are never permanent and the problems eventually recur.

- There will be no guarantee that a person will receive the required inputs to do the job and uncertainty as to whether the outputs were sent to the correct destination.

In business, everything is constrained by requirements, targets, objectives and standards, otherwise businesses would not be businesses for long!

Inconsistency of requirements

- There are requirements for quality system procedures rather than for all the documentation used in the system. The only procedures required are those which are required to be established and maintained by the various clauses of the standard. All other documents should be derived from the established procedures since no other provisions are included in ISO 9001.

- Documented procedures are not required to design and develop the quality system. If it can be shown that the review and approval process produces documents of an inconsistent standard then a nonconformity exists with clause 4.5.2, which addresses the adequacy of documentation.

- Documented procedures are not required to reference the quality records. If the absence of record compilation instructions or cross-references to quality records cause errors in the implementation of the system then a nonconformity is justified on the basis that the procedures are not being effectively implemented, as required by clause 4.2.2b.

• Procedures have to be prepared consistent with the requirements of the standard and the *supplier's quality policy* which conflicts with clause 4.2.1 – which only requires the quality system to ensure that (intended) product conforms with specified requirements. If the quality policy imposes obligations beyond the scope of the standard (for example, personnel safety and environmental issues etc.) then procedures also have to go beyond the standard.

• Documented procedures have to be prepared which are consistent with the requirements of the standard. This could be interpreted as implying that only where the standard requires documented procedures need documented procedures be prepared, or where a procedure is needed to implement a requirement.

• There is an implication that where documented procedures are required they should respond to the requirements of the relevant clause but since it is not explicitly stated, there is no nonconformance if procedures do not respond to every requirement of the relevant clause.

• Suppliers have to implement effectively the quality system and its documented procedures, which could mean that some suppliers might limit their procedures to the requirements of the standard and others might go beyond the requirements of the standard, thereby creating inequality in quality system audits. If the procedures go beyond measures to achieve customer satisfaction then these areas are of no concern to the auditor.

• There is a requirement to implement effectively the quality system and its documented procedures but no requirement to maintain documentary evidence of compliance with the standard. If documentary evidence is not available at the time of the audit there is no nonconformity. The only exception is where the standard requires specific quality records through a cross reference to clause 4.16 and where the stated retention time is more than the period between the creation of the records and the date of the audit.

Tasks for developers

These are addressed in Part 2.

Questions for developers

1 How do you prepare the quality system procedures?
2 How is the degree of documentation required determined?
3 How do you ensure your quality system procedures are consistent with the requirements of ISO 9001 and your quality policy?
4 How do you ensure the documented system is implemented effectively?

Questions for auditors

Procedure development

1 What was your strategy regarding the degree of documentation needed to satisfy ISO 9000?
2 To what extent does the present system utilize documented procedures produced prior to commencing ISO 9000 implementation?
3 In which areas have new practices been introduced?
4 In which areas did you merely document current practices?
5 Who is responsible for maintaining the procedures?
6 Who is responsible for maintaining the job instructions?
7 Who maintains the master list of quality system documentation?
8 How are forms and labels controlled?

Procedure implementation

1 How were the procedures introduced into the organization?
2 What training was given to the staff?
3 What involvement did senior management have in introducing the quality system?
4 To what extent do the staff refer to procedures when carrying out work?
5 What instructional aids are employed to convey the policies and procedures to the staff?
6 What channels of communication are open to staff who have difficulty in understanding the procedures?
7 This requirement is also checked everywhere usually by the questions: 'Would you please show me an example of ...?', 'May I examine the records that ...?' 'Could you produce evidence to demonstrate that ...?'

8 Quality planning

Requirements of ISO 9001 clause 4.2.3

The supplier is required to:

1 Define and document how requirements for quality will be met.

2 Ensure that quality planning is consistent with all other requirements of the quality system.

3 Document quality planning in a format to suit the method of operation.

4 Give consideration to the preparation of quality plans.

5 Give consideration to the identification and acquisition of any controls needed.

6 Give consideration to the identification and acquisition of any processes needed.

7 Give consideration to the identification and acquisition of any equipment and fixtures needed.

8 Give consideration to the identification and acquisition of any resources needed.

9 Give consideration to the identification and acquisition of any skills needed.

10 Give consideration to ensuring the compatibility of the design and applicable documentation with specified requirements.

11 Give consideration to the compatibility of the production, installation and servicing process and applicable documentation with specified requirements.

12 Give consideration to the compatibility of inspection and test procedures with specified requirements.

13 Give consideration to the updating of quality control, inspection and test techniques.

14 Give consideration to the development of new instrumentation.

15 Give consideration to the identification of any measurement capabilities.

16 Give consideration to the identification of appropriate verification.

17 Give consideration to the clarification of standards of acceptability.

18 Give consideration to the identification and preparation of quality records.

Purpose of requirements

The purpose of quality planning is to determine the provisions required to ensure that particular requirements for products and services will be achieved by the organization and to identify where the provisions of the existing quality system may need to be changed.

Guidance on interpretation

Applicability

The requirements apply to the organization's management responsible for executing orders, contracts or projects. They apply where the quality system has to be tailored to meet customer requirements. They only apply to product or service quality, not to internal quality improvement programmes. These are covered (indirectly) by the corrective and preventive action requirements.

Application

The quality system developed to meet the requirements of ISO 9000 is likely to be a generic system, not specific to any particular product, project or contract other than the range of products and services which your organization supplies. By implementing the policies and procedures of the documented quality system, product-, project- or contract-specific plans, procedures, specifications etc. are generated. For a given product, project or contract there will be specific product, project or contract requirements and it is these requirements to which this clause of the standard refers.

Requirements for quality

The requirements for quality are the objectives which the organization is committed to achieve through the contract. See also ISO 8402.

Giving consideration

The standard requires that *the supplier gives consideration* to a number of activities as appropriate but it does not define when such consideration should be given. If you intend to submit a fixed price tender to a customer, then preparing detailed plans of what you are going to do for the price *before* you submit your bid is giving appropriate consideration to planning. Likewise, identifying controls, ordering equipment and materials, etc. in good time, before you need them, is giving appropriate consideration. That is, anticipating what you may need and initiating its acquisition beforehand will prevent you from having delays and problems when you embark upon the work.

Quality plans

Quality plans are needed when the work you intend to carry out requires detailed planning beyond that already planned for by the quality system. The quality system documentation will not specify everything you need to do for every job. You will need to define the specific documentation to be produced, tests, inspections and reviews to be performed and resources to be employed.

Consequences of failure

Failing to plan for quality will result in requirements for quality being achieved by chance and not design. The required tasks will not be assigned, customer requirements will be unlikely to be conveyed to the point of implementation effectively and processes, equipment, tooling, skills etc. may not be appropriate to enable you to meet specific customer requirements. Failing to plan is likely to result in delays and rejection of product or service by the customer as it becomes clear that you have not supplied what the customer required. In your contract, or agreement, you make a promise to the customer – failing to plan for quality is likely to result in you not fulfilling your promise. In other words you will not have done what you said you would do.

Inconsistency of requirements

- Documented procedures are not required for quality planning. If it can be shown that the review and approval process produces quality planning documents of an inconsistent standard which reduces system effectiveness then a nonconformity exists with clause 4.5.2 which addresses the adequacy of documentation.

- If a supplier's quality system included provisions beyond the standard then the quality planning requirements require that the quality planning be consistent with the quality system and it therefore cannot be restricted to compliance with the standard. If the quality system addresses typical contract requirements which are beyond the standard, where quality planning does not address these requirements, there is a nonconformity.

- The standard requires that the supplier gives consideration to several activities in meeting specified requirements for products, projects or contracts but does not require that the result of giving such consideration be defined and documented. The auditor has to obtain reasoned argument from the auditee that consideration was given to the topics in clause 4.2.3 and, for reasons given, that the course of action taken was decided.

Tasks for developers

1 Don't produce project/product specific procedures which conflict with the established quality system.

2 Create a mechanism for preparing quality plans if your quality system has to be tailored to suit each product, contract or project.

3 Produce and agree resource budgets for implementing the quality plan.

4 Review quality plans at each stage of the product/project life cycle for continued suitability.

Questions to stimulate policies

1 In what manner do you define and document how the requirements for quality will be met?

2 How do you ensure that quality planning is consistent with other requirements of the quality system?

3 How do you determine whether a quality plan is required for products, projects or contracts?

4 How do you ensure that standards of acceptability for all features, including those containing a subjective element, are clarified before work commences?

5 How do you ensure that the design, production process, installation, servicing, inspection and test procedures and applicable documentation are compatible with the specified requirements?

6 How do you identify and acquire any controls, processes, equipment, fixtures, resources and skills that may be needed to achieve the required quality?

7 How do you identify whether any quality control, inspection and testing techniques and instrumentation requires updating to meet specified requirements?

8 How do you identify measurement requirements involving a capability that exceeds the known state of the art in sufficient time for the capability to be developed?

9 How do you identify verification requirements and plan their implementation at the appropriate stages?

10 How do you identify and prepare any new quality records that are needed to meet specified requirements?

Questions for auditors

1 Who is responsible for determining how the requirements for quality are to be met?

2 How is the quality system applied when you receive customer orders?

3 What provision have you made to permit deviations from the system documentation to meet variations in customer needs?

4 What planning activities are carried out before work on a new contract commences?

5   In what documents are the planning provisions defined?

6   What new controls, processes, equipment, resources and skills did you identify as being needed to meet this contract?

7   How did you go about identifying the risk areas and what do you do about them?

8   How do you ensure compatibility between design, production and inspection documentation for this contract?

9   What standards and regulations do you normally have to comply with to meet your customer's requirements?

10 Where a contract invoked a new standard or regulation, how do you ensure these requirements are conveyed to the point of implementation?

11 What provisions have you made for planning reviews by the implementers prior to commencement of work?

12 How do you identify a need to change your inspection and test techniques for particular contracts?

13 How do you identify whether any new measurement capability will be required?

14 Where a new measurement capability is required, how is the capability acquired?

15 How do you identify the verification measures needed to confirm that customer requirements have been met?

16 In what documents are the verification requirements defined?

17 How do you ensure these requirements are implemented at appropriate stages of product development and production?

18 How are these requirements conveyed to staff assigned to verification activities?

19 How are standards of acceptability for the product or service established?

20 What provisions have been made for any new quality records needed to capture objective evidence of conformity with the contract requirements?

9 Contract review procedures

Requirements of ISO 9001 clause 4.3.1

The supplier is required to:

1 Establish and maintain documented procedures for contract review.

2 Establish and maintain procedures for the co-ordination of contract review activities.

Purpose of requirements

The purpose of contract review procedures is to implement policy and regulate processes which are essential to the business.

Guidance on interpretation

Applicability

The requirements apply to the organization's management. No tailoring is needed for specific industries although the content will vary and this is addressed in the next chapter. They do not apply to ordering product from your suppliers – this activity is governed by the purchasing requirements of the standard.

Application

Where an organization does not operate through formal customers' orders or contracts the requirements should be interpreted as applying to the transaction between the organization and its 'customers': i.e. the people who use its services and the people or authorities who dictate what services will be provided. Such transactions may be verbal or written.

The customer does not have to document the contract but you do. Often the person in the organization receiving the request takes the responsibility for defining and documenting it.

Co-ordination of reviews

A person charged with taking orders over the telephone can make this decision alone providing he/she is provided with the necessary criteria such as a listing of the company's products and services and minimum delivery times and prices. Procedures should detail the method for dealing with exceptions.

Consequences of failure

Without a procedure for reviewing tenders and contracts, you are more likely either to make promises you can't fulfil or not to respond to the needs of the customer. Documented procedures for this activity will bring about consistency in the decisions on whether to submit a tender or accept a contract. They are a means of conveying to those responsible the policies and practices that will prevent expensive mistakes.

Inconsistency of requirements

Procedures have to be established for contract review and for the co-ordination of these activities but not to achieve any particular purpose. The contract review procedures should ensure that the only contracts that are accepted are those which the supplier has the capability of executing to the customer's satisfaction.

Tasks for developers

- Prepare a procedure for conducting formal contract reviews.

- Determine which functions in the organization should participate in contract reviews.

- Decide how you will obtain input, comment and participation in contract reviews.

- Determine who should receive copies of the contract.

- Establish criteria for determining whether sufficient information has been provided in the contract.

- Establish a means for the reviewers to determine whether your organization has the capability to meet the contract requirements.

Questions to stimulate policies

1 What procedures have been established and documented for contract review?

2 How do you co-ordinate contract reviews?

Questions for auditors

1 How are potential customers persuaded to place orders or invitation to tender?

2 Who is responsible for handling customer enquiries?

3 What types of enquiries are received?

4 What is the process that is followed on receipt of a customer enquiry?

5 In what form are customer requirements conveyed to the organization?

6 How are contracts negotiated?

7 Who is involved in the negotiation process?

8 How do you co-ordinate the inputs from those who will be involved in the execution of a contract?

9 Who has authority for accepting contracts or orders?

10 In what document is this process defined?

10   Contract and tender review

Requirements of ISO 9001 clause 4.3.2

The supplier is required to:

1   Review tenders before submission.

2   Review contracts before acceptance.

3   Ensure that requirements are adequately defined and documented before acceptance.

4   Ensure that order requirements are agreed before acceptance.

5   Ensure that differences between tender and contract/order requirements are resolved before acceptance.

6   Ensure capability to meet contract/order requirements before tender submission or contract acceptance.

Purpose of requirements

The purpose of these requirements is to prevent the organization from entering into a commitment with its customers that it may fail to meet.

Guidance on interpretation

Applicability

The requirements apply to the organization's management with responsibility for order input. Tailoring is necessary for specific industries. They do not apply to purchase orders you send to your suppliers – this activity is governed by the purchasing requirements of the standard.

Application

This is one of the most important requirements of the standard as its implementation should result in a definition of requirements that will enable both customer and supplier to determine the quality of the products and services supplied.

The review should verify that you understand the customer requirements and have the capability of meeting them. To do this you need to ensure that those performing the review have access to sufficient reliable information on which to make the decision.

The review may be conducted with the customer over the telephone, may be a meeting between those involved in the execution of the contract, or may be carried out remotely by sending the information received from the customer to those involved and by requesting comment on its acceptability.

In service organizations, the review may be scheduled at defined intervals and not on receipt of each request for service. Agreed requirements may be documented in *Service Level Agreements* in which both parties agree on the services to be provided and the criteria for judging an acceptable level of service.

It is your responsibility to ensure you understand what the customer wants, not that of the customer.

Consequences of failure

Failure to review tenders before submission and contacts before acceptance is likely to result in you making promises you can't fulfil or not responding to the needs of your customer. If you don't know your capability, you can't make promises that you can fulfil. If you don't document your agreement with your customer, you may find that the customer complains that you have not supplied what was asked for. If you don't take the time to find out what the customer wants and what the product or service will be used for, you may find the goods are returned or request of payment refused. Without a definition of requirements, the question of what is acceptable or unacceptable quality becomes subjective and open to interpretation.

Inconsistency of requirements

The standard requires the supplier to have the ability to meet contract requirements rather than meet specified requirements for the product. Where evidence is found that the supplier does not have the ability to meet a contract requirement, regardless of it affecting product quality, a non-conformity is justified against clause 4.3.2c.

Tasks for developers

1 Define what constitutes a contract for your organization.

2 Determine when a formal review of a contract is necessary.

3 Determine what constitutes a review of a contract.

4 Don't accept any contract unless you have established that you have the capability to satisfy its requirements, you have agreement on the payment to be made on completion and when completion is required.

5 Don't allow your sales people to make promises the factory cannot fulfil.

6 If the customer has not given precise details of what he/she wants, do establish how the customer intends to use the product or service before accepting the order.

7 Establish what constitutes acceptance by the customer.

8 Ensure that those determining compliance with contracts have access to current versions of the contract.

9 Read the small print and any reference documents before you accept the contract.

10 Declare any areas where your offer differs from that required and state the reasons in terms advantageous to the customer.

11 Establish the boundaries affecting what you and the customer are responsible for.

12 Don't make promises to your customer that your staff will not be able to honour.

13 Check your sources of data, prices, technical specification etc. that they are current and applicable to the specific terms of the contract.

Questions to stimulate policies

1 How do you ensure that tenders are reviewed before submission?

2 How do you ensure that contracts are reviewed before acceptance?

3 How do you ensure that requirements are adequately defined and documented before accepting a contract?

4 How do you ensure that requirements differing from those in the tender are resolved before accepting a contract?

5 How do you ensure that you have the capability to meet the contractual requirements before accepting a contract?

6 What do you do if the customer cannot specify exactly his/her requirements?

Questions for auditors

Definition of requirements

1 In what documents are the customer requirements defined?

2 What criteria do you use to establish that the requirements are adequately defined prior to their acceptance?

3 What action is taken should the requirements be inadequately defined or be unacceptable?

4 Who participates in the review process?

5 In what document are the responsibilities of the participants defined?

6 How are the customer requirements conveyed to those involved in the review?

7 How do the review participants indicate their acceptance of the conditions?

8 What action is taken should a participant query or not accept any conditions of the contract?

9 Who is authorized to communicate directly with the customer?

10 How you do indicate acceptance of customer requirements?

11 Should you receive verbal orders, how might these be dealt with?

12 How do you indicate that verbal orders have been accepted?

13 Under what circumstances would a contract be accepted without formal review?

14 How often is the contract review process repeated?

Resolving differences

1 In what situations would you submit tenders before award of a contract?

2 How are tenders processed?

3 What checks are carried out on receipt of a contract resulting from a tender you submitted?

4 In what documents are the anomalies defined?

5 How are differences between the tender and the contract resolved with the customer?

6 At what stage in the negotiations is work permitted to proceed?

7 What action is taken should the differences between the tender and the contract not be resolved?

Capability

1 How do the personnel reviewing tenders or contacts determine the organization's capability needed to meet customer requirements?

2 How do the personnel accepting contracts or orders know whether the organization has the capability to meet the customer's requirements?

3 How is this information conveyed to these personnel?

4 What action is taken should the necessary capability not be available?

5 What risks, limitations or unusual demands have been identified in the execution of this contract?

6 How are staff made aware of the risks, limitations and unusual demands of a contract?

7 During the duration of a contract, what measures are taken to ensure the company remains capable of satisfying the customer's requirements?

8 How would the customer become aware of circumstances that adversely affect your obligations under a contract?

9 In what document are these processes defined?

11   Contract amendment

Requirements of ISO 9001 clause 4.3.3

The supplier is required to:

1   Identify how contract amendments are made.

2   Identify how contract amendments are correctly transferred to the functions concerned.

Purpose of requirements

The purpose of controlling the contract amendment process is two-fold: to prevent unauthorized changes being made to agreed contracts thus resulting in a situation in which neither the customer or the company benefit, and to ensure that any required changes to the product, service or process are implemented promptly.

Guidance on interpretation

Applicability

A contract amendment is any change to the original agreement that is conveyed to you from the customer's designated representative.

Application

Amendments to contract need to be legitimate by being issued by the customer's designated representative. If changes come from other customer representatives you need to ensure that they are legitimate and the best way to do this is for the changes to carry the signature of the authorized person.

Consequences of failure

If you don't control the contract-amendment process you may find that changes have been accepted by your staff without proper authorization – resulting in commitments that cannot be honoured within the original price. If you don't ensure that amendments get to the place where they are implemented, the customer may well reject the supplies as nonconforming.

Inconsistency of requirements

- Suppliers have to identify how an amendment to a contract is made but not define this in documented procedures. As a contract, if documented, is governed by the requirements for document and data control, procedures for changing contracts are required by virtue of the requirements of clause 4.5.1.

- There is no requirement for contract amendments to be documented. An amendment to a contract is a change to a document which relates to the requirements of the standard and therefore comes within the provisions of clause 4.5.3 on changes to documents. Whilst the amendment itself does not have to be documented the change to the document does have to be approved prior to issue.

- There is no requirement to review the amendment to contract before acceptance, only to review it prior to issue, as stated in clause 4.5.2. An amendment to a contract creates a different contract and therefore it is required to be reviewed before acceptance.

Tasks for developers

1   Make provision in your procedures for verifying the legitimacy of contract amendments before processing them.

2   Issue contract amendments on the same distribution list as the original contract.

3 Don't imply acceptance of a change to contract in any communication other than a formal contract amendment.

4 Prepare a contract amendment procedure covering incoming and outgoing amendments.

Questions to stimulate policies

1 How are changes in tender requirements conveyed to those preparing the tender?

2 How are amendments to contracts made?

3 How do you ensure that contract amendments are correctly transferred to the functions concerned?

Questions for auditors

1 In what form are contract amendments conveyed to the organization?

2 What action is taken on receipt of a contract amendment?

3 Under what circumstances would an amendment not be processed through the contract review procedure?

4 How is the existence of a contract amendment denoted in the contract documentation?

5 How are staff made aware of an amendment to contract?

6 How do you indicate to your customer that you have accepted a contract amendment?

12 Contract and tender review records

Requirements of ISO 9001 clause 4.3.4

The supplier is required to

1 Maintain records of contract reviews.

Purpose of requirements

The purpose of maintaining records of contract and tender reviews is to document the basis on which the contract was accepted or tender submitted so that it serves as a legitimate point of reference for commencing and conducting work and delivering supplies.

Consequences of failure

Without a record of the tender or contract review, you have no objective evidence to show what was agreed. Without this evidence, you are reliant on memory. The documents you have may well define all the requirements but unless you have evidence that these documents are the ones that were reviewed and accepted, you may be working to the wrong documents and hence may not meet customer requirements or initiate work for which there is no requirement.

Guidance on interpretation

Applicability

The requirement applies to the records of a formal review of tenders, contracts or orders received from external customers. They do not apply to records of a review of purchase orders you send to your suppliers – this activity is governed by the purchasing requirements of the standard.

Application

The tender and contract review record may be as simple as a signature on the contract by your authorized representative. It may also take the form of minutes of a meeting or a completed questionnaire or the documented comments of those involved in the review process. If a combination of these methods is used, you need to retain all the results, not just the contract with a signature.

Inconsistency of requirements

The content of contract review records is not specified so it can be an acceptance mark on a contract/order or a file of contract negotiations. The records need to demonstrate that the requirements of clause 4.3.2 were met as applicable, otherwise they do not conform to the definition of quality records in ISO 8402.

Tasks for developers

1 Establish who will hold the records of contract reviews, where they will be filed and who will have access to them.

Questions to stimulate policies

1 In what documents do you record the results of tender reviews?

2 In what documents do you record the results of contract reviews?

3 Where are the channels of communication and interface with the customer's organization defined?

Questions for auditors

1   What records are maintained of tender/contract review?

2   Where are the records stored?

3   Who has access to these records?

4   Where does it define the requirements that were agreed?

5   Where does it indicate who was involved in the review process?

6   Where does it indicate the conclusion that the organization has the capability to meet the customer requirements?

7   Where does it indicate who accepted the tender for submission?

8   Where does it indicate who accepted the contract?

13 Design control procedures

Requirements of ISO 9001 clause 4.4.1

The supplier is required to:

1 Establish and maintain documented procedures to control the design of product.

2 Establish and maintain documented procedures to verify the design of product.

Purpose of requirements

The purpose of design control is to prevent design commencing without agreed requirements and to prevent the release of designs that do not meet user needs and/or requirements.

The purpose of design control procedures is to implement policy and regulate processes which are essential to the business.

Guidance on interpretation

Applicability

The requirements apply to the core products or services designed by the organization for sale to its customers (its outputs) and not to any support or ancillary products which are not offered for sale, such as tools and test equipment or internal services. All the requirements of element 4.4 apply to the same core products and services and should not be indiscriminately applied to internal outputs of the organization. They do not, for instance, apply to the design tooling, test equipment, internal training courses unless of course these are offered for sale to external customers. Tailoring is necessary for specific industries.

Application

Design control procedures should control the design process and not inhibit creativity. Design is a process with discrete steps that are not necessarily intuitive to designers. The actual design activity is but one step in a process from design input through to design output. The design is not complete until it has been verified as meeting the input requirements. It should not be assumed that because an individual is a qualified designer, he/she will know intuitively the sequence of activities that are required to create a design that meets customer requirements and company standards and to design a product that is saleable, economical to produce, safe, maintainable and reliable, etc. such that it is ready for production by the date specified.

Scope of procedures

The design control procedures required should cover all the requirements of element 4.4. There could be one procedure to cover the complete process or several procedures, either one for each clause (which would be unusual) or a number of procedures that addressed the various stages and activities of the design process (which is more common). Separate procedures may be necessary for hardware, software and service design.

To control any design activity there are ten primary steps in the design process:

1 Establish the customer needs.

2 Convert the customer needs into a definitive specification of the requirements.

3 Plan for meeting the requirements.

4 Organize resources and materials for meeting the requirements.

5 Conduct a feasibility study to discover whether accomplishment of the requirements is feasible.

6 Conduct a project definition study to discover which of the many possible solutions will be the most suitable.

7 Develop a specification which details all the features and characteristics of the product or service.

8 Produce a prototype or model of the proposed design.

9   Conduct extensive trails to discover whether the product or service which has been developed meets the design requirements and customer needs.

10 Feed data back into the design and repeat the process until the product or service is proven to be fit for the task.

Consequences of failure

Without procedures for controlling design you are at the mercy of the designer who, without constraints, may not deliver a design that is economical to produce when you want it. Without procedures there is a distinct possibility that others working on the design will not receive the right information, do the right things or provide the right inputs. Without control of design, costs will escalate and time-scales will be exceeded. And finally, you may be provided with a design for which there is no requirement, no market or no capability to deliver.

Inconsistency of requirements

- The standard requires procedures for design control and verification implying that design control does not include verification. In principle design control does include design verification and validation because the design verification and validation is the measurement component of the design process.

- The design control element covers design verification and design validation but the procedures only have to cover design verification. This is an oversight since the design output has to be expressed in terms that can be verified and validated so procedures should cover both.

Tasks for developers

1   Set standards for design documentation and stick to them.

2   Identify the types of products and services which the organization designs.

3   Determine the processes by which customer requirements or market needs are translated into a set of specifications for a particular product or service.

4   Analyse these processes and identify the discrete tasks which are performed.

5   Prepare procedures to control these tasks and the interfaces between them.

6   Prepare or select guides and standards which assist designers to select proven technologies, parts, materials, methods etc.

7   Determine a methodology for identifying and specifying the documentation requirements for design activities covering system design, hardware design, software design, service design etc.

8   Determine a methodology for design and development which integrates the major design tasks from the feasibility phase to the production phase.

9   Determine the design controls you intend to impose over the design of test equipment, tools, test rigs and other articles.

Questions to stimulate policies

1   What procedures have been established and documented to control and verify product design?

2   How do you control and verify product design?

Questions for auditors

1   What is the scope of design activities within the company?

2   What products and services does the organization design specifically for its customers?

3   Who is responsible for the organization's design activities?

4   What is the process for translating customer requirements into a set of specifications for a particular product or service?

5   In what way does the process differ when designing products for the market in general?

6   Where is test equipment, plant and other supporting equipment designed?

7   In what document is your design capability defined?

8   To what extent are design staff involved in the contract review process?

9   What action is taken when a contract requires a design capability beyond that available in the organization?

10 In what document are the design processes defined?

14   Design and development planning

Requirements of ISO 9001 clause 4.4.2

The supplier is required to:

1   Prepare plans for each design and development activity.

2   Describe or reference design and development activities in the design and development plans.

3   Define the responsibility for design and development activities in the design and development plans.

4   Assign design and development activities to qualified personnel.

5   Equip design and development personnel with adequate resources.

6   Update design and development plans as the design evolves.

Purpose of requirements

The purpose of these requirements is to provide a means of defining the activities needed to produce, verify and validate a design which meets the specified requirements.

Guidance on interpretation

Applicability

These requirements apply to any preparatory activities carried out before commencing design of a product or service. You should prepare a design and development plan for each new design and also for any modification of an existing design which radically changes the performance of the product or service. For modifications which marginally change performance, control of the changes required may be accomplished through your design change procedures.

Application

One plans in order to achieve objectives – the objectives in this case are the design input requirements.

The plans should identify as a minimum:

- The design requirements.

- The design and development programme showing activities against time.

- The work packages and names of those who will execute them. (Work packages are the parcels of work that are to be handed out either internally or to subcontractors.)

- The work-breakdown structure showing the relationship between all the parcels of work.

- The reviews to be held for authorizing work to proceed from stage to stage.

- The resources in terms of finance, manpower and facilities.

- The risks to success and the plans to minimize them.

- The controls (quality plan or procedures and standards) that will be exercised to keep the design on course.

Supplementary plans

Your design and development plans may also have to be subdivided into plans for special aspects of the design, such as reliability plans, maintainability plans, safety engineering plans, electromagnetic compatibility plans, configuration management plans, software development plans etc.

Updating the plan

It is not unusual for plans to be produced and then, as design gets underway, problems are encountered which require a change in direction. When this occurs the original plans should be changed. Assessors will be looking to see that your current design and development activities match those in the approved plans.

Consequences of failure

Without a development plan, the design will proceed informally and may never reach a conclusion; it may be under-resourced, late and the various groups involved will have no common point of reference to guide them in what they have to do and when their outputs are to be delivered. Staff will be unprepared for reviews and the project will lose its direction. By not keeping the plan current, you run the risk of staff working to obsolete information – by using other means to convey change, you run the risk of staff using the wrong information.

Inconsistency of requirements

- The standard requires the supplier to prepare plans for each design and development activity but does not require that these plans be documented and implemented. As the system has to be documented it follows that design and development plans have to be documented as they are part of the system and clause 4.2.2a requires the system to be implemented.

- Design and development activities are required to be assigned to qualified personnel equipped with adequate resources which duplicates the combined requirements of clause 4.1.2.2 and 4.18. If a nonconformity is detected on the assignment of qualified or trained personnel or the adequacy of resources the best clause should be chosen but the auditor should not prepare separate nonconformity statements against clauses 4.4.2, 4.1.2.2 and 4.18.

Tasks for developers

- Involve the specialists as soon as possible, since the later they start the more redesign will result.

- Allow for designs to fail design verification in your development plans – never assume designs can be produced right first time.

- Don't assume that a proven design will necessarily be suitable for other applications.

- Don't use unproven material, components or processes in new designs unless you plan to evaluate and qualify them before production commences.

- Determine who is to carry out which design task before you start design.

- Establish a mechanism of reviewing progress through the design and development process for in-house designs and subcontracted designs.

- Create a procedure for controlling the allocation of work packages to various design groups and to subcontractors.

- Prepare procedures for the preparation and maintenance of design and development plans.

- Prepare procedures for creating speciality plans covering reliability, safety, environmental engineering etc.

- Prepare standard requirements for subcontracted design activities which specify the documentation requirements.

Questions to stimulate policies

1   In which documents have you identified the responsibility for each design and development activity?

2   How do you ensure that the design and development plans are updated as the design evolves?

3   How do you ensure that design and verification activities are planned and assigned to qualified personnel equipped with adequate resources?

Questions for auditors

Design plans

1   How is design work initiated?

2   How do you determine the resources and activities required to produce a design which meets customer requirements?

3   How do you determine how long a design project will take?

4   How are funds allocated to new designs?

5   What are the means for granting approval for designs to continue through the various phases of design?

6   How do you determine which group in the organization is to be involved in the design?

7   In what documents are the provisions made to produce and verify a design documented?

8   How are these plans conveyed to those concerned and commitment to their accomplishment obtained?

Allocation of design work

1   How do you allocate design work to groups and individual designers?

2   How do you know these groups and individuals are qualified to do the work?

3   How do you know that these groups and individuals have adequate resources to accomplish the design work in the time allocated?

Design monitoring

1   What measures are taken to ensure design projects proceed as planned?

2   How do you know whether design activities are on schedule?

3   How often are progress meetings held on a design?

4   What action is taken should the programme slip behind schedule?

Changes to design plans

1   Under what circumstances is the design plan changed?

2   How often is the plan updated?

3   How do you make changes to the plan and convey these to those concerned?

15 Organization and technical interfaces

Requirements of ISO 9001 clause 4.4.3

The supplier is required to:

1 Define and document the organizational interfaces between groups in the design process.

2 Define and document the technical interfaces between groups in the design process.

3 Transmit organizational interface information to groups which input to the design process.

4 Transmit technical interface information to groups which input to the design process.

5 Regularly review organizational interface information.

6 Regularly review technical interface information.

Purpose of requirements

The purpose of these requirements is to communicate organizational and technical requirements to those assigned to execute them.

Guidance on interpretation

Applicability

Organizational interfaces refer to the relationships between organizations both internal and external to the organization. Technical interfaces refer to the relationships between components within the end product and between the end product and those it will interface with in-service

Organizational interfaces

In your design procedures you should identify where work passes from one organization to another and the means you use to convey the requirements, such as work instructions.

Technical interfaces

Within each development specification the technical interfaces between systems, subsystems, equipment etc. should be specified so they function properly.

Consequences of failure

By not defining the organizational interfaces, staff on the project will be unaware of where their inputs come from and their output go and where to obtain information and send it. Document distribution then becomes a hit or miss process with those with the greater need possibly not receiving the right data, thus causing project delay.

By not defining the technical interfaces, the components may not fit together when assembled – physical inputs may not match, resulting in incompatibility and, hence, product failure.

Inconsistency of requirements

Organizational and technical interface information is required to be documented but the resources to implement the design and development plan do not have to be documented. Clause 4.4.2 requires the design and development activities to be assigned to qualified personnel equipped with adequate resources. Such resources should be identified to meet the requirements of clause 4.1.2.2 so, if they are not documented, their adequacy cannot be verified.

Tasks for developers

1 Give all relevant groups in the organization the opportunity to contribute to the design process.

2 Produce procedures and standards governing technical interface specifications, their preparation, promulgation and maintenance.

3 Set up an interface control board to review and evaluate technical interface data.

Questions to stimulate policies

1 How do you identify, document, transmit and regularly review the organizational and technical interfaces between different design groups?

Questions for auditors

Organizational interfaces

1 Which departments participate in the design process?

2 What measures are taken to co-ordinate the interfaces between the various design groups?

3 To what extent are design subcontractors employed?

4 How do you select your design subcontractors?

5 How are design responsibilities allocated to subcontractors?

6 How are the design activities of subcontractors monitored?

7 How is design information conveyed to internal design personnel?

8 In what documents are these organizational interfaces defined?

9 How often is this organizational interface information reviewed?

10 Who reviews the organizational interface data?

Technical interfaces

1   How do you ensure that no incompatibility of technical interfaces arise during the design process?

2   How are designers made aware of product features being created by others that may affect their design?

3   In what documents are the technical interfaces defined?

4   How often are these interface documents reviewed?

5   Who reviews the technical interface data?

6   Should changes be required, how are these conveyed to those affected?

16   Design input

Requirements of ISO 9001 clause 4.4.4

The supplier is required to:

1   Identify and document design input requirements relating to the product.

2   Identify and document statutory and regulatory requirements relating to the product.

3   Review for adequacy the selection of design input information.

4   Resolve incomplete, ambiguous or conflicting requirements with those responsible.

5   Take into consideration the results of contract reviews in documenting design input requirements.

Purpose of requirements

The purpose of these requirements is to provide a means of establishing design requirements for determining the acceptability of the design solution.

Guidance on interpretation

Applicability

The requirements apply to the requirements imposed upon the design – the design requirements for the product or service. They are more than a statement of function – they are details that will constrain the design and so result in an output that is fit for its purpose.

Application

The design input requirements may be specified in a contract or other agreement or in standards and other documents referenced in the contract or agreement. As a supplier, you have a responsibility to establish your customer requirements and expectations.

To identify design input requirements you need to identify:

- The purpose of the product or service

- The conditions under which it will be used, stored and transported

- The skills and category of those who will use and maintain the product or service

- The countries to which it will be sold

- The special features and characteristics which the customer requires the product or service to exhibit

- The constraints in terms of time-scale, operating environment, cost, size, weight or other factors

- The standards with which the product or service needs to comply

- The products or service with which it will directly and indirectly interface and their features and characteristics

- The documentation required of the design output necessary to manufacture, procure, inspect, test, install, operate and maintain a product or service

Statutory and regulatory requirements

Statutory and regulatory requirements are those which apply in the country to which the product or service is to be supplied. Just because such requirements are not specified in the contract doesn't mean you don't have to meet them. Regulatory requirements may apply to health and safety, environmental emissions and electromagnetic compatibility and these often require accompanying certification of compliance. If you intend exporting the product or service, it would be prudent to determine the regulations which would apply before you complete the design requirement.

Consequences of failure

Failing to define the design input requirements will almost inevitably result in a design that does not fulfil the need. The need has to be defined in terms that enable the right product or service to be designed – brevity, whilst economic, often results in misunderstanding. Failure to identify statutory and regulatory requirements can result in a refusal to grant an export licence or imprisonment in certain cases if you are found noncompliant following shipment of the product.

Inconsistency of requirements

- The design input requirements do not have to be reviewed for adequacy before implementation. Whilst not explicitly stated in this clause of the standard, since design input documents are those which relate to the requirements of the standard, the requirements of clause 4.5.2 do apply.

- There is no requirement for design input requirements to include user needs and/or requirements although the design output has to meet design input and must be expressed in terms that can be validated against user needs. This is an oversight and any approved and issued design input documentation that did not include user needs and/or requirements would be inadequate under clause 4.5.2.

- There is no requirement for design input requirements to include design verification requirements. Where verification requirements are absent from contracts, the supplier needs to have established that there are no customer verification requirements as part of the contract review process. This is all part of establishing that they have the capability of meeting the customer's requirements. Auditors therefore need to verify that design verification was considered during the contract review if verification requirements were omitted from the design input documents.

Tasks for developers

1   Don't commence design without a written and agreed requirement.

2   Don't give designers a wish list – be specific about the purpose of the product/service.

3   Maintain the design requirement document even after you have produced the product specification.

4   Produce procedures and standards governing the specification of development requirements for components of the design.

5   Produce procedures which regulate the specification of design (input) requirements and the documentation of product specifications and drawings.

6   Determine how you will establish what regulatory requirements apply in the countries to which you expect your products to be exported.

Questions to stimulate policies

1   How do you identify, document and review design input requirements including applicable statutory and regulatory requirements?

2   How do you ensure that the selection of design input requirements is reviewed for adequacy.

3   How do you resolve incomplete, ambiguous or conflicting design input requirements?

4   How do you ensure that design inputs take into consideration the results of contract reviews?

Questions for auditors

1   How do you determine the design input requirements for a particular product or service?

2   What factors constitute design input requirements?

3   How do you determine your customer's needs and expectations regarding product design features?

4   How are you made aware of the results of contract reviews?

5 What statutory and regulatory requirements do you normally have to comply with for these designs?

6 What additional requirements does the company impose beyond those imposed by the customer?

7 What action would be taken should applicable national and international standards not be invoked in a contract?

8 What measures are taken to ensure that the design input requirements are adequate before design work commences?

9 Who reviews and approves design input requirements?

10 What action is taken should the requirements be incomplete, ambiguous or in conflict?

11 In what documents are these requirements defined?

12 To whom are the design input requirement documents distributed?

17 Design output

Requirements of ISO 9001 clause 4.4.5

The supplier is required to:

1 Document design output.

2 Express design output in terms that can be verified and validated against design input requirements.

3 Ensure that design output meets design input requirements.

4 Ensure design output contains or makes reference to acceptance criteria.

5 Identify characteristics that are crucial to the safe and proper functioning of the product.

6 Review design output documents before release.

Purpose of requirements

The purpose of these requirements is to provide a means for describing the design solution and preventing its release before its acceptability has been established.

Guidance on interpretation

Applicability

The requirements apply to the product of the design process – all of the results not only the specifications and drawings needed to make the product or deliver the service, but also the reports, analyses, calculations and other outputs that serve to demonstrate that the design meets the requirements. The product descriptions, handbooks, operating manuals, user guides and other documents which support the product or service in use are as much a part of the design as the other product requirements.

Application

Expressing the requirements in terms that can be verified and validated has two meanings. You have to be able to verify that both design input requirements and user requirements (if different) have been achieved in the product, so they need to be expressed in appropriate terms. The vehicle to contain such requirements is usually a Product or Service Specification. You also need to be able to verify that the design output meets the design input and to achieve this you will need to document your calculations and analyses.

Product specifications

Product specifications should specify requirements for the manufacture, assembly and installation of the product in a manner that provides acceptance criteria for inspection and test. Where there are several documents which make up the product specification there should be an overall listing which relates documents to one another.

Design calculations

In performing design calculations, it is important that the status of the design on which the calculations are based is recorded. When there are changes in the design these calculations may need to be repeated.

Design analyses

Analyses are types of calculations but may be comparative studies, predictions and estimations. Examples are stress analysis, reliability analysis, hazard analysis. Analyses are often performed to detect whether the design has any inherent modes of failure and to predict the probability of occurrence. The analyses assist in design improvement and the prevention of failure, hazard, deterioration and other adverse conditions.

Acceptance criteria

Acceptance criteria are the requirements which, if met, will deem the product acceptable. Every requirement should be stated in such a way that it can be verified. Characteristics should be specified in measurable terms with tolerances or min/max limits. These limits should be such that will ensure that all production versions will perform to the product specification and that such limits are well within the limits to which the design has been tested.

Consequences of failure

A failure to adequately document the design output is likely to result in a product that is not fit for purpose. A lack of attention to acceptance criteria, crucial characteristics, design analyses etc. will give rise to problems in design verification. The measures are intended to prevent problems later when their correction is costly.

Inconsistency of requirements

Design output documents are not required to be approved before release. Auditors should verify that design output documents are governed by the document and data control procedures which should require both their review and approval before being released.

Tasks for developers

1   Produce procedures which govern the generation, proving and publication of product/service support documents such as handbooks, operating instructions etc.

Questions to stimulate policies

1   How do you document design output requirements?

2   What evidence is there to show that design output can be verified and validated against the design input requirements?

3   How do you ensure that the design output contains or references acceptance criteria?

4   How do you identify those characteristics of the design that are crucial to the safe and proper functioning of the product?

5   How do you ensure that design output documents are reviewed before release?

Questions for auditors

1 In what documents are the design output requirements defined?

2 Which functions contribute to the design output documentation?

3 How are the requirements conveyed to these functions?

4 What standards and procedures are used to govern the format and content of design output documents?

5 What is the process for producing, reviewing and approving design output documentation?

6 What types of documents comprise the total design output documentation?

7 In what documents are the product characteristics specified?

8 In what documents are the acceptance criteria specified?

9 In what documents are the installation requirements specified?

10 In what documents are the user and maintenance requirements specified?

11 In what documents are the safety, handling, storage and disposal requirements specified?

12 What calculations and analyses are performed to verify that the design output documents reflect a product that meets the input requirements?

13 In what documents are the results of these checks recorded?

14 What checks are performed to verify that the design documentation reflects a product that can be manufactured, inspected, tested, installed and serviced?

15 When are the design output checks performed?

16 What measures are taken to alert users of the design documentation to critical characteristics?

17 How is the release of design documentation denoted following its approval?

18   Design review

Requirements of ISO 9001 clause 4.4.6

The supplier is required to:

1   Plan formal documented reviews of the design results at appropriate stages.

2   Conduct formal documented reviews of the design results at appropriate stages.

3   Include representatives of all functions concerned with the design stage at each design review.

4   Include specialist personnel as required at each design review.

5   Maintain records of each design review.

Purpose of requirements

The purpose of these requirements is to prevent design continuing beyond prescribed stages before its acceptability has been established. It should also determine whether the documentation for the next phase is adequate before further resources are committed.

Guidance on interpretation

Applicability

Design review is a method of design verification. In some cases it is the only method used (for example, by an architect or structural engineer). If so, it has to address all the requirements of clause 4.4.7 of the standard.

Design review is that part of the design control process which measures design performance, compares it with pre-defined requirements and provides feedback so that deficiencies may be corrected before the design is released to the next phase. Although design documents may have been through a vetting process, the purpose of the design review is not to review documents but to subject the design to an independent board of experts for its judgement as to whether the most satisfactory design solution has been chosen.

Types of design review

In some cases there will need to be only one design review, after completion of all design verification activities. However, depending on the complexity of the design and the risks, you may need to review the design at some, or all, of the following intervals:

- *Design Requirement Review.* To establish that the design requirements can be met and reflect the needs of the customer before commencement of design.

- *Conceptual Design Review.* To establish that the design concept fulfils the requirements before project definition commences.

- *Preliminary Design Review.* To establish that all risks have been resolved and development specifications produced for each sub-element of the product/service before detail design commences.

- *Critical Design Review.* To establish that the detail design for each sub-element of the product/service complies with its development specification and that product specifications have been produced before manufacture of the prototypes.

- *Qualification Readiness Review.* To establish the configuration of the baseline design and readiness for qualification before commencement of design proving.

- *Final Design Review.* To establish that the design fulfils the requirements of its development specification before preparation for its production.

Participants

The review team should have a collective competency greater than that of the designer of the design being reviewed. For a design review to be effective it has to be conducted by someone other than the designer.

Conducting the review

Before any meeting of the design review panel, the design documentation should have been submitted to the panel so that they may review it without the constraints of a meeting and come prepared to ask questions and challenge decisions and assumptions the designer has taken. A good method is to employ a series of check lists that have evolved over time to capture the combined expertise of the organization. The design review should present the design, explaining the rationale and indicating the extent of compliance with the design input requirements.

Design review records

The results of the design review should be documented in a report rather than minutes of a meeting, since it represents objective evidence that may be required later to determine product compliance with requirements, investigate design problems and compare similar designs. The report should have the agreement of the full review team and include:

- The criteria against which the design has been reviewed.

- A list of the documentation which describes the design being reviewed and any evidence presented which purports to demonstrate that the design meets the requirements.

- The decision on whether the design is to proceed to the next stage.

- The basis on which confidence has been placed in the design.

- A record of any outstanding corrective actions from previous reviews.

- The recommendations and reasons for corrective action, if any.

- The members of the review team and their roles.

Consequences of failure

By not conducting design reviews there is a distinct possibility that the design will not fulfil the defined requirements. The designer may have been too close to the design to notice aspects that have not been addressed. If designs are not reviewed prior to verification, prototypes may have to be modified and tests repeated when errors are detected. Some errors may not be detected until the results of the validation trials have been completed.

Inconsistency of requirements

The content of design review records is not a specified requirement of the standard. As with the management review records, the design review records should represent the results of the review rather than a record of a meeting convened to discuss the results of the review. Auditors should examine the records against the ISO 8402 definition and, if inadequate, declare a nonconformity against this standard.

Tasks for developers

1   Establish design review procedures which operate at various levels within the design hierarchy, including subcontractors.

Questions to stimulate policies

1   What criteria are employed to determine the stages of design where design reviews are required?

2   How are formal design reviews planned, conducted and documented?

3   How are the results of design reviews recorded?

Questions for auditors

1   What is the policy on design reviews?

2   In what document is this policy defined?

3   How do you distinguish between formal and informal design reviews?

4   At what stages in the design process are formal design reviews carried out?

5   In what document is the design review schedule defined?

6   Who plans design reviews?

7   How are staff notified of the design review schedule?

8   What input data is required for each of the design reviews?

9   What is the process for obtaining this data and ensuring that it is reviewed by appropriate parties?

10 Who participates in design reviews?

11 In which document are the responsibilities of these participants defined?

12 What topics are discussed at a design review?

13 In what form are the results of the review documented?

14 What happens after the review?

15 How are actions tracked?

16 What action is taken should an actionee not carry out the agreed action on time?

17 In what circumstance would a design be released when there are actions outstanding?

19   Design verification

Requirements of ISO 9001 clause 4.4.7

The supplier is required to:

1   Perform design verification at appropriate stages.

2   Ensure that design stage output meets design stage input.

3   Record design verification measures.

Purpose of requirements

The purpose of these requirements is to provide a means of establishing objective evidence that the design output meets the design input.

Guidance on interpretation

Applicability

The requirements apply to all designs but design review may be the only practical method of verification. If so, it has to address all the requirements of clause 4.4.7 of the standard.

Design verification may not be possible for services until they are in use, unless modelling is employed to test theories.

Application

Design verification needs to be performed when there is a verifiable output. When designing a system there should be design requirements for each subsystem, each equipment, each unit, and so on, down to component and raw material level. Each of these design requirements represents acceptance criteria for verifying the design output of each stage.

Verification measures

You need to cover all the requirements, those that can be verified by test, by inspection, by analysis, by simulation or demonstration or simply by validation of product records. For those requirements to be verified by test, a test specification will need to be produced.

The verification plan needs to cover some or all of the following details as appropriate:

- A definition of the product design standard which is being verified.

- The objectives of the plan. You may need several plans covering different aspects of the requirements.

- Definition of the specifications and procedures to be employed for determining that each requirement has been achieved.

- Definition of the stages in the development phase at which verification can most economically be carried out.

- The identity of the various models that will be used to demonstrate achievement of design requirements. Some models may be simple space models, others laboratory standard or production standard depending on the need.

- Definition of the verification activities that are to be performed to qualify or validate the design and those which need to be performed on every product in production as a means of ensuring that the qualified design standard has been maintained.

- Definition of the test equipment, support equipment and facilities needed to carry out the verification activities.

- Definition of the time-scales for the verification activities in the sequence in which the activities are to be carried out.

- Identification of the venue for the verification activities.

- Identification of the organization responsible for conducting each of the verification activities.

- Reference to the controls to be exercised over the verification. Provision should also be included for dealing with failures, their remedy, investigation and action on design modifications.

Development tests

Where tests are needed to verify conformance with the design specification, development test specifications will be needed to specify the test parameters, limits and operating conditions. For each development test specification there should be a corresponding development test procedure. The models used to conduct the tests should be representative of those that will enter production.

Demonstrations

Tests exercise the functional properties of the product. Demonstrations on the other hand, serve to exhibit usage characteristics, such as access and maintainability, including interchangeability, reparability and serviceability. One of the most important characteristics which need to be demonstrated is producibility. Can you actually make the product in the quantities required economically?

Consequences of failure

By not conducting design verification properly, you run the risk of the product failing production tests and failing to fulfil customer requirements. If design is proven on uncontrolled models then it is likely that there will be little traceability to the production models.

Inconsistency of requirements

The standard requires design verification measures to be recorded but it is unclear whether design verification requirements are to be specified or design verification results are to be recorded. As clause 4.16 is referenced the implication is that there is no requirement for design verification requirements to be defined and documented since design verification is not addressed in the clause on design input. If design verification requirements are not specified by the supplier, then the auditor has to decide whether the product characteristics and conditions of use are sufficiently detailed without additional verification requirements. If not, then the nonconformity is against the adequacy of design control procedures in ensuring that specified requirements are met.

Tasks for developers

1 Increase safety factors if verification by analysis is performed in lieu of test.

2 Record the design documentation status used in the performance of calculations and analyses.

3 Don't start making prototypes until the interface dimensions have been confirmed.

4 Don't start pre-production until the design has been functionally proven.

5 Decide on a method of identifying ways of verifying that the design meets each of the requirements.

6 Prepare procedures governing the construction of models for use in proving the design.

7 Establish standards for preparation of development and production test specifications and procedures

8 Decide on the methods to be employed to make the transition from development to pre-production and from pre-production to production.

9 Prepare procedures for the conduct of design verification activities.

Questions to stimulate policies

1 How do you ensure that design stage output meets design stage input requirements?

2 In what documents are the design verification measures defined?

3 Under what circumstances would alternative calculations be performed?

4 Under what circumstances would design verification by similarity be valid?

5 When would tests and demonstrations be an appropriate verification method?

6 How do you ensure that design stage documents are reviewed before release?

Questions for auditors

1 Who is responsible for conducting design verification?

2 At what stages of design is verification carried out?

3 In what document are the design verification requirements defined?

4 In what documents are the plans for carrying out design verification defined?

5 What standards govern the content of design verification plans?

6 What is the verification philosophy for *this* design?

7 Which requirements are verified by analysis and simulation rather then by test?

8 Which functions participate in design verification?

9 In which document are the responsibilities of the participants defined?

10 What are the processes for producing the development models used for design verification?

11 What checks are carried out on development models to validate their conformity prior to use in design verification?

12 What records are maintained of the design standard before, during and after design verification?

13 In what documents are the design verification methods and recording requirements defined?

14 What checks are performed to validate the test equipment and test methods prior to commencing design verification?

15 What action would be taken should a design input requirement not be demonstrated satisfactorily?

16 What records are maintained of the results of design verification?

17 What controls are exercised over subcontracted design verification activities?

20   Design validation

Requirements of ISO 9001 clause 4.4.8

The supplier is required to:

1   Perform design validation.

2   Ensure that product conforms to defined user needs and/or requirements.

Purpose of requirements

The purpose of these requirements is to provide a means for confirming that the design reflects a product which conforms to user needs and/or requirements.

Guidance on interpretation

Applicability

Design validation is a process of evaluating a design to establish that it fulfils the intended use requirements. It goes further than design verification in that validation tests and trials may stress the product of such a design beyond operating conditions in order to establish design margins of safety and performance. Design validation can also be performed on mature designs in order to establish whether they will fulfil user requirements different to the original design input requirements.

Application

Design validation may take the form of qualification tests which stress the product up to and beyond design limits:

- *Beta tests* where products are supplied to several typical users on trial in order to gather operational performance data.

- *Performance trials* and *reliability and maintainability trails* where products are put on test for prolonged periods to simulate usage conditions.

During the design process many assumptions may have been made and will require proving before commitment of resources to the replication of the design. Some of the requirements, such as reliability and maintainability, will be time-dependent. Others may not be verifiable without stressing the product beyond its design limits.

Procedures for controlling design validation should provide for:

- Test specifications to be produced which define the features and characteristics that are to be verified for design qualification and acceptance.

- Test plans to be produced which define the sequence of tests, the responsibilities for their conduct, the location of the tests and test procedures to be used.

- Test procedures to be produced which describe how the tests specified in the test specification are to be conducted, together with the tools and test equipment to be used and the data to be recorded.

- All measuring equipment to be within calibration during the tests.

- The test sample to have successfully passed all planned in-process and assembly inspections and tests prior to commencing qualification tests.

- The configuration of the product in terms of its design standard, deviations, nonconformances and design changes to be recorded prior to and subsequent to the tests.

- Test reviews to be held before tests commence to ensure that the product, facilities, tools, documentation and personnel are in a state of operational readiness for verification.

- Test activities to be conducted in accordance with the prescribed specifications, plans and procedures.

- The results of all tests and the conditions under which they were obtained to be recorded.

- Deviations to be recorded, remedial action taken and the product subject to re-verification prior to continuing with the tests.

- Test reviews to be performed following qualification tests to confirm that sufficient objective evidence has been obtained to demonstrate that the product fulfils the requirements of the test specification.

Consequences of failure

If you don't carry out design validation, you will be uncertain how the product will perform under actual operating conditions. The variation in materials, dimensions and finishes, etc. present in production models may lead to products that fail in service because the design margins were not established through design validation.

Inconsistency of requirements

- The user needs and/or requirements are not required to be specified in the design input or the contract although the design output has to meet design input and must be expressed in terms that can be validated against user needs. This is an oversight and any approved and issued design input documentation that did not include user needs and/or requirements would be inadequate under clause 4.5.2.

- There is no requirement for design validation requirements to be defined and documented. The lack of design validation requirements can be dealt with in the same way as for design verification requirements.

- There is no requirement for design validation results to be recorded. This is an oversight. ISO 9001 is usually invoked in contracts for design; therefore, the catch-all requirement in clause 4.16 for quality records covers this.

Tasks for developers

1   Plan for validation as part of your product development planning.

2   Establish how user characteristics are to be demonstrated.

3 Establish the model philosophy for carrying out validation trials.

4 Prepare detail plans for specific trials.

5 Produce test specifications and procedures.

6 Provide demonstration models that are fully representative of those that will be supplied to customers.

7 Organize the resources necessary to carry out the trials.

8 Acquire the equipment, facilities, sites etc. for carrying out the trials.

9 Conduct pre-trial reviews to establish the validation baseline and confirm readiness for test.

10 Conduct the trials in accordance with the approved documentation.

11 Record all the results including any on-site changes, nonconformities and test conditions.

12 Conduct post-trial reviews to establish that the objectives have been met.

13 Return all materials, products to the factory and quarantine until required for further test.

14 Don't permit modifications without authorization.

15 Don't use previous models unless you know their history and you are in possession of the records.

17 Feed back all modifications into the design process so that future models can be built to the same standard.

Questions to stimulate policies

1 What criteria are employed to determine the need for design validation?

2 How is the degree of design validation determined?

3 How do you ensure that design validation activities are carried out under controlled conditions?

4 What records are maintained to demonstrate that designs meet user needs and requirements?

Questions for auditors

1   How do you distinguish between design verification and design validation activities?

2   At what stages is design validation carried out?

3   Who is responsible for design validation?

4   In what documents are the design validation requirements specified?

5   What measures are taken to ensure that the design validation requirements are compatible with user needs and requirements?

6   How are design validation activities planned and controlled?

7   In what documents are the design validation methods defined?

8   How are the actual operating conditions determined?

9   What measures are taken to ensure that operating conditions are replicated in the laboratory?

10 Where conditions cannot be replicated in the laboratory, how are the conditions simulated?

11 What records of design validation activities are maintained?

12 What action would be taken in the event of a failure to validate the design?

21 Design changes

Requirements of ISO 9001 clause 4.4.9

The supplier is required to:

1 Identify all design changes.

2 Identify all modifications.

3 Document all design changes.

4 Document all modifications.

5 Review all design changes before their implementation.

6 Ensure all design changes are approved by authorized personnel before their implementation.

Purpose of requirements

The purpose of these requirements is to provide a means for ensuring that only approved design changes are implemented. Another reason for controlling design changes is to restrain the creativity of designers and keep the design within the budget and timescale.

Guidance on interpretation

Applicability

Design changes are simply changes to the design and can occur at any stage in the design process from the stage at which the requirement is agreed to the final certification that the design is proven. Modifications are changes made to products to incorporate design changes and occur only after the first product is built.

Application

Once the design requirements have been agreed, any changes in the requirements should be subject to formal procedures. When a particular design solution is complete and has been found to meet the requirements at a design review it should be brought under change control. Between the design reviews the designers should be given complete freedom to derive solutions to the requirements.

Design changes will result in changes to documentation but not all design documentation changes are design changes. This is why design change control should be treated separately from document control.

At each design review a design baseline should be established which identifies the design documentation that has been approved. The baseline should be recorded and change control procedures employed to deal with any changes.

Change documentation

- *Change Request* forms contain the reason for change and the results of the evaluation. These were described previously as they are used to initiate the change and obtain approval before being implemented.

- *Change Notices* provide instructions defining what has to be changed. A Change Notice is issued following approval of the change as instructions to the owners of the various documents that are affected by the change.

- *Change Records* describe what has been changed. A Change Record usually forms part of the document that has been changed and can be either in the form of a box at the side of the sheet (as with drawings) or in the form of a table on a separate sheet (as with specifications).

Modification documentation

Prior to commencement of production, design changes do not require any modification documentation. When product is in production, instructions need to be provided so that the modification can be embodied in the product. These modification instructions should detail:

- Which products are affected, by part number and serial number.

- The new parts that are required.

- The work to be carried out to remove obsolete items and fit new items.

- The work to be carried out to salvage existing items and render them suitable for modification.

- The markings to be applied to the product and its modification label.

- The tests and inspections to be performed to verify that the product is serviceable.

- The records to be produced as evidence that the modification has been embodied.

Review and approval of changes

The change proposals need to be evaluated to:

- Validate the reason for change.

- Determine whether the proposed change is feasible.

- Judge whether the change is desirable.

- Determine the effects on performance, costs and timescales.

- Examine the documentation affected by the change and programme their revision.

- Determine the stage at which the change should be embodied.

Review and approval of modifications

During production the change control board will need to make four decisions:

- Whether to accept or reject the change

- When to implement the change in the design documentation

- When to implement the modification in new product

- What to do with existing product in production, in store and in service

Consequences of failure

If you don't control design changes you won't control your costs and schedules and you may find agreed changes have not been made and undesirable changes have been made. If you don't control modifications, you may find that agreed changes have not been embodied in production models wherever they are and, also, unauthorized changes may be made rendering the product unsafe, unreliable, unmaintainable etc.

Inconsistency of requirements

The title is 'Design changes' whereas the text addresses design changes and modifications and there is no definition in ISO 8402 of the difference between a design change and a modification. Auditors should take the view that design changes are changes to a design and modifications are changes to a product as a result of a design change.

Tasks for developers

1   Produce procedures governing the preparation, review, approval and distribution of modification instructions.

2   Decide on the conventions to be used for identifying the issue status of design documents during development and following design certification.

3   Decide on the conventions to be used to identify the modification status of products or services.

4   Decide on the criteria for judging when design changes should be incorporated into design documentation.

5   Decide on a mechanism for establishing the design baseline and for controlling changes to the baseline.

6   Set up a design change control board to review, evaluate and approve or reject design changes.

7   Commence change control immediately after the design requirement has been agreed and issued.

8   Assess the calculations and analysis when the design changes.

9   Incorporate all design changes before any product is delivered.

10 Don't accept changes to requirements from your customer without a change to the contract and always get them in writing.

11 Don't allow designers to change approved designs without prior approval.

Questions to stimulate policies

1 How do you identify, document, review and approve design changes?

2 How do you identify, document, review and approve modifications?

3 How do you ensure that no change is made to the design without prior approval of authorized personnel?

4 How do you ensure that no modification is made to the product without prior approval of authorized personnel?

Questions for auditors

Change proposals

1 At what stages in the design process are design changes brought under formal control?

2 What is the process for changing a design at any stage during development?

3 In what way does this process differ following production launch?

4 Who is responsible for co-ordinating proposed changes to designs?

5 How are proposed changes identified and documented?

Change evaluation

1 Who is authorized to review and approve design changes?

2 What measures are taken to ensure that the impact of any design change on related documentation, products, equipment, costs and contractual requirements is fully taken into account?

3 Where the need to change a design is detected in production or field operations, what measures are taken to gather complete evidence for the change?

4 Where changes affect subcontracted designs, how does the subcontractor seek approval to make the changes?

5 Where the designs are under customer control, how is approval to change secured from the customer?

6 In what documents are these processes defined?

Change implementation

1 How is the process of implementing the approved change proposals managed?

2 How are changes to designs identified following their approval?

3 In what documents are approved design changes recorded?

Modifications

1 How are approved design changes promulgated to users of design data?

2 What measures are taken to control the implementation of a design change to products in production, in stock and in service?

3 Where a design change has a safety and environmental impact, what measures are taken to alert users and recall product?

4 How is the modification status of product identified?

5 In which document is the modification record of product defined?

6 In which documents are these processes defined?

22 Document and data control procedures

Requirements of ISO 9001 clause 4.5.1

The supplier is required to:

1 Establish and maintain document control procedures for documents of internal origin.

2 Control all documents that relate to the requirements of the standard.

3 Establish and maintain data control procedures.

4 Control all data that relates to the requirements of the standard.

5 Establish and maintain document control procedures for documents of external origin.

6 Control all documents of external origin that relate to the requirements of the standard.

Purpose of requirements

The purpose of these requirements is to prevent the inadvertent use of incorrect, invalid or obsolete documents and data.

These requirements apply to all documents and data that relate to the requirements of the standard, not just the quality system procedures.

Guidance on interpretation

Applicability

More than one control procedure may be required to meet this requirement. Measures should be taken to ensure the control procedures cover all types of documents, policies, procedures standards, guides, derived documents (plans, specifications, contracts, orders etc.) and reference documents (including external documents such as manuals, whether supplied by customers, suppliers or obtained from other sources). Data may be in the form of information contained in documents or in electronic storage, such as a database on a computer. The requirements do not apply to documents and data which record the results of activities performed or results achieved, such as test results. The requirements also do not apply to the activities performed prior to submission of documents and data for review and approval. No tailoring is needed for specific industries.

Scope of control procedures

Your document and data control procedures should cover the following topics:

- Planning new documents, funding, prior authorization, establishing need etc.

- Preparation of documents, who prepares, drafting process, text, diagrams, forms etc.

- Standards for the format and content of documents, forms and diagrams

- Document identification conventions

- Issue notation, draft issues, post approval issues

- Dating conventions, date of issue, date of approval or date of distribution

- Document review: who reviews and what evidence is retained

- Document approval: who approves and how approval is denoted

- Document proving prior to use

- Printing and publication: who does it, who checks it

- Distribution of documents: who decides, who does it, who checks it

- Use of documents, limitations, unauthorized copying and marking

- Revision of issued documents, requests for revision: who approves the request, who implements the change

- Denoting changes, revision marks, re-issues, sidelining, underlining

- Amending copies of issued documents, amendment instructions, amendment status

- Indexing documents, listing documents by issue status

- Document maintenance, keeping them current, periodic review

- Document accessibility inside and outside normal working hours

- Document security, unauthorized changes, copying, disposal, computer viruses, fire, theft

- Document filing, masters, copies, drafts, custom binders

- Document storage, libraries and archive, who controls, location, loan arrangements

- Document retention and obsolescence

External documents

The control which you exercise over external documents is somewhat limited. You cannot, for instance, control the revision of such documents therefore all the requirements concerning document changes will not apply. You can, however, control the use and amendment of external documents.

Consequences of failure

Failing to provide adequate procedures to control internal and external documents will result in an inconsistent approach through the organization, such that you will not be able to prevent invalid documents being used.

Inconsistency of requirements

- The requirements apply to external documents but not to external data. External data may be in the form of tables, technical information or statistics taken from external publications. The auditor should establish what external data is being used and verify that provisions have been made for capturing data changes.

- The term 'data' and how it differs from a 'document' is not defined in ISO 8402. Data is information organized in a form suitable for manual or computer analysis. The data does not have to be documented for it to constitute data. Verbal data that is not subsequently documented in some form cannot be controlled.

Tasks for developers

1 Keep 'insurance copies' at a remote location.

2 Protect computer access from unauthorized users.

3 Use computer virus protection practices.

4 Don't impose presentation standards that are costly to meet and maintain.

5 Secure the masters of documents.

6 Identify the types of document that you need to control.

7 Classify these documents so that you can apply controls appropriate to their classification.

8 Ensure your quality system procedures identify all the types of documents requiring control.

9 Specify appropriate requirements for each of the controlled documents.

10 Produce procedures for preparing, reviewing, approving, issuing and changing controlled documents.

11 Establish numbering, dating and revision status conventions.

Questions to stimulate policies

1 What procedures have been established for controlling documents and data that relate to the requirements of ISO 9001?

2 How do you control documents and data that relate to the requirements of ISO 9001?

3 How do you control documents of external origin?

Questions for auditors

Document control procedures

1 Who is responsible for controlling internally-generated documentation and data?

2 How do you control documents that relate to the requirements of ISO 9000?

3 In what documents are these methods defined?

4 What types of data do you generate or use in your work?

5 How is this data controlled?

6 In what documents are these methods defined?

7 How do you distinguish between draft and approved documents?

Control of external documents

1 Who is responsible for controlling documents of external origin?

2 What documents of external origin do you use?

3 In what documents are these external documents specified?

4 How do you know these documents are of current revision?

5 What procedure specifies the controls you exercise over external documents?

6 What action is taken on receipt of a change to an external document?

23   Document and data review and approval

Requirements of ISO 9001 clause 4.5.2

The supplier is required to:

1   Review documents for adequacy prior to release.

2   Review data for adequacy prior to release.

3   Ensure that documents are approved by authorized personnel prior to release.

4   Ensure that data is approved by authorized personnel prior to release.

5   Establish and maintain a master list or document control procedure for identifying the current revision status of documents.

6   Ensure that the master list or document control procedure is readily available.

7   Preclude the use of invalid and/or obsolete documents.

8   Ensure that the pertinent issues of appropriate documents are available at all essential locations.

9   Prevent unintended use of invalid and/or obsolete documents.

10 Identify any retained obsolete documents.

Purpose of requirements

The purpose of these requirements is to provide a means for preventing invalid documents and data being issued or selected for use.

Guidance on interpretation

Applicability

These requirements apply to all internal documents and data identified or intended for use in your quality system. They do not apply to documents that are outside the scope of the quality system. To ensure this happens you need a policy that prohibits staff using documents and data that are not specified in the system. Text books and other helpful literature is normally for guidance only and does not need to be controlled. The requirement also applies to external documents, although in a limited sense. Whilst you cannot change external documents, you can establish that those issued to you are suitable before issue to those who need them.

Document review

Users, particularly, should participate in the preparation process so that the resultant document reflects their needs and is fit for the intended purpose. You will need to be able to demonstrate that your documents have, in fact, been reviewed prior to issue. You can do this by showing that nominated personnel have been issued with drafts for comment and that they have provided comments which have been considered by the approval authorities.

The review should establish that the document is adequate but the term *adequacy* is a little vague. It should be taken as meaning that the document is fit for its purpose.

Data review

All data should be examined before use, otherwise you may inadvertently introduce errors into your work.

Document approval

Documents have to be approved by authorized personnel. In the procedure which requires the document to be produced you should identify who the approval authorities are by their role or function, rather than their job title and certainly not by their name, as both can change. Approval can be denoted directly on the document, on a change or issue record, in a register or on a separate approval record. You should always print the name and position of the person who signed the document so that you can verify it was signed by the authorized person.

Data approval

Regarding approval of data, you will need to define which data needs approval before issue, as some data may well be used as an input to a document which itself is subject to approval. Approval before issue should be taken to mean 'issue to someone else'. Therefore if you use data which you have generated then it does not need review and approval prior to use. If you issue data to someone else then it should be reviewed and approved beforehand.

Issuing documents

The term *issue* in the context of documents means that copies of the document are distributed. You will of course wish to *issue* draft documents for comment but obviously they cannot be reviewed and approved beforehand. The sole purpose of issuing draft documents is to solicit comments.

Master lists of documents

Staff should have a means of being able to determine the correct revision status of documents they use. You can do this through the work instructions, specification or planning documents, or by controlling the distribution, if the policy is to work to the latest issue. However, both these means have weaknesses. Documents can get lost, errors can creep into specifications and the cost of changing documents sometimes prohibits keeping them up to date unless the documents are accessible through a computer network. The issuing authority for each range of documents should maintain a register of documents showing the progression of changes that have been made since the initial issue. With electronic documents, this may be unnecessary as you can arrange the controls to prohibit staff to view any document that is not current.

Revision notation

The revision status of a document may be indicated by date, by letter or by number or may be a combination of issue and revision state. A pertinent issue is a document of the correct revision state. Every change to a document should increment the revision status or version. Changes may be major, causing the document to be re-issued or re-released, or they may be minor, causing only the affected pages to be revised. Conventions vary but a common approach is to identify draft documents as Issue or Version A, B, C up to first approval and 1A, 1B, 1C etc. afterwards. Approved versions can be identified as 1, 2, 3 etc. with minor revisions as 1.1, 1.2, 1.3 and major revisions incremented by a whole number.

If you choose to revise documents at page level then the revision status only applies to the pages affected. For example, Page 1 is Issue 1 Rev 0, Page 2 is Issue 1 Rev 1, etc.

Availability of documents

In order to make sure that documents are available you should not keep them under lock and key. If there is a need for access out of normal working hours then access has to be provided. The more copies there are the greater the chance that documents will not be maintained so keep the number of copies to a minimum. Documents stored on a computer network can provide greater flexibility for access and availability.

Obsolete documents

It is unnecessary to remove invalid or obsolete documents if you provide staff with the means of determining the pertinent issues of documents to use. If documents carry the revision status on the front, further identification is unnecessary providing the previously mentioned conditions are applied. If you want to retain obsolete documents and there is no date or revision status noted on the document, you should mark the document as SUPERSEDED or OBSOLETE. If the documents apply to equipment or products you no longer provide then even this is unnecessary as there will be no requirement in your system that invokes their use.

Consequences of failure

The use of any documents and data that is not valid, because it is obsolete, unapproved, of the wrong revision status or incomplete, may result in the wrong actions and decisions being taken and thus directly result in a failure to meet customer requirements or company policy (including legal requirements). The degree of impact depends upon the nature of the information that was invalid. Sometimes the effect is cosmetic but on other occasions the effect might be quite serious – the problem is that the user may not be able to distinguish between the trivial and the vital issues either because they are not trained or simply because they lack sufficient information to make a judgement.

Inconsistency of requirements

- There is no requirement for documents and data to be reviewed and approved prior to use or release if they are not issued. Auditors need to establish what the documents and data are being used for and make a judgement as to whether adequate controls exist to prevent the use of invalid or obsolete documents and data.

- There is no requirement for the master list or document control procedure to identify the current revision status of data. Data often doesn't have any revision status but can be identified by its source and date. Where data is inserted into documents, the source should be stated. A list of data sources should therefore be maintained where such data is relevant to product/service quality. Data in specification, procedures, standards etc. used to generate product characteristics should be of known status.

- There is no requirement for the preclusion of obsolete data or for obsolete data to be promptly removed or otherwise identified. Data can exist in documents but also in a computer database. Control of the database is important and therefore the general requirement for data control applies.

- There is no requirement for pertinent issues of data to be available at all locations. The same argument as applied to obsolete data applies to the availability of data.

Tasks for developers

1 Don't state the issue status of reference documents in your procedures and specifications unless absolutely necessary.

2 Don't put the distribution list on controlled documents – keep it separate.

3 Don't issue documents to individuals – use titles.

4 Provide labelled binders for ranges of documents as they are more easily traced.

5 Don't ignore written comments to draft documents.

6 Don't purge every office in search of obsolete documents.

7 Don't keep all your documents in one place.

8 Limit distribution lists to a 'need to know' basis.

9 Review controlled documents periodically to determine whether they remain relevant.

10 Identify the issuing authorities for the controlled documents.

11 Determine where each type of document is to be stored.

12 Decide how you will indicate the approval status on documents.

13 Determine who will review and who will approve the controlled documents.

14 Decide how you will safeguard approved documents from unauthorized change, copying and removal.

15 Create controlled lists of documents which denote the revision status.

16 Create distribution lists for controlled documents.

17 Provide document custodians with stamps to mark obsolete documents upon receipt of instructions.

Questions to stimulate policies

1 How do you ensure that documents and data are reviewed for adequacy by authorized personnel prior to issue?

2 How do you ensure that documents and data are approved for adequacy by authorized personnel prior to issue?

3   How do you ensure that the pertinent issues of appropriate documents are available at all locations where operations essential to the effective functioning of the quality system are performed?

4   How do you ensure that information on the current revision status of documents is readily available?

5   How do you ensure that invalid and/or obsolete documents are assured against inadvertent use?

6   What means are used to identify obsolete documents retained for legal and/or knowledge preservation purposes?

Questions for auditors

Review and approval

1   What methods do you employ to release documents for use?

2   Who has reviewed this document before it was issued?

3   Who are the approval authorities for this document?

4   How do you know that the person who has signed this document has authority to do so?

5   What evidence is there that this unsigned document has been approved?

6   What criteria have been employed to judge the adequacy of this document?

Revision status

1   How do you determine the pertinent revision level of a document?

2   When did the changes denoted in this document take effect?

Availability of documents

1   How do you determine which documents are required to be used when performing this work?

2   Where are the documents located?

3   What measures are employed to prevent loss of these documents?

4   How can you obtain the necessary documents outside normal working hours?

5   Who is responsible for maintaining this set of documents?

6   Where are the master documents held from which this copy was taken?

7   What happens if you inadvertently delete a document on screen?

Invalid and obsolete documents

1   How do you determine whether or not a document is authorized for use?

2   On whose authority were these changes made to this document?

3   What happens to the old document when you are issued with a new version?

4   Should you retain an old document, how do you indicate that it is obsolete?

5   When products are phased out of production, what happens to the related documentation?

24 Document and data change

Requirements of ISO 9001 clause 4.5.3

The supplier is required to:

1   Ensure that changes to documents are reviewed by the same functions that performed the original review.

2   Ensure that changes to documents are approved by the same functions that performed the original approval.

3   Provide the designated functions with access to pertinent background information upon which to base their review and approval.

4   Identify the nature of change in the document or appropriate attachment.

Purpose of requirements

The purpose of these requirements is to provide a means for preventing unauthorized changes to approved documents and data, of ensuring that those authorizing the documents make sound decisions and those using the changed documents know what has changed.

Guidance on interpretation

Applicability

These requirements apply to the documents and data that form part of the system only, as described in Chapter 23.

Changes to documents

If you have a copy of a document and make pencil marks upon it, you have not changed it but defaced it. If you need to make changes that alter the meaning or parameters specified you can mark up a document providing the changes are covered by an approved change instruction. The change instructions should detail the changes to be made and then authorized by the appropriate authorities. On receipt of the change instructions the recipients make the changes in manuscript or by page replacement, and annotate the changes with the serial number of the instruction.

In order that a change be reviewed it has to be proposed and the most common method is to employ Document Change Requests. Using a formal change request allows anyone to make a request for a change to the appropriate authorities. Your change requests need to identify: the document to be changed, who is proposing the change, why the change is necessary, what needs to be changed and, where known, the text that is to be inserted.

Changes to data

Data that has not been issued to anyone does not require approval if changed. Only the data that has be issued to someone other that its producer needs to be brought under change control. If you are using data provided by someone else then, in principle, you can't change it without that person's permission. However, there will be many circumstances where formal change control of data is unnecessary and many where it is vital – as with scientific experiments, research, product testing etc.

The nature of a change

The nature of a change is principally the intrinsic characteristics of the change. You should therefore indicate not only what has changed but also give the reasons for change. This can be accomplished in a change record forming: part of the document, a footnote at the end of the document or an amendment instruction issued with the revised document or pages.

Consequences of failure

If you don't control document and data changes you won't control your costs, as is the case with design change control. Therefore failing to adequately control changes to documents and data may well incur unnecessary costs and delays as work is reworked to meet the valid requirements. If you don't inform staff what has changed, you run the risk that they may think nothing has changed that affects what they do, when the purpose of the change was to cause a change in work practices. If different functions than the original functions approve the change, insufficient consideration may be given to the consequences of the change which may result in a serious breach of contract or legal requirements.

Inconsistency of requirements

There is no requirement to identify the nature of change in data whether or not it is practicable. Data changes can be more difficult to detect if not identified. For example, a new table of parameters may look the same as the old table, only the decimal place may have been moved. Auditors should verify that the data control procedures cover this aspect. Where data changes are not identified, the data controls would not be adequate to cause the use of the changed data.

Tasks for developers

1   Don't change a controlled document without an approved change notice.

2   Don't use concessions to change documents – change the document or use a change note.

3   Don't create a complex change control mechanism – it should represent the easiest way of changing a document.

4   Inform staff why changes have been made.

5   Give all change requests a unique identity.

6   Provide for amending the document index before revised documents are issued.

7   Create a formal change request mechanism for initiating changes to controlled documents.

8   Provide a fast route to change documents.

9   Provide an economic means of changing a range of documents affected by a single change.

10 Provide a means of withdrawing and disposing of documents when the product, organization, service or process becomes obsolete.

11 Provide a means of evaluating the effects that a change in one document has on other documents.

Questions to stimulate policies

1 How do you ensure that changes to documents are reviewed by the same functions or organizations that performed the original review?

2 How do you ensure that changes to documents are approved by the same functions or organizations that performed the original approval?

3 How do you ensure that designated organizations have access to pertinent background information upon which to make their review and approval of changes to documents?

4 How do you identify the nature of changes within documents or their attachments?

Questions for auditors

Review and approval

1 How are changes to documents identified?

2 To whom do you submit a request for change?

3 What method is employed to process a change to an approved document?

4 In what documents are these methods defined?

5 What action would be taken if the change affected a range of documents?

6 Who is responsible for processing documentation changes?

7 What method is used to make small changes?

8 What instructions do you receive on incorporating a change to a document?

9   What method is employed to make changes to approved data?

10 In what documents are these methods defined?

11 What action do you take on receipt of a changed document?

Access to background information

1   How are changes initiated to approved documents?

2   What information is submitted to those charged with conducting a review of changes to documents?

3   How do the approval authorities determine whether the change is necessary?

4   How are the changed documents conveyed to the users?

5   How do you ensure all users receive the revised document or data?

Nature of change

1   What conventions are used to indicate changes in documents?

2   What conventions are used to indicate changes in data?

3   In which documents are these methods defined?

4   On receipt of a changed document, how do users determine what has changed?

25 Purchasing procedures

Requirements of ISO 9001 clause 4.6.1

The supplier is required to:

1 Establish and maintain documented purchasing procedures.

2 Ensure that purchased product conforms to specified requirements.

Purpose of requirements

The purpose of the purchasing requirements is to prevent the purchase and acceptance of product or service that does not meet specified requirements. The purpose of purchasing procedures is to implement policy and regulate processes which are essential to the business.

Guidance on interpretation

Applicability

No tailoring is needed for specific industries. These requirements apply to products and services purchased from external suppliers for use in connection with the products and services offered for sale to external customers. They do not apply to purchases that have no bearing on the saleable product unless such items are used in a way which would affect it.

They also apply to the purchasing process wherever that process commences – be it in design, in production or elsewhere. They do not only apply to the purchasing function.

Scope of purchasing procedures

There are four key processes for which you should prepare procedures:

- The *specification process*, which starts once the need has been identified and ends with a request to purchase. This is covered by clause 4.6.3 of ISO 9001.

- The *evaluation process*, which starts with the request to purchase and ends with the placement of the order or contract. This is covered by clause 4.6.2 of ISO 9001.

- The *surveillance process*, which starts with placement of order or contract and ends upon delivery of supplies. This is covered by clause 4.6.2 and 4.6.4 of ISO 9001.

- The *acceptance process*, which starts with delivery of supplies and ends with entry of supplies onto the inventory. This is covered by clause 4.10.2 of ISO 9001.

Types of purchasing procedures

Whatever you purchase, the processes will be very similar although there will be variations for purchased services such as subcontract labour, computer maintenance, legal services etc. Where the purchasing process is relatively simple, one procedure may suffice but where the process varies you may need separate procedures so as to avoid all purchases – regardless of value and risk – going through the same process.

Consequences of failure

Failing to provide adequate documented procedures to control purchasing processes will result in an inconsistent approach through the organization such that you will not be able to prevent expenditure on items which do no meet the organization's requirements. Purchases or varying quality will result and adversely impact the quality of the products and services supplied to customers. Even though you may not have designed or manufactured the purchased items, you have a responsibility to ensure that such items are fit for their purpose if you sell them onto your customer (either directly or as part of another product) since you selected them.

Inconsistency of requirements

The standard does not specify whether the specified requirements with which the purchased product has to conform should be the customer, purchaser or supplier requirements or all three. Since the standard addresses a system which will ensure conforming product is supplied to customers, the specified requirements are those of the customer, in this case. A definition of specified requirements is given in ISO 9000-2: 1997.

Tasks for developers

1   Be sure that purchasing staff and technical staff operate to the same standards and procedures.

2   Identify the broad categories of products and service which you procure.

3   Classify products and services into groups according to their potential effect on end-product quality.

4   Prepare procedures for purchasing those products and services, the quality of which affects end-product quality.

5   Provide forms for staff to request the procurement of goods.

Questions to stimulate policies

1   What procedures have been established and documented for ensuring purchased product conforms to specified requirements?

2   How do you ensure that purchased product conforms to specified requirements?

Questions for auditors

1   What is the policy regarding the procurement of products and services?

2 Who is responsible for placing orders on subcontractors and suppliers?

3 What types of products and services are procured?

4 How are procurement needs identified?

5 What method is used to convey procurement requirements to the purchasing authority?

6 What methods are used to procure materials and equipment for use in deliverable equipment?

7 What methods are used to procure services used in the development and production of product?

8 In which document are these methods defined?

26   Evaluation of subcontractors

Requirements of ISO 9001 clause 4.6.2

The supplier is required to:

1   Evaluate subcontractors.

2   Select subcontractors on the basis of their ability to meet subcontract requirements.

3   Define the type and extent of control exercised over subcontractors.

4   Base subcontractor controls upon the type of product.

5   Base subcontractor controls upon the impact of subcontract product on the quality of the final product.

6   Base subcontractor controls on the quality audit reports and/or quality records of the previously demonstrated capability and performance of subcontractors.

7   Establish and maintain quality records of acceptable subcontractors.

Purpose of requirements

The purpose of these requirements is to prevent use of suppliers for which there is no objective evidence of their ability to meet the purchaser's requirements. The requirements also serve to ensure that chosen subcontractors will deliver supplies that meet the purchaser's requirements.

Guidance on interpretation

Applicability

The requirement applies to all suppliers of products and services that impact the quality of the products and services you supply to your customers.

Subcontract requirements

The requirements you pass to your subcontractors need to include:

- The terms and conditions of the contract.

- The required delivery date or schedule.

- A specification of the product or service that you require which transmits all of the relevant requirements of the main contract from your customer.

- A specification of the means by which the requirements are to be demonstrated.

- A statement of work that you require the subcontractor to perform. It might be design, development, management or verification work. You need to be clear as to the interfaces – both organizationally and technically (see Chapter 4).

- A specification of the requirements that will give you an assurance of quality. This might be a simple reference to the appropriate ISO 9000 standard but, since this standard does not give you any rights, you will probably need to amplify the requirements.

Evaluating suppliers

There are four types of supplier in the market place:

- Those that are interested only in relieving you of your money

- Those with good intentions but poor capability

- Those with intentions that match their capability but are too expensive or can't deliver in the required time frame

- Those with the capability to supply what you want when you want it ecomonically

The purpose of supplier evaluation is to select a supplier of the fourth type and this requires a rigorous process that eliminates unsuitable suppliers. This process may cover the following:

- Preparation of tender documents

- Selection of suppliers that will be invited to tender

- Issue of Invitations to Tender (ITT) (the ITT serves to discover which suppliers have the required capability to meet your requirements)

- Evaluation of tenders (this will eliminate suppliers that do not have the required capability)

- Creation of short list of capable suppliers

- Preparation and issue of Request for Proposal (RFP)

- Evaluation of proposals (this will eliminate suppliers that offer a solution to your requirements that is either noncompliant, too costly or cannot be delivered in the time-frame you require)

- Selection of compliant supplier

Controlling suppliers

The degree of control you need to exercise over your subcontractors and suppliers depends on the confidence you have in their ability to meet your requirements. In determining the degree of control to be exercised you need to establish whether:

- The quality of the product or service can be verified by you on receipt using your normal inspection and test techniques or whether additional equipment or facilities are necessary.

- The quality of the product can be verified by you witnessing the final acceptance tests and inspections on the subcontractor's premises.

- The verification of the product could be contracted to a third party.

- The quality of the product can only be verified by the subcontractor during its design and manufacture.

Records of suppliers

This requirement does not mean that you have to maintain a list of approved suppliers. A list of names and addresses is not a quality record – the quality record is the evidence you have gathered for justifying the decision to select and continue to use certain suppliers. You should monitor subcontractor performance and classify each according to prescribed guidelines.

If you use a computerized supplier database, you can design it such that it won't allow orders to be placed on unacceptable suppliers.

Consequences of failure

Failure to evaluate your suppliers and select only those that meet your requirements will inevitably impact your ability to meet your customer requirements. If you don't know anything about a supplier other than the price of the goods or services offered, you may be wasting your money. Even discounting the unethical suppliers, a supplier may not understand what you want and offer you the wrong supplies or mislead you over their capability to meet your requirements. If you do not have confidence in a supplier, you may be delivered products or services that fall well below your expectations and too late to correct the deficiencies. If your receiving checks are not effective, the defective goods may well escape detection and result in severe problems with your customers – even to the extent of breaching your legal obligations.

Inconsistency of requirements

- There is no requirement for the criteria for selecting subcontractors to be defined and documented. This may be included in the purchasing procedures. Auditors should verify that the selection criteria are compatible with the criteria specified in the purchasing documents.

- There is no requirement for the type and extent of control exercised by the supplier over subcontractors to be defined and documented. This too may be documented in the purchasing procedures or the receipt inspection procedures.

- The requirement to establish and maintain quality records of acceptable subcontractors is ambiguous since there is no requirement to maintain records which demonstrate why the subcontractors are acceptable. A list of names is insufficient without the acceptance criteria and performance record.

Tasks for developers

1   Perform pre-award surveys of potential subcontractors.

2 Keep records of both supplier and subcontractor performance whether it be good or bad.

3 Maintain only one list of assessed suppliers and subcontractors.

4 Don't constrain yourself to purchase only from approved suppliers – compensate for poor performers through subcontractor/supplier controls.

5 Obtain proposals as to how the subcontractor proposes to control the quality of the product or service before acceptance of tender.

6 Don't change the documents in the tender until after you are in a position to negotiate with the winner.

7 Obtain documentation of the subcontractor's processes so as to aid problem investigations in-house.

8 Don't permit subcontractors to further subcontract the work without your approval and assessment of the proposed subcontractors.

9 Maintain a record of any articles you furnish to your subcontractors.

10 Establish a means of promptly responding to subcontractor queries and problem reports.

11 Provide feedback to subcontractors and suppliers of their performance.

12 Maintain records of all meetings and visits with suppliers and subcontractors.

13 Compile a list of preferred suppliers and subcontractors.

14 Prepare procedures for assessing your subcontractors and suppliers.

15 Decide on the criteria for selecting subcontractors and suppliers.

16 Provide for assessment of subcontractors to be carried out before award of contract.

17 Prepare procedures for producing and maintaining subcontract requirements and letting tenders.

18 Prepare procedures for evaluating tenders and selecting subcontractors.

19 Provide those responsible for the preparation of subcontract requirements to approve them prior to issue to the subcontractor.

20 Provide resources for the control of subcontractors.

21 Prepare procedures covering the planning of subcontractor control activities.

22 Provide a means for purchasing staff to gain access to current technical data to pass on to suppliers and subcontractors.

23 Provide a means of adding and removing subcontractors and suppliers from the list of preferred suppliers and subcontractors.

24 Provide a means for changing subcontract requirements during the contract.

25 Provide a means for monitoring the subcontractor's progress in meeting the requirements.

Questions to stimulate policies

1 How do you evaluate and select your subcontractors and suppliers?

2 How do you establish the capability of your subcontractors and suppliers?

3 How do you determine the control to be exercised over you subcontractors/suppliers?

4 Where are your subcontractor controls defined?

5 In what documents do you record those subcontractors/suppliers that are acceptable?

Questions for auditors

Tendering

1 How are potential suppliers and subcontractors identified?

2 What documents are issued to potential suppliers when invitations to tender are issued?

3 What measures are taken to ensure that these documents are accurate prior to release for tendering purposes?

4 Who is responsible for controlling the tendering process?

5 How are potential suppliers and subcontractors evaluated?

6 What criteria are used to select suppliers and subcontractors?

7 In what documents are these criteria defined?

8 To what extent is previous supply history taken into account?

9 In what documents are these supplier selection decisions recorded?

10 Who participates in decisions on supplier selection?

11 What responsibilities do these participants have?

Supplier control

1 How do you determine the type of controls to be exercised over subcontractors and suppliers?

2 What factors are taken into account when determining supplier controls?

3 Who determines the controls that are required?

4 In what document are these controls defined?

5 What records of previously demonstrated capability are maintained of suppliers and subcontractors?

6 What records are maintained that indicate the acceptability of suppliers and subcontractors?

7 What is the process for deselecting a previously acceptable supplier/subcontractor?

27   Purchasing data

Requirements of ISO 9001 clause 4.6.3

The supplier is required to:

1   Ensure that purchasing documents clearly describe the product ordered.

2   Describe the type, class, grade of product ordered in purchasing documents.

3   In purchasing documents, define the identity and applicable issues of relevant technical data for product ordered.

4   In purchasing documents, define requirements for approval or qualification of product, procedures, process equipment and personnel.

5   In purchasing documents, define the title, number and issue of the quality system standard to be applied.

6   Review and approve purchasing documents for adequacy of specified requirements prior to release.

Purpose of requirements

The purpose of these requirements is to provide a means of communicating purchasing requirements to subcontractors and for establishing the acceptability of supplies provided by the same subcontractors.

Guidance on interpretation

Applicability

The requirement applies to all purchases for supplies that impact the product or service supplied to customers. It applies whether your purchasing system relies on telephone orders or formal purchase orders.

Orders by telephone

With orders placed by telephone to the supplier, there is little documentary evidence that a transaction has taken place. In order to provide adequate control in such circumstances you need to adopt the following practices:

- Provide buyers with read-only access to approved purchasing data in the database.

- Provide buyers with read-only access to a list of approved suppliers in the database.

- Provide a computer file containing details of purchasing transactions with read and write access.

- Provide a procedure which defines the activities, responsibilities and authority of all staff involved in the process.

- Train the buyers in the use of the database.

- Route purchase requisitions only to trained buyers for processing.

Purchasing data

Purchasing data includes the purchase order and any other reference document used to identify the product or service and the conditions under which it is to be supplied. You do not have to impose ISO 9000 requirements on your suppliers. You have to ensure your suppliers meet your requirements and you have a choice of how this is done. Chapter 26 shows that you can use poor suppliers providing you compensate for their inadequacies – you may have little choice if they are the sole supplier of the product or service your require.

Approval of purchasing data

Not only does the purchase order need to be approved but also any reference data that may, or may not be, supplied to the supplier. Approval of this data can denoted in many ways:

- By signature on each document

- By signature on an approval record that is traceable to the document concerned

- By storing the data in a database that has data entry approval controls

- By selecting external documents such as standards and catalogues from an approved list

Your purchasing procedure should identify which personnel have the authority to approve purchasing data.

You can control the adequacy of the purchasing data in four ways:

- Provide the criteria for staff to operate under self control.

- Check everything they do.

- Select those orders which need to be checked on a sample basis.

- Classify orders according to risk and only review and approve those which present a risk.

Consequences of failure

Failure to convey your requirement to suppliers adequately will result in you being supplied products and services that do not fulfil your needs. Reliance on verbal orders may result in the supplier misunderstanding your requirements. They may also result in unsuitable goods being accepted or suitable goods being rejected, if the person placing the order is not the one accepting the delivery. Urgent supplies may be held up until it can be shown that deliveries match requirements.

Inconsistency of requirements

- There is no requirement to establish and maintain purchasing documents only a requirement for what they should contain. This is an oversight. Information passed over telephone lines is data, it is therefore governed by the element 4.5.

- There is no requirement to issue purchasing documents to subcontractors. The phrase 'prior to release' can mean release to subcontractors or release for use (as in the case of a database that is used for purchasing purposes).

Tasks for developers

1 Ensure that the requirements placed on subcontractors are compatible with those of the main contract.

2 Afford the same rights to your subcontractor on contract review as you wish afforded to you by your purchaser.

3 Provide a means of apportioning the requirements of the main contract to the subcontract.

4 Prepare procedures and standards which govern the specification of items to be purchased.

5 Provide standard conditions for subcontracts.

6 Provide a means for adjusting the standard conditions according to the nature of the work subcontracted.

Questions to stimulate policies

1 How do you ensure that purchasing documents clearly describe the product ordered?

2 How do you ensure that purchasing documents are reviewed and approved for adequacy of specified requirements prior to release?

Questions for auditors

Product/service identification

1 What sources of reference data are used to identity purchased product/service?

2 What methods are used to ensure the correct identity of the product/service purchased?

Procurement specifications

1   Who specifies the technical requirements for purchased product and services?

2   In what documents are these requirements defined?

3   What measures are taken to ensure that these specifications remain compatible with current designs?

4   What standards govern the content of procurement specifications?

Quality system requirements

1   Who specifies the quality system and quality assurance requirements to be placed upon suppliers and subcontractors?

2   In which documents are these requirements specified?

3   What criteria are used to determine which conditions apply?

Order approval

1   Who is responsible for reviewing and approving orders before their release?

2   How is approval status denoted on purchase orders?

3   What criteria are used to determine the adequacy of purchasing documents prior to release?

28 Supplier verification at subcontractor's premises

Requirements of ISO 9001 clause 4.6.4.1

The supplier is required to:

1 Specify verification arrangements in purchasing documents where purchased product is to be verified at subcontractor's premises.

2 Specify method of product release in purchasing documents where purchased product is to be verified at subcontractor's premises.

Purpose of requirements

The purpose of these requirements is to prevent subcontractors prohibiting the purchaser from gaining access to their premises to carry out legitimate verification activities.

Guidance on interpretation

These requirements only apply when confidence in supplies cannot be obtained solely by remote means.

Consequences of failure

Failing to specify the verification arrangements and method of product release in the contract may result in a supplier refusing you entry to their premises. This will make your supplier control plan ineffective and, hence, reduce your confidence in the product being supplied.

Inconsistency of requirements

There is no requirement for the supplier to plan and implement any proposed subcontractor verification, only a requirement to specify it. The subcontractor control plans form part of the documented quality system although they are not procedures. Clause 4.2.2b requires that the quality system be implemented so a failure to implement the plans would be a nonconformity with the clause.

Tasks for developers

1 Identify those subcontractors which you intent to subject to on-site surveillance.

2 Prepare a surveillance plan, indicating the activities you will perform and the deliverables required of the subcontractor.

3 Specify the amount of notice the subcontractor will provide before commencing acceptance tests.

4 Establish what constitutes delivery – acceptance on-site or at your premises.

5 Establish how you will accept/reject products or services.

6 Resource the surveillance plan before it becomes contractual.

7 Don't make commitments that you cannot honour.

8 Ensure that the requirement for on-site surveillance and product/service acceptance is stated in the purchase order or subcontract.

9 Obtain the agreement of the subcontractor before commencing surveillance.

Questions to stimulate policies

1 How do you determine the necessity for verifying product at subcontractor's premises?

2 How are your subcontractor verification requirements and methods of product release conveyed to subcontractors?

Questions for auditors

1 How are supplier verification requirements conveyed to the supplier/subcontractor?

2 At what stage in the procurement process are these requirements made known to the supplier/subcontractor?

3 What action is taken should the supplier/subcontractor not agree to the proposed requirements?

4 In the event that changes are necessary following placement of order, how are these handled?

5 What records are maintained to demonstrate that the proposed supplier controls have been correctly applied?

29 Customer verification of subcontracted product

Requirements of ISO 9001 clause 4.6.4.2

The supplier is required to:

1 Afford customers the right to verify at subcontractor's premises that subcontracted product conforms to specified requirements.

Purpose of requirements

The purpose of these requirements is to provide a means for the purchaser's customer to verify purchased product prior to shipment to the supplier.

Guidance on interpretation

These requirements only apply in cases where customers need added confidence in the supplier's control over its subcontractors. Such instances will be specified in the contract with the customer, when they are necessary.

When customers visit your subcontractors, or inspect product on receipt, they have the right to reserve judgement on the final acceptance of the product since it is not under their direct control and they may not be able to carry out all the test and inspections that are required to gain sufficient confidence. Customer visits are to gain confidence and not to accept product.

Consequences of failure

Failure to afford the right of your customers to your supplier's premises may result in your customer rejecting your product, owing to their inability to verify its quality.

Inconsistency of requirements

There is no requirement for the rights afforded to customers to verify subcontracted product to be specified in purchasing documents and conveyed to subcontractors. This is an option for the supplier and if such rights are not conveyed to the subcontractor, problems with customer access may occur. The auditor should establish how the supplier intends to deal with this.

Tasks for developers

1 Establish the purpose of any specified customer visits to your subcontractors.

2 Provide your customer with a copy of your subcontractor surveillance plan.

3 Endeavour to get the customer to agree to accompany you on your visits to the subcontractors.

4 Specify in your subcontract that your customer be given access to verify product.

5 Ensure your customer does not issue visit reports to your subcontractors without them first being screened by you.

Questions to stimulate policies

1 How do you enable customers to verify purchased product at source or upon receipt?

2 What do you do with any evidence of conformity or nonconformity obtained by customers verifying subcontracted product?

Questions for auditors

1 How are customer requirements for verification at supplier's premises conveyed to the supplier?

2 What action is taken should the supplier refuse access to your customers for verification purposes?

3 What arrangements are made to permit customers to enter supplier premises at the agreed times?

4 What records are maintained of customer visits to your suppliers?

5 What action is taken should the customer detect nonconformities to product from a batch that has already been delivered?

30 Control of customer supplied product

Requirements of ISO 9001 clause 4.7

The supplier is required to:

1 Establish and maintain documented procedures for controlling the verification of customer supplied product.

2 Establish and maintain documented procedures for controlling the storage of customer supplied product.

3 Establish and maintain documented procedures for controlling the maintenance of customer supplied product.

4 Record any customer supplied product that is lost, damaged or otherwise unsuitable for use.

5 Report to the customer any customer supplied product that is lost, damaged or otherwise unsuitable for use.

Purpose of requirements

The purpose of these requirements is to prevent loss, damage or deterioration of product not owned by the organization and to prevent the use of any such product that is unsuitable.

Guidance on interpretation

Applicability

These requirements apply to product furnished by the external customer either for incorporation into product that will be subsequently sold back to the customer or for use in executing the contract and which will be subsequently returned to the customer following completion of the contract.

Not all the requirements can be applied to customer supplied services. Product may be tangible goods or may be information (such as personal details provided to banks, credit card agencies etc.) which has to be protected. In education, training, health care etc. the customer supplied product is the pupil, student, delegate, patient etc. In a law practice or financial institution it is any document furnished by the client which will ultimately be returned.

Application

If the customer supplied product is hardware you should maintain a register containing the following details, as applicable:

- Name of product, part numbers, serial numbers and other identifying features

- Name of customer and source of product if different

- Delivery note reference, date of delivery

- Receipt inspection requirements

- Condition on receipt, including reference to any rejection note

- Storage conditions and place of storage

- Maintenance specification if maintenance is required

- Current location and name of custodian

- Date of return to customer or embodiment into supplies

- Part number and serial number of product embodying the customer supplied product

- Dispatch note reference of assembly containing the product

If the customer supplied product is people you should keep registers also with details about the person. In a training class this may be limited to the name and address of the sponsor and the person. In hospitals the register will be much more detailed and include details sufficient to ensure correct diagnosis and prevent incorrect treatment.

Consequences of failure

Failing to provide adequate control over customer supplied product could result in legal action being taken by your customer. If you damage it, lose it or fail to maintain it in accordance with your contractual obligations you could face a demand for compensation in addition to any other penalty that may arise due to your inability to deliver the service or end product to your customer on time.

Inconsistency of requirements

There is no requirement for records of customer supplied product to be maintained only records of such product that is lost, damaged or is unsuitable. The contract should identify the products being supplied by the customer but, if not, the auditor should verify that the inspection records under clause 4.10.5 include such details.

Tasks for developers

1 Don't lose track of customer supplied product.

2 Make sure that users are aware that it is not company property.

3 Give customer supplied product an identity which denotes its source.

4 Establish the condition of customer supplied product before use.

5 Report back to the customer any performance variation of customer supplied product following its embodiment in your product.

6 Provide a register of all products supplied by customers and keep it under central control.

7 Make provision for customer supplied product to be processed through receipt inspection.

8 Prepare procedures for inspecting customer supplied product and notifying the customer of any problems.

9 Provide separate storage areas for customer supplied product.

10 Provide procedures for the receipt and removal of product from stores.

11 Make provision in your contract procedures for requiring customers to supply handling, operating and maintenance instructions as necessary for any product they supply.

12 Provide a form for conveying to the customer the results of any defects detected during receipt inspection, maintenance or operational use.

13 Provide a mechanism for gathering change of use and location of customer supplied product.

Questions to stimulate policies

1 What procedures have been established and documented for controlling customer supplied product?

2 How do you verify customer supplied product?

3 How do you store customer supplied product?

4 How do you maintain customer supplied product?

5 How do you ensure that any lost or unsuitable customer supplied product is recorded and reported to the customer?

Questions for auditors

Preparation

1 What types of customer supplied product are issued to you?

2 What prior arrangements are made to receive customer supplied product?

3 How do you determine the documentation and resources needed to control customer supplied product?

4 In what documents are these arrangements defined?

5 Who is responsible for control of customer supplied product?

Verification

1   What action is taken on receipt of customer supplied product?

2   What checks are performed?

3   In what documents are the acceptance criteria defined?

4   What action is taken should problems be encountered?

5   What records are maintained of the condition of customer supplied product on receipt?

6   How are customers made aware of problems detected on receipt?

7   In what documents are the procedures defined for controlled receipt of customer supplied product?

Storage

1   In what areas is customer supplied product stored prior to and after use?

2   What measures are taken to preserve the integrity of customer supplied product during storage?

3   How are customer supplied products segregated from other products during storage?

4   In what documents are the procedures defined for controlled storage of customer supplied product?

Maintenance

1   How are maintenance requirements for customer supplied product determined?

2   In what documents are these requirements defined?

3   How is maintenance of customer supplied product planned and controlled?

4   What procedures govern maintenance activities on customer supplied product?

Reporting

1 How are customers made aware of problems with product they have supplied?

2 What details are reported to the customer?

3 How are unserviceable customer supplied products identified?

4 Who is responsible for reporting problems to the customer?

5 What records are maintained for determining the location and condition of customer supplied product for the duration of a contract?

31 Product identification and traceability

Requirements of ISO 9001 clause 4.8

The supplier is required to:

1 Establish and maintain documented procedures, where appropriate, for identifying the product from receipt and during all stages of production, delivery and installation.

2 Establish and maintain documented procedures, when specified, for unique identification of individual product or batches.

3 Record the unique identification of product or batches.

Purpose of requirements

The purpose of these requirements is to prevent inadvertent use or installation of incorrect product and to enable the recurrence of nonconformities to be prevented. Tailoring is necessary for specific industries.

Guidance on interpretation

Applicability

These identification requirements apply to products or services supplied to customers after receipt of the component parts or materials and through to delivery and installation. They also apply to support products, materials and equipment, etc. used to produce the deliverable product where absence of identification would cause product nonconformity. They apply only where products cannot be distinguished from one another without additional markings or labels.

The traceability requirements apply only when is it necessary to recall product following the identification of defects and only apply to the traceability of the product and not to the activities carried out on it, such as tests, heat treatment etc. Other requirements in clause 4.14.2 imply a need for traceability in order to establish the cause of nonconformity.

Application

Product identification and traceability requirements need to be established at the design stage so that products are built bearing appropriate identification that will enable them to be distinguished from other products.

Identification

Product identity is vital in many situations to prevent inadvertent mixing, to enable re-ordering, to match products with documents that describe them and to do that basic of all human activities: communicate. Without codes, numbers, labels, names and other forms of identification we cannot adequately describe the product or service to anyone else. We use terms such as 'thingummybob', 'widget', 'you know what I mean, it's a ...' Using names, labels etc. conveys meaning precisely.

Traceability

Traceability, on the other hand, is a notion of being able to trace something through a process to a point along its course either forwards through the process or backwards through the process. One needs traceability to find the root cause of problems. Traceability is key to corrective action and, although the standard only requires traceability when required by contract, assessors will seek an audit trail to determine compliance with the standard. This trail can only be laid by using the principles of traceability.

Consequences of failure

Failing to identify product when its identity is not inherently obvious may result in inadvertent mixing of product or processing and use or shipment of incorrect product. The consequences of such events may be minor but may also damage the organization to the extent of forcing it out of business and in addition may cause severe impact on society and the environment.

Failing to trace a product either backwards to its source or forwards to its user may cause a recurrence of a failure that is preventable. An inability to trace a defective component in a product may result in successive accidents and again force an organization out of business as well as cause the loss of life.

Inconsistency of requirements

- There is no requirement to identify product, only to establish and maintain procedures where appropriate. This is an oversight, however; unless the quality system provides for product to be identified, it will not cause the supply of conforming product and therefore is nonconforming with clause 4.2.1.

- The standard does not specify the circumstances where product identification is required. The auditor needs to establish whether the supplier's controls will prevent the supply of nonconforming product and if identity of the product is not obvious, the system is ineffective and nonconforming with clause 4.2.1.

- The requirement for traceability is limited to where it is a specified requirement but the standard does not indicate whether the specified requirements in this case are those of the customer or those of the supplier. There are, in some cases, legal requirements for traceability; for example, pharmaceuticals, components of public transport vehicles, etc. The auditor needs to establish the regulations that apply and verify that the system makes provision for compliance.

Tasks for developers

1 Centralize the identification system so as to prevent duplication of codes.

2 Specify the product identification details in the product specification and denote where, and with what materials, identification is to applied.

3 Don't claim a higher level of traceability than is necessary for the type of business.

4 Make it a routine that identification data is checked at each inspection and test stage.

5   Don't use product that has lost its identity.

6   Don't mix product as a safeguard against loss of identity.

7   Place identification labels where the product user can see them.

8   Provide a means of tracing the results of verification activities to the characteristics specified in the product specification.

9   Establish an identification system for products and services.

10 Provide registers or other devices for allocating identification numbers to documents which describe products or services.

11 Prepare standards or process specifications for applying identification details to products and services.

12 Decide on which types of product will be given serial numbers.

13 Provide registers for allocating serial numbers to individual products.

14 Make provision on all product records for the product identification to be recorded.

15 Decide on the convention for denoting modification status.

16 Provide specifications for producing and fixing modification plates to product.

17 Make provision in product and process records to capture source details of component parts and materials.

18 Make provision in inspection and test records to capture details of inspection, test and measuring equipment used.

19 Provide registers for allocating batch numbers, date codes and other identification data when appropriate.

20 Make provision on tags, labels etc. for recording product identification details.

21 Provide data storage systems that enable rapid retrieval of records by product identification.

22 Provide for remnant material to retain its identity.

23 Decide who will allocate serial numbers, batch numbers etc.

24 Provide for separated lots or batches to be identified to the original lot or batch.

25 Decide on the minimum level of traceability that is to be maintained for your products.

Questions to stimulate policies

1 What procedures have been established and documented for identifying product?

2 How do you enable products to be identified from receipt and during all stages of production, delivery and installation?

3 How do you ensure traceability of product to original material identification, quality status and the unit responsible for both its supply and verification?

4 How do you identify and record individual product and batches?

Questions for auditors

Identification

1 Who determines the product identification methods?

2 What methods are employed to identify product on receipt?

3 When is the method of product identification determined?

4 What methods are used to identify product during manufacture?

5 What method is used to identify material cut from stock?

6 Who is responsible for applying the appropriate identity to products?

7 How are split batches and materials identified during production?

8 How are products identified which are too small to carry labels?

9 How are differences in specification identified when parts look alike?

10 In what documents are the product identification methods defined?

11 If a product should lose its identity, what action is taken?

12 What happens to the identification labels when they are removed prior to assembly?

13 If a product has been removed following its assembly, how is it identified?

Traceability

1 What traceability requirements have been specified by the customer?

2 How have these requirements been conveyed to the point of implementation?

3 In what documents are these methods defined?

4 When are these requirements conveyed to production?

5 Which assemblies contain parts from this batch?

6 What is the manufacturing history of this part?

7 To which customers have parts from this batch been delivered?

8 What supplier supplied these parts?

9 Where did these parts come from?

10 Where are these parts going to?

11 What records are maintained to indicate the specific identification applied to provide traceability?

32   Process control

Requirements of ISO 9001 clause 4.9

The supplier is required to:

1   Identify and plan the production, installation and servicing processes which directly affect quality.

2   Carry out processes directly affecting quality under controlled conditions.

3   Document those procedures that define the manner of production, installation and servicing.

4   Use suitable production, installation and servicing equipment.

5   Use a suitable working environment.

6   Comply with reference standards/codes, quality plans and/or documented procedures.

7   Monitor and control suitable process parameters.

8   Monitor and control suitable product characteristics.

9   Approve production, installation and servicing processes.

10   Approve production, installation and servicing equipment.

11   Stipulate criteria for workmanship in the clearest practical manner.

12   Provide suitable maintenance of equipment to ensure continuing process capability.

13   Use only qualified operators for special processes or employ continuous monitoring of process parameters.

14   Specify requirements for any qualification of process operations, equipment and personnel.

15   Maintain records for qualified processes, equipment and personnel.

Purpose of requirements

The purpose of these requirements is to prevent variation in result-producing processes from exceeding defined limits. Tailoring is necessary for specific industries.

Guidance on interpretation

Applicability

These requirements apply to production, installation and servicing processes and not to the supporting processes or other processes dealt with in other elements of the standard, such as design, purchasing and delivery. In the service sector they apply to the processes needed to deliver the service, whether activated by a specific customer or not. If the product is a design rather than a product of a design, the requirements will apply to the design process.

Application

There are two ways in which product quality can be controlled: by controlling the product which emerges from the producing processes or by controlling the processes through which the product passes. Process control relies upon control of the elements which drive the process, whereas product control relies upon verification of the product as it emerges from the process.

Production, installation and servicing planning

The planning of production, installation and servicing processes requires three levels:

- Identifying which processes are required to produce, install and service the product

- Designing, commissioning and qualifying these processes for operational use

- Routing the product through the appropriate qualified processes

To ensure that the processes are carried out under controlled conditions the production plans need to define the following as appropriate:

- Identify the product in terms of the specification reference and its issue status.

- Define the quantity required.

- Define which section is to perform the work.

- Define each stage of manufacture and assembly.

- Provide for progress through the various processes to be recorded so that you know what stage the product has reached at any one time.

- Define the special tools, processing equipment, jigs, fixtures and other equipment required to produce the product. General purpose tools and equipment need not be specified because your staff should be trained to select the right tool for the job.

- Define the methods to be used to produce the product either directly or by reference to separate instructions.

- Define the environment to be maintained during production of the product in anything other than ambient conditions.

- Define the process specifications and workmanship standards to be achieved.

- Define the stages at which inspections and tests are to be performed.

- Define any special handling, packaging, marking requirements to be met.

- Define any precautions to be observed to protect health and safety.

- Define the procedures for disposing of any waste or defective product.

Installation plans need to cover in addition:

- Site surveys and site preparation

- Transport and delivery of materials and equipment

- Inspection of equipment entering the site

- Storage of equipment awaiting installation

- Installation of equipment

- Commissioning and acceptance tests

- On-site maintenance before handover

- Handover to customer

- Return of surplus and defective goods

Servicing plans need to cover in addition to production plans:

- The service to be performed

- The consumable materials and spares required

Documented procedures

The standard only requires procedures where their absence would adversely affect quality. Any operation which relies on skills doesn't need a procedure. However, an operator is not clairvoyant and so you may need to provide procedures for simple tasks to convey special safety, handling, packaging and recording requirements. The setting up of equipment, other than equipment typical of the industry, may also need to be specified to ensure consistent results. In fact, any operation which requires tasks to be carried out in a certain sequence to obtain consistent results should be specified in a procedure.

Suitable equipment

This means equipment that is fit for its purpose. In selecting such equipment you should determine whether it is capable of producing, maintaining or handling conforming product consistently. You need to ensure that the equipment is capable of achieving the specified dimensions within the stated tolerances; process capability studies serve this purpose.

Suitable working environment

This means an environment in which product quality will not be impaired by the environmental conditions prevailing when it is produced. It has nothing to do with comfortable conditions for the workers or even safe conditions for the operators. Environmental conditions that may need to be controlled include: temperature, pressure, humidity, cleanliness, vibration, light and electromagnetic field.

Reference documents

The reference documents and codes of practice referred to are those pertaining to the production of the product, not the running of the business. These will normally be the documents referenced in the production drawings, specifications and quality plans.

Monitoring process and product characteristics

The purpose of monitoring the process is, firstly, to establish its capability of producing product correctly and consistently and, secondly, to alert the process operators to conditions which indicate that the process is becoming incapable of producing the product correctly and consistently. This requires process capability studies.

Approval of processes and equipment

All processes and equipment should be proven capable of performing the task for which they were designed and so should either be subject to qualification tests or process capability tests. In the process industries, the plant is specially designed and so needs to be commissioned and qualified by the user.

Workmanship criteria

The results of some processes cannot be directly measured using gauges, tools, test and measuring equipment and so an alternative means has to be found of determining what is conforming product. The term given to such means is *workmanship criteria*, criteria that will enable producers and inspectors to gain a common understanding of what is acceptable and unacceptable. Situations where this may apply in manufacturing are soldering, welding, brazing, riveting, deburring etc. It may also include criteria for finishes, photographs, printing, blemishes and many others.

Maintenance of equipment

In a manufacturing environment, this requirement applies to the process plant, machinery and any other equipment upon which process capability depends. The requirement for documented procedures in 4.9a implies that you will need procedures for maintaining this equipment and this means that you will need:

- A list of the equipment upon which process capability depends

- Defined maintenance requirements specifying maintenance tasks and their frequency

- A maintenance programme which schedules each of the maintenance tasks on a calendar

- Procedures defining how specific maintenance tasks are to be conducted

- Procedures governing the decommissioning of plant prior to planned maintenance

- Procedures governing the commissioning of plant following planned maintenance

- Procedures dealing with the actions required in the event of equipment malfunction

- Maintenance logs that record both the preventive and corrective maintenance work carried out

Special processes

There are some processes where the output is totally dependent upon the personnel, the equipment and the facilities used in their production and which cannot be fully verified by examination of the end product at any stage of assembly. If any of these factors is less than adequate, deficiencies may not become apparent until long after the product enters service. Among such processes are welding, soldering, adhesive bonding, casting, forging, forming, heat treatment, protective treatments, and inspection and test techniques such as X-ray examination, ultrasonics, environmental tests, mechanical stress tests etc.

Consequences of failure

Failing to control the production, installation and servicing processes will result in the variation of product quality being unpredictable. The impact of failure in any one of the attributes of process control will vary from a minor loss of control to a complete breakdown of the process where no conforming products are produced. Inspection may detect the nonconformities but this is a costly way of controlling product quality. Inspection should be used to detect those variations that cannot be adequately controlled within predetermined limits.

Inconsistency of requirements

- The heading to this element does not wholly reflect the scope as the requirements do not refer to inspection as the method of measuring product characteristics. This is not intended to imply that inspection and test are not part of process control but an explanation in this clause would have been useful.

- There is no requirement for the supplier to document the plan of the production, installation and servicing processes. As the plan forms part of the quality system which has to be documented (clause 4.2.1) it follows that the plans for production, installation and servicing processes need to be documented.

- There is no requirement for production, installation and servicing plans to define responsibility for their implementation, unlike the requirement on design and development plans in clause 4.4.2. Responsibilities for such tasks have to be documented as defined in clause 4.2.2.1, whether in these plans or in other documents.

- There is no requirement for production, installation and servicing activities to be assigned to qualified personnel equipped with adequate resources, unlike the requirements for design and development activities of clause 4.4.2. Clause 4.18 requires personnel performing activities to be qualified only. The auditor needs to draw together the requirements of clause 4.1.2.2 and 4.18 and verify that competent personnel, equipped with adequate resources, are assigned to carry out these activities.

- Whereas this clause requires only documented procedures for servicing, where their absence could adversely affect quality, clause 4.19 requires documented procedures regardless of such conditions. There are two types of procedure: control procedures and operating procedures. Clause 4.9 deals with the operating procedures and clause 4.19 with the control procedures.

- There is no requirement to record the results of monitoring and controlling process and product parameters. Depending on the process, records may not be necessary since an on-line monitoring activity may cause the data to be refreshed continually. The absence of records does not indicate a lack of control providing the inspection and test records required by clause 4.10.5 are maintained.

- There is no requirement for records of the equipment used and the environmental conditions provided. The same argument as applied to process monitoring applies in this case. The auditor needs to establish whether a lack of records adversely affects the ability to control the process.

- There is no requirement for records of approved processes and equipment. Without a record of some kind, the supplier will not be able to demonstrate that the processes and equipment in use have been approved. The process controls have to be documented by virtue of clause 4.2.1 and such documentation should include the process and equipment approval method. The 'as appropriate' in the requirement refers to the processes and equipment that need approval.

- There is no requirement for workmanship criteria to be defined and documented, only that they be stipulated. The term *stipulated* means to lay down as a condition of an agreement. The agreement in this case is the procedure. Either the procedure needs to specify the criteria or should make reference to the model, illustration, sample etc. which is to be used.

- There is no requirement for records of equipment maintenance and process capability to be maintained. The same argument as applied to process monitoring applies to this situation.

- There is no requirement for process capability to be determined prior to commencement of production, installation or servicing, unlike the requirements in clause 4.11.1 for the use of measuring devices which have to be proven prior to release. This is an oversight. The requirements for maintenance of equipment to ensure continuing process capability is premature if process capability had not been previously established.

- There is no requirement for the requirements for process qualification to be defined and documented, only that they be specified. The implication is that such process qualification be specified in the production plan or the documented procedures.

Tasks for developers

1 Record the issue status of documents used to fabricate product.

2 Don't destroy labels attached to product when removed for assembly or installation – transfer data to assembly records before destroying the labels.

3 Don't permit product to exit from the production process without having a plan for the operations to be carried out until its return.

4 Don't inspect product until it reaches the planned inspection stage.

5 Don't work to instructions unless provided in the quality system procedures, product specification, production plan or in approved change notices or by the nonconformance review board.

6 Don't countenance informalities, work-around plans or unwritten tips as they create problems when those who know them are absent.

7 Don't work to marked-up specifications unless covered by an approved change note.

8 Don't use parts which have lost their identity.

9 Don't skip operations without considering the effects and obtaining planning approval.

10 Gain set-up approval before commencing long production runs.

11 Delegate as much control to the operator as possible but provide the means for enabling self control.

12 Don't put dots on charts without knowing what causes the results.

13 Monitor the effects of adjusting the process.

14 Don't conduct experiments on the production line.

15 Don't give control of the process to inspection.

16 Display process flowcharts in strategic areas to remind staff of the relationships.

17 Identify the result-producing processes.

18 Provide for the production requirement to be documented and made available to the production planners.

19 Prepare procedures for planning production of product lines and batched and single products.

20 Prepare procedures for providing instructions governing production activities, where necessary.

21 Prepare procedures for provisioning tools, equipment and facilities needed for production.

22 Establish standards of workmanship, where appropriate, and provide means for their control.

23 Provide suitable environments for the conduct of production operations.

24 Provide libraries, or other areas, where staff can gain access to the documentation needed to produce the product.

25 Install controls to enable operators to monitor production processes.

26 Provide travellers or route cards to route product through the production process into stores.

27 Carry out pre-production runs on new designs to prove the production set-up and debug the design.

28 Qualify all new process plant and equipment prior to use in production.

29 Train and qualify operators working with special processes.

30 Prepare and maintain a list of special processes and records of these processes.

31 Provide designated work-in-progress areas for holding product waiting further processing.

32 Provide designated areas, or bins, for product waiting inspection.

33 Provide equipment and containers for the safe transportation of product between operations.

34 Provide separate areas for reworking, repairing or modifying product.

35 Provide a means of distributing parts from stores to assembly stations.

36 Provide security and protection for workmanship standards.

37 Identify any equipment which is vital to your operation and make provision for its maintenance, or replacement, in the event of failure.

Questions to stimulate policies

1 How do you ensure that production, installation and servicing processes that directly affect quality are identified, planned and carried out under controlled conditions?

2 In which documents do you define the manner of production, installation and servicing?

3 In which documents do you define the production, installation and servicing equipment?

4 In which documents do you define the production, installation and servicing working environments?

5 In which documents do you define the reference standards, codes of practice, quality plans and procedures to be complied with during production, installation and servicing?

6 How do you monitor and control process and product characteristics during production, installation and servicing?

7 How do you approve processes and equipment?

8 How do you define criteria for workmanship?

9 How do you ensure continued process capability?

10 In which documents do you define how process equipment is maintained?

11 In which documents do you identify the processes which produce results that cannot be fully verified by subsequent inspection and testing of product?

12 How do you ensure that the results of these processes comply with specified requirements?

13 How are the requirements for process qualification specified?

14 In what documents do you record those processes, personnel and equipment that have been qualified?

Questions for auditors

Manufacturing planning

1 Who is responsible for identifying manufacturing/installation requirements?

2 What types of processes are employed to produce the product or deliver the service?

3 What documents are used to plan the production operations?

4 How is the status of these documents controlled throughout production?

5 How is the sequence of production operations determined?

6 In which documents is the sequence of production operations defined?

7 In which documents is the sequence of inspection and test operations defined?

Workmanship

1 What provisions have been made to ensure consistency in workmanship standards?

2 How are the models/samples/aids for judging workmanship controlled?

3 Who is responsible for controlling workmanship standards?

Environment

1 In which documents are the environmental conditions specified?

2 How would staff be made aware of a deterioration in the prescribed environmental conditions?

Special processes

1 What processes are employed where the quality of the output cannot be verified by subsequent inspection or test?

2 What provisions have been made to qualify these special processes?

3   In which documents are these provisions defined?

4   What records are maintained of qualified processes?

Maintenance

1   What provisions have been made to minimize downtime of production plant due to failure?

2   How are the maintenance requirements conveyed to the process operators?

3   What records are maintained of preventive and corrective maintenance carried out?

Process capability

1   What measures are taken to prevent mistakes in the production process?

2   What measures are taken to minimize errors that may be introduced by the variability in measuring systems?

3   What measures are taken to bring processes under statistical process control before production launch.

4   What measures are taken to determine and improve process capability?

Pre-production/installation

1   What measures are taken to prove production/installation equipment, materials, tooling and processes prior to production launch?

2   In which document are the tools, equipment, jigs and gauges specified for producing, handling and verifying product?

3   What criteria are employed to release products into full production?

Production planning

1   Who is responsible for production planning?

2   In which documents are the quantities required and scheduling of production operations defined?

3   How is the bill of materials determined to meet production demands?

4   How is production allocated to machines/staff?

5   How are changes in the production schedule handled?

6   What checks are carried out to verify that production rates are meeting order requirements?

7   What measures are taken to compensate for failure of products and processes during production?

Production

1   Who is responsible for controlling the processes that produce the product?

2   Who has authority to stop the production process?

3   What instructions have been issued to staff defining the sequence of operations, the methods of manufacture and the equipment and tools to be used?

4   How are critical characteristics identified in production/installation documentation?

5   What monitoring of product and process characteristics is carried out by process operators?

6   What sensors have been installed to provide operators with the information needed to monitor the processes under their control?

7   What records are maintained to show that the processes are under control and within the defined statistical limits?

8   What action do staff take on detecting an abnormal condition?

9   What actions are taken to maintain plant and equipment in a serviceable condition?

10 What action is taken by operators should the plant/equipment malfunction?

11 What action is taken should staff detect errors or ambiguities in the documentation being used?

33 Inspection and test procedures

Requirements of ISO 9001 clause 4.10.1

The supplier is required to:

1 Establish and maintain documented procedures for inspecting and testing activities to verify that specified requirements for the product are
   met.

2 Detail the required inspection and testing in the quality plan or documented procedures.

3 Detail the inspection and test records to be established in the quality
   plan or documented procedures.

Purpose of requirements

The purpose of these requirements is to prevent the release of nonconforming product to a subsequent stage in the process. The purpose of
inspection and test procedures is to implement policy and regulate
processes which are essential to the business. Tailoring is necessary for
specific industries.

Guidance on interpretation

Applicability

Whilst entitled 'Inspection and testing' these requirements apply to all verification activities carried out to determine whether products and services,
and parts thereof, comply with specified requirements. The verification
method can be an analysis, a simulation or a comparison.

These requirements apply to the process of generating the inspection and
test requirements. This process may be part of a design, development or

planning process rather than an inspection process. Many such requirements may be included in the manufacturing drawings, specifications or quality plan but they may also be supplemented with additional requirements for sampling, etc. These documents would define which tests are to be carried out rather than how the test should be performed. They also apply to the procedures used for controlling inspection and test activities as well as those used for performing specific inspections and tests.

Application

To meet this requirement for documented procedures you will need two types of procedure:

- Procedures that provide for the necessary inspections and tests to be planned and carried out at the appropriate stage of the process

- Procedures for carrying out the specific inspections and tests

Also there are two types of record to be considered:

- Records that show which inspections and test have been performed

- Records that show the results of the inspections and tests carried out

Inspection planning

Your inspection and test plans should:

- Identify the product to be inspected and tested.

- Define the specification and acceptance criteria to be used and the issue status which applies.

- Define what is to be inspected at each stage: is it all work between stages or only certain operations? The parameters to be verified should include those which are known to be varied by the manufacturing processes. Those that remain constant from product to product need verifying only once – usually during design proving.

- Define the inspection aids and test equipment to be used. There may be jigs, fixtures, gauges and other aids to inspection that are needed. Standard measuring equipment would not need to be specified as your inspectors and testers should be trained to select the right tools for the job. Any special test equipment should be identified.

- Define the environment for the measurements to be made if critical to the measurements to be made (see Chapter 11).

- Identify the organization that is to perform the inspections and tests

- Make provision for the results of the inspections and test to be recorded.

Consequences of failure

Failing to plan for inspection will result in you not detecting error when its detection is most economic. Failing to provide adequate documented inspection procedures will create conditions in which you will not be able to rely on inspections detecting the errors or adequately identifying and segregating nonconforming product. Failing to provide for inspection records will result in you being reliant on the whim of individual inspectors as to what they record, if anything.

Inconsistency of requirements

Unlike the process control requirements, there is no requirement for inspection to be planned and, unlike the design control requirements, there is no requirement for an inspection plan to be prepared. Requiring inspection to be detailed in a quality plan or documented procedures is too vague to ensure consistent interpretation.

Tasks for developers

1 Prepare procedures for inspection and test planning.

2 Prepare specifications defining the product and process characteristics to be verified and the acceptable limits.

3 Prepare procedures for inspecting and testing incoming goods.

4 Produce procedures for in-process inspection and test.

5 Produce procedures for final inspection and test.

6 Produce blank forms for recording the results of inspections and tests.

Questions to stimulate policies

1   What procedures have been established and documented for inspection and testing activities?

2   How do you establish the inspections and tests required to verify that the specified requirement for product are met?

3   In which documents are the inspecting and testing requirements defined?

4   In which document do you specify the inspection and test records to be established?

Questions for auditors

Procedures for inspection and test

1   Who is responsible for the preparation of inspection and test procedures?

2   What procedures are employed to accept incoming product?

3   What procedures are employed to carry out in-process inspection and test?

4   What procedures are employed for final inspection and test?

5   In which documents are the specific inspection and test methods defined?

6   For what situations do you employ external inspection resources?

7   What measures have been taken to ensure that such resources are adequate?

Inspection and test requirements and records

1   Who determines the inspection and test requirements?

2   In which documents is the sequence of inspections and test specified?

3 In which document are the inspection and test requirements for specific products defined for each stage in the production process?

4 What methods are employed to determine the number of samples required for acceptance inspections/tests?

5 How are the samples required for inspection selected?

6 How and when are these requirements conveyed to the inspectors and testers performing these activities?

7 What records are required to be produced of these inspections and tests?

8 What instructions are provided concerning the recording of inspection and test results?

9 What are the acceptance criteria used in your sampling plans?

10 What visual standards are used to accept product?

11 In what documents are these standards defined?

12 What evidence exists to show that these standards have been approved by the customer, prior to use?

34 Receiving inspection and test

Requirements of ISO 9001 clause 4.10.2

The supplier is required to:

1 Ensure that incoming product is not used or processed until it has been verified as conforming to specified requirements.

2 Conduct receiving verification in accordance with the quality plan or documented procedures.

3 Give consideration to the amount of control exercised at subcontractor premises and the recorded evidence of conformance provided when determining the amount and nature of receiving inspection.

4 Positively identify product which is to be released for urgent production purposes prior to receipt verification.

5 Record products released for urgent production purposes prior to receipt verification.

Purpose of requirements

The purpose of these requirements is to ensure that purchased product and service is deemed acceptable before use and, hence, prevent the release of unacceptable products and services into storage or production.

Guidance on interpretation

Applicability

These requirements apply to product received by the supplier but may be satisfied before receipt. Just-in-time techniques are therefore acceptable providing there is evidence justifying the confidence the supplier has to omit inspection on receipt.

Application

The only way to make certain that no nonconforming product is released for use is to install a *gate* through which only conforming items may pass. You need to register the receipt of items and then pass them to an inspection station equipped to determine conformance with your purchasing requirements. If items would normally pass into stores following inspection, then, as a safeguard, you should also make provision for the storeperson to check that all items received have been through inspection, rejecting any that have not.

When purchasing subcontract labour, you need to ensure, however, that the labour conforms with your requirements before deployment. Such checks will include verification that the personnel provided have the requisite qualifications, skills and knowledge and they are who they say they are. These checks can be made on the documentary evidence provided (such as certificates) but you will probably wish to monitor their performance since it is the effort you have purchased, not the people.

Receipt inspection procedures

The main aspects to cover are as follows:

- Define how the receipt inspection personnel obtain current purchasing requirements.

- Categorize all items that you purchase so that you can assign levels of receipt inspection based on given criteria.

- For each level of inspection, define the checks that are to be carried out and the acceptance criteria to be applied.

- Where dimensional and functional checks are necessary, define how the receipt inspection personnel obtain the acceptance criteria and how they are to conduct the inspections.

- Define the action to be taken when product, the packaging or the documentation is found acceptable.

- Define the action to be taken when the product, the packaging or the documentation is found unacceptable.

- Define the records to be maintained.

Premature release

If you do release a batch of product prior to verification being performed and one out of the batch is subsequently found to be nonconforming, you will need to retrieve all others from the same batch.

Consequences of failure

If no measures were taken to assure product quality before receipt, failing to inspect incoming product could result in the use, processing or shipment of defective product to customers, as characteristics which have not been verified on receipt may never be verified. To neglect to carry out adequate incoming inspection and test may result in you forfeiting your rights to return product later if found defective or nonconforming.

Inconsistency of requirements

There is no requirement for the recorded evidence of conformance obtained through subcontractor controls to be treated as a quality record as there is no reference to clause 4.16. Such evidence does constitute a quality record and thus is an oversight in the standard. If such recorded evidence is not maintained in accordance with clause 4.16, the auditor has to establish how the receiving inspection can be carried out on the basis of such data.

Tasks for developers

1 Attach labels to products on receipt to indicate their inspection status.

2 Don't mix inspected product with uninspected product.

3 Don't permit the release of incoming product until it has either passed inspection or a sample has been taken for inspection.

4 Keep a check on the criteria your inspectors are using to accept product.

5 Ensure current purchasing data is available at the place of receipt inspection.

6 Don't place product back in the receipt inspection area once it has been released.

7 Keep a register of the articles placed in quarantine.

8 Don't permit articles to be removed from quarantine without authorization, a record of why they have been removed and who has removed them.

9 Establish a receipt inspection area for processing incoming goods.

10 Classify goods so as to apply inspection and test according to the need.

11 Define the criteria for acceptance of goods into the organization.

12 Appoint an authority for releasing incoming product to stores or for use.

13 Establish means of dealing with nonconforming product.

14 Provide measuring facilities and equipment for use in the receipt inspection area and measures for their control.

15 Provide a quarantine area to place nonconforming product pending disposition.

16 Establish a means of tracing product back to its inspection on receipt.

Questions to stimulate policies

1 How do you ensure that product is not used or processed until verified as conforming with specified requirements?

2 How do you ensure that product is not dispatched until verified as conforming with specified requirements?

3 How is the amount and nature of receipt inspection determined?

4 When you need to release incoming product for urgent processing, how do you enable immediate recall and replacement in the event of nonconformances being revealed?

5 How do you ensure that incoming product released for urgent production purposes is identified and the identification recorded?

Questions for auditors

Receiving controls

1 Where does incoming product enter the facility?

2 Who is responsible for releasing product into the facility?

3 How do you know that an incoming product does not require receipt inspection?

4 What means are employed to distinguish between products that require inspection and those that do not?

5 For those items requiring receipt inspection, what inspections are carried out?

6 In what documents are these requirements specified?

Receiving inspection requirements

1 Who carries out inspection on incoming goods?

2 How are you made aware of the purchasing requirements?

3 What mechanism is used to keep you informed of any changes in these requirements?

4 How are the receiving inspection and test requirements determined?

5 Who determines these requirements?

6 How are you made aware of the measures taken to control particular subcontractors?

7 How are you informed of the results of any audits or acceptance tests carried out on subcontractor premises?

8 What documentation is required to be supplied with shipments from subcontractors?

9 What action is taken should the required documents not be provided?

Premature release of product

1 What is your policy regarding the release of product into production prior to completing receipt verification?

2 In the event that premature release is required, what action is taken to enable immediate recall should problems be encountered later on?

3 Who is authorized to release product without incoming verification being completed?

4 How do you distinguish between product that has been released under normal conditions and product that has been released prior to incoming verification?

5 In which documents are these methods defined?

35   In-process inspection and test

Requirements of ISO 9001 clause 4.10.3

The supplier is required to:

1   Inspect and test product as required by quality plan and/or documented procedures.

2   Hold product until the required inspection and tests have been completed or reports have been received and verified.

Purpose of requirements

The purpose of these requirements is to detect variation at stages in production where product characteristics are accessible to measurement and ensure that batches that may contain nonconforming product are not released until deemed conforming.

Guidance on interpretation

Applicability

These requirements apply at any stage between receipt and final inspection.

Application

In-process inspection is carried out in order to verify those features and characteristics that would not be accessible to verification by further processing or assembly.

Held product

In continuous production, product is inspected by taking samples from the line which are then examined whilst the line continues producing product. In such cases you will need a means of holding product produced between sampling points until the results of the tests and inspections are available. You will also need a means of releasing product when the results indicate that the product is acceptable. So a Product Release Procedure, or Held Product Procedure, may be necessary.

Consequences of failure

Failing to perform in-process inspection may enable defects to escape detection on final inspection when they may be inaccessible to verification. If such defects can be detected at the final stage, eliminating in-process inspection increases the cost of removing the defect.

Inconsistency of requirements

There is no requirement to perform in-process inspection, only to carry out any in-process inspection in accordance with documented procedures. In-process inspection is only necessary when product characteristics may not be accessible for verification at subsequent stages. The auditor has to establish that where in-process inspections are not performed, all the product characteristics can in fact be verified on final inspection.

Tasks for developers

1 Don't permit product to skip planned inspections and tests without the prior authorization of the planners.

2 Don't mix inspected product with uninspected product.

3 Re-plan inspection and test in the event of rework, repair or modification action.

4 Don't accept product back into the inspection flow without verification that previous inspection stages have not been invalidated.

5 Don't delegate inspection and test operations to others without confirming that they meet the criteria for trained inspectors and testers.

6 Don't permit designers to tinker with deliverable product.

7 Re-validate processes which have been stopped for remedial action before running product.

8 Don't use gauges or other tools for inspection and test purposes unless verified accurate.

9 Don't release nonconforming product until remedial action has been authorized and taken.

10 Don't permit inspectors to rework product unless they produced it.

11 Train operators to inspect and test their own work.

12 Monitor inspection errors, classify them and act on those that are under your control.

13 Protect product after inspection operations.

14 Keep a check on the criteria your inspectors are using to accept product.

15 Provide for inspection and test plans to be produced for verifying product through the various stages of production.

16 Provide a means for progressing the inspections and tests and for identifying those responsible for carrying them out.

17 Provide inspection stations in-process to which product is passed for inspection.

18 Provide inspection aids, tools and measuring equipment appropriate for the task.

19 Provide environmental controls for inspection and test areas where measurement accuracy requires them.

20 Provide facilities for inspectors to obtain current versions of all relevant product specification, drawings and process specifications.

21 Provide areas for held product pending results of final inspection.

22 Provide for products to re-enter the inspection flow following rework, repair or modification.

Questions to stimulate policies

1 How do you ensure that product is inspected, tested and identified as required by the quality plan or documented procedures?

2 How do you ensure product is held until the required inspections and tests or necessary reports have been received and verified?

Questions for auditors

Inspection procedure

1 Who carries out in-process inspections and tests?

2 In what documents are the required in-process inspections and tests specified?

3 What measures are employed to ensure that each product is subjected to the prescribed inspections and tests?

4 If the item under inspection contains a component that was released under positive recall procedures, what additional actions are taken?

5 What records of in-process inspections are created?

6 How is product release indicated?

7 In what documents are these methods defined?

Held product

1 When is sampling used as a means of product acceptance?

2 Where sampling is used, what happens to the batch from which the sample has been taken?

3 What measures are employed to prevent this batch from entering the next process before the results of inspection are notified?

4 Who is responsible for releasing held product?

5 When inspection and test is complete, how is this information transmitted to those holding the rest of the batch?

6 If the results of sampling inspection indicate that the batch is defective, what action is taken?

7 In which documents are these methods defined?

36 Final inspection and test

Requirements of ISO 9001 clause 4.10.4

The supplier is required to:

1   Carry out final inspection and testing in accordance with the quality plan and/or documented procedures.

2   Require all specified inspection and tests to be carried out and results to meet specified requirements.

3   Hold dispatch of product until all activities specified in the quality plan and/or documented procedures have been satisfactorily completed.

4   Hold dispatch of product until all the associated data and documentation is available and authorized.

Purpose of requirements

The purpose of these requirements is to detect nonconformities before products are designated for delivery to customers.

Guidance on interpretation

Applicability

These requirements apply to the last inspection and test stage for a particular product. This may be prior to delivery to an internal stock room, dispatch to a customer or, where responsibilities extend to installation, final inspection will be prior to handover to the customer. There may be several final inspections before ownership of the product passes to the customer.

Final inspection plans

Final inspection plans should contain, as appropriate, some or all of the following:

- Identity of the product to be inspected and tested.

- Definition of the specification and acceptance criteria to be used and the issue status which applies.

- Definition of the inspection aids and test equipment to be used.

- Definition of the environment for the measurements to be made.

- Provision for the results of the inspections and test to be recorded. These need to be presented in a form that correlates with the specified requirements.

Final inspection procedure

There are two aspects to final inspection. One is checking what has gone before and the other is accepting the product.

Final inspection and test checks should detect whether:

- All previous inspections and checks have been performed.

- The product bears the correct identification, part numbers, serial numbers, modification status etc.

- The as-built configuration is the same as the issue status of all the parts, sub-assemblies, assemblies etc. specified by the design standard.

- All recorded nonconformances have been resolved and remedial action taken and verified.

- All concession applications have been approved.

- All inspection and test results have been collected.

- Any result outside the stated limits is either subject to an approved concession, an approved specification change or a retest which shows conformance with the requirements.

- All documentation to be delivered with the product has been produced and conforms to the prescribed standards.

Product release decisions

You need four things before you can release product, whether it be to the stores, to the customer, to the site for installation or elsewhere:

● Sight of the product

● Sight of the requirement with which the product is to conform

● Sight of the objective evidence which purports to demonstrate that the particular product meets the requirement

● Sight of an authorized signatory or the stamp of an approved stamp holder who has checked that the particular product, the evidence and the requirement are in complete accord

Consequences of failure

Unless your processes are capable of only yielding conforming product, failing to subject the product to a final inspection is likely to result in delivery of nonconforming product to customers.

Inconsistency of requirements

● There is a requirement for the results of final inspection to meet specified requirements and not to demonstrate that the product meets specified requirements. The intention here is that the results are within the tolerances range specified in the contract for the particular parameters. The auditor needs to check inspection and test results to verify that none are outside specified limits.

● The requirement for no product to be dispatched until all activities in the quality plan or documented procedures have been completed is inconsistent with the inspection and test requirements. Such plans and procedures may specify activities which do not constrain product dispatch. The auditor needs to establish what activities are required to be carried out and then judge whether any affecting the product remain incomplete.

Tasks for developers

1   Don't mix inspected product with uninspected product.

2   Keep a check on the criteria your inspectors are using to accept product.

Questions to stimulate policies

1   In which document do you define the inspections and tests required to complete the evidence of conformance of the finished product to specified requirements?

2   In which documents do you require all the specified inspections and tests to have been carried out and require the results to meet specified requirements at the final inspection stage?

3   How do you ensure that product is not dispatched until all the specified activities have been satisfactorily completed and the associated data and documentation is available and authorized?

Questions for auditors

Completing evidence of conformity

1   At what stage is final inspection carried out?

2   In which document are the final inspection requirements defined?

3   Who is responsible for final inspection?

4   What evidence is provided at final inspection which indicates the status of previous inspection and test stages?

Ensuring no incomplete dispatch of product

1   How do you ensure that no product is dispatched until all the specified activities have been completed?

2   How are you made aware of the status of the activities specified in the control plan?

3   What authorization is required for the documentation and data that relates to these activities?

4   Who is responsible for the release of product?

5   What action would be taken should any of these activities be incomplete or documents or data be unauthorized?

6   How often is layout inspection and functional verification performed?

7   In which documents are these requirements specified?

8   What records of the results are maintained?

9   Where are these records located?

37   Inspection and test records

Requirements of ISO 9001 clause 4.10.5

The supplier is required to:

1   Establish and maintain records which provide evidence that product has been inspected and/or tested.

2   Ensure that records show clearly whether the product has passed or failed the inspection criteria.

3   Subject failed product to procedures for control of nonconforming product.

4   Record the identify of the inspection authority responsible for release of product.

Purpose of requirements

The purpose of these requirements is to document the basis upon which products or services are released into the organization for storage or processing, or released to customers.

Guidance on interpretation

Applicability

These requirements apply to all records of product and process verification activities at any stage in the development, production, installation or servicing of the product or service.

Types of records

Your inspection and test records or verification records should be of two forms: one which indicates what inspections and tests have been carried out and the other which indicates the results of such inspections and test.

What to record

Don't assume that because a parameter is shown in a specification that an inspector, or tester, will record the result. A result can be a figure, a pass/fail or just a tick. Be specific in what you want recorded. All inspection and test records should define the acceptance criteria, the limits between which the product is acceptable and beyond which the product is unacceptable and, therefore, nonconforming.

Inspection authority

The inspection authority is the organization that decided whether the product was conforming or nonconforming. It may be an individual or an organization.

Action on nonconforming product

The standard emphasizes that a nonconforming product is one which has failed a planned inspection and/or test. Up to that stage, the product is neither conforming nor nonconforming – it is merely in-process.

Consequences of failure

Without records of the verification activities there will be doubt as to what was checked, what criteria were employed and what the result actually was; therefore, disputes may arise either internally or with customers and suppliers. In a dispute, the party with the accurate inspection and test records wins the day.

Inconsistency of requirements

- The cross-reference to clause 4.16 implies that only the records which identify the authority for the release of product have to meet the requirements of clause 4.16 and not the other records referred to in this clause. This unfortunate cross-reference is incorrectly placed and should have been on the first line of this clause.

- There is no requirement for details of the measuring devices used to carry out the inspections and tests to be recorded although, in some cases, it may be impossible to comply with clause 4.11.2f if this were not done.

Tasks for developers

1   Provide a means of recording inspection and test results so that any omissions can be checked at subsequent inspections.

2   Provide secure areas for storing inspection and test records.

Questions to stimulate policies

1   Which documents record the evidence that product has passed inspection and test with defined acceptance criteria?

2   What measures are taken when a product fails to pass any inspection and/or test?

3   In which documents do you identify the inspection authority responsible for the release of conforming product?

Questions for auditors

1   Who determines the type of inspection and test data to be recorded?

2   Where do the acceptance criteria originate that appear on these test records?

3   What mechanism is employed to ensure that the data required on the inspection and test records remains compatible with that in the product specification?

4 Where is the evidence to demonstrate that this particular parameter of the customer specification has been achieved and verified?

5 What provision has been made to identify the release authority for product?

6 How do you indicate whether product has passed or failed the inspections and test specified?

7 What measures are taken to prevent the alteration of these records?

8 What action is taken should the recorded data be found incorrect?

38 Inspection, measuring and test equipment

Requirements of ISO 9001 clause 4.11.1

The supplier is required to:

1 Establish and maintain documented procedures to control inspection, measuring and test equipment.

2 Establish and maintain documented procedures to calibrate inspection, measuring and test equipment.

3 Establish and maintain documented procedures to maintain inspection, measuring and test equipment.

4 Establish and maintain documented procedures to control test software.

5 Establish and maintain documented procedures to calibrate test software.

6 Establish and maintain documented procedures to maintain test software.

7 Use inspection, measuring and test equipment in a manner which ensures that the measurement uncertainty is known.

8 Ensure that measurement uncertainty is consistent with the required measurement capability.

9 Check comparative references to prove that they are capable of verifying the acceptability of product prior to release for use during production, installation and servicing.

10 Recheck comparative references at prescribed intervals.

11 Establish the extent and frequency of checks on comparative references.

12 Maintain records of checks on comparative references.

13 Cause technical data of inspection, measuring and test equipment to be available to the customer, when required.

Purpose of requirements

The purpose of the procedural requirements of this clause are to implement policy and regulate processes which are essential to the business.

The purpose of the hardware and software requirements of this clause is to prevent devices being used for product, service and process verification that will not yield accurate and precise results.

Guidance on interpretation

Applicability

Although the heading implies tangible equipment only, these requirements apply to any device used to determine the acceptability of products and services. The device may be an item of equipment but can also be a piece of software or a reference material when measuring quantitative characteristics. The device can also be a technique such as a written examination or a questionnaire when measuring achievement of qualitative characteristics. Clearly, in such circumstances many of the requirements of this element could not be applied to non-physical measurement techniques and would therefore not be applicable. Tailoring is necessary for specific industries.

If you rely on jigs, tools, fixtures, templates, patterns etc. to form shapes or other characteristics and have no other means of verifying the shape achieved, then these devices become a means of verification. If you use software to control equipment, simulate the environment or operational conditions or carry out tests and you rely on that software doing what it is supposed to do without any separate means of checking the result, then the quality of such software becomes critical to product verification.

Controlling verification devices

You know nothing about an object until you can measure it, but you must measure it accurately and precisely. Hence the devices you use need to be controlled. Control in this instance can mean several things:

• Knowing what devices are used for product verification

- Knowing where the equipment is located

- Knowing who the current custodian is

- Knowing what condition it is in

- Knowing when its accuracy was last checked

- Knowing what checks have been made using the instrument since it was last checked

- Knowing that the measurements made using it are accurate

- Knowing that it is only being used for measuring the parameters for which it was designed

You may not need to know all these things about every device used for product verification but you should know most of them. This knowledge can be gained by three means:

- By controlling the selection of measuring devices

- By controlling the use of measuring devices

- By controlling the calibration of measuring devices

Calibration

Calibration is concerned with determining the values of the errors of a measuring instrument and often involves its adjustment, or scale graduation, to the required accuracy. You should not assume that just because a device was once accurate it will remain so forever.

It is not necessary to calibrate all test and measuring equipment. Some equipment may be used solely as an indicator, such as a thermometer, a clock or a tachometer. Other equipment may be used for diagnostic purposes, to indicate if a fault exists. If such devices are not used for determining the acceptability of products and services or process parameters, their calibration is not essential. However, you should identify such devices as for 'Indication Purposes Only' if their use for measurement is possible. You don't need to identify all clocks and thermometers fixed to walls unless they are used for measurement.

Calibration and verification

There are two systems used for maintaining the accuracy and integrity of measuring devices. The calibration system determines the accuracy of measurement and the verification system determines the integrity of the device. If accuracy is important then the device should be included in the calibration system. If accuracy is not an issue but the device's form, properties or function is important then it should be included in the verification system.

Maintenance

In addition to calibrating the devices you will need to carry out preventive and corrective maintenance in order to keep them in good condition.

Software

To control test software you need to control its use, modification, location (in terms of where it is installed), replication and disposal. Use is controlled by specifying the software by type designation and version in the development and production test procedures. Modifications should be controlled in a manner which complies with the requirements of clauses 4.4.9 and 4.5 of the standard. The location could be controlled by index, register, inventory or other such means, and replication and disposal could be controlled by secure storage and prior authorization routines.

Measurement uncertainty

There is uncertainty in all measurement processes. There are uncertainties attributable to the measuring device being used, the person carrying out the measurements and the environment in which the measurement are carried out. When repeated measurements are taken with the same device on the same dimension of the same product and the results vary, this is measurement uncertainty. Variation in measurement systems arises due to bias, repeatability, reproducibility, stability and linearity (see *Glossary*).

Consequences of failure

Failure to provide accurate verification devices may result in delivery of nonconforming product or service. However, as important, components may nor fit or function together if verified using inaccurate devices and, hence, delay production/delivery. There is little point in measuring anything unless the instrument used is capable of measurement with the required accuracy and precision.

Inconsistency of requirements

This requirement addresses more than the measurement devices referred to as it contains requirements for measurements to be made which may be defined during design. Auditors should be aware that suppliers may misinterpret these requirements.

Tasks for developers

1   Don't bring devices under control of the measurement system if they are not used in performing measurements.

2   Take account of measurement uncertainty in determining the acceptability of product.

3   Don't continue using measuring equipment that has sustained damage even if it appears to have had no effect.

4   Verify that your subcontractors have an adequate calibration system.

5   Produce and maintain a list of the devices which will be used for measuring product and process characteristics.

6   Produce and maintain a list of all tools, jigs, fixtures etc. that will be used as a means of inspection.

7   Produce a list of the software that will be used to verify product or process characteristics and to control equipment that is used to verify product and process characteristics.

8   Prepare procedures controlling the development and maintenance of software used in measurement systems.

9   Validate software used for measurement purposes or that drives measuring equipment.

Questions to stimulate policies

1 What procedures have been established and documented to control, calibrate and maintain inspection, measuring and test equipment (including test software)?

2 How do you control devices used to demonstrate conformance of product with specified requirements?

3 How do you calibrate devices used to demonstrate conformance of product with specified requirements?

4 How do you maintain devices used to demonstrate conformance of product with specified requirements?

5 How do you ensure that measurement uncertainty is known and consistent with the required measurement capability?

6 How do you ensure that devices used as suitable forms of inspection are proven capable of verifying the acceptability of product prior to their release for use during production and installation?

7 What periodic checks are performed on such devices to ensure they remain capable of verifying the acceptability of product?

8 What records are maintained of the checks carried out on devices used as suitable forms of inspection?

9 In which documents do you define your measurement design data?

Questions for auditors

Control of verification devices

1 What types of verification devices are used in this facility?

2 Who is responsible for controlling these devices?

3 How do you ensure that the correct devices are available when needed?

4 How do you distinguish between devices that require control and those that do not?

5   How do users know which device to use for a particular task?

6   What action is taken should a device be found damaged or due for calibration?

7   In which documents are these provisions defined?

Calibration of verification devices

1   Who is responsible for calibrating measuring devices?

2   How do you decide whether or not a device requires calibration?

3   Where are the devices requiring calibration specified?

4   How do you indicate that a measuring device does not require calibration?

5   How do you ensure that devices are submitted for calibration when due?

6   How are new devices brought into the calibration system?

7   How are old devices taken out of the calibration system?

8   What is the policy on the calibration of personal measuring devices?

9   How do you establish the intervals of calibration?

10 In which document are the calibration procedures defined?

Maintenance of verification devices

1   Who is responsible for maintaining inspection, measuring and test equipment?

2   What equipment is subjected to maintenance?

3   Where is this equipment specified?

4   In which documents are the maintenance requirements specified?

5   What action is taken to prevent the failure of equipment?

6   How often is preventive maintenance carried out?

7   What action is taken on detecting that a device has failed in service?

8   What records are maintained of the maintenance carried out?

9 How are devices subjected to preventive or corrective maintenance released back into service?

10 In what documents are the maintenance procedures defined?

Control of test software

1 What test software is used in this facility?

2 Who is responsible for the development of test software?

3 Who is responsible for controlling the use of test software?

4 How is the suitability of test software validated?

5 Who carries out the validation tests?

6 In which documents are the test software control procedures defined?

7 How is test software validation status indicated?

8 What control is exercised over the test software replication process?

9 How is the distribution of test software controlled?

10 How are modifications to test software handled?

11 How is obsolete test software dealt with?

12 How do users know which version of test software to use?

Measurement uncertainty

1 Who is responsible for determining the measurement system for the parameters to be measured?

2 How is measurement uncertainty determined?

3 How have the effects of the operators and the environment been taken into account?

4 What measures have been taken to stabilize the measurement system?

5 How is this information conveyed to those performing the measurements?

6 What studies have been carried out to analyse the variation present in the result of each type of measuring system?

7 Who performed these studies?

Comparative references

1 What verification tasks are performed using comparative references?

2 How has the accuracy of these references been validated?

3 How do you determine when comparative references require checking?

4 How often is the accuracy of these devices rechecked?

5 How is the frequency of such checks determined?

6 What method is used to ensure such devices are submitted for checks at the prescribed time?

7 How are the validation checks performed?

8 Who performs these checks?

9 What records are maintained of these checks?

10 In which documents are these provisions defined?

Measurement data

1 What non-standard measurement systems are employed?

2 What requirements have been specified by the customer for the availability of measurement data?

3 In which documents has the basis of measurement been defined?

4 Where are these documents located?

5 Who is responsible for maintaining these documents?

39 Inspection, measuring and test equipment control procedures

Requirements of ISO 9001 clause 4.11.2

The supplier is required to:

1 Determine the measurements to be made and the accuracy required to demonstrate conformance of product to specified requirements.

2 Select the appropriate inspection, measuring and test equipment that is capable of the necessary accuracy and precision to demonstrate conformance of product to specified requirements.

3 Identify all inspection, measuring and test equipment that can affect product quality.

4 Calibrate and adjust all inspection, measuring and test equipment that can affect product quality.

5 Calibrate devices at prescribed intervals or prior to use.

6 Calibrate devices against certified equipment having a known relationship to internationally or nationally recognized standards.

7 Document the basis of calibration where no recognized standards exist.

8 Define the process employed for the calibration of inspection, measuring and test equipment.

9 Define equipment type and unique identification.

10 Define the location of equipment.

11 Define the frequency of checks and the check method.

12 Define the acceptance criteria.

13 Define the action to be taken when results are unsatisfactory.

14 Identify inspection, measuring and test equipment with a suitable indicator or approved identification record to show the calibration status.

15 Maintain calibration records for inspection, measuring and test equipment.

16 Assess and document the validity of previous inspection and test results when inspection, measuring and test equipment is found to be out of calibration.

17 Carry out calibration in a suitable environment.

18 Carry out inspection, measurements and tests in a suitable environment.

19 Maintain the accuracy and fitness for use of inspection, measuring and test equipment.

20 Safeguard inspection, measuring and test facilities from adjustments which would invalidate the calibration setting.

Purpose of requirements

The purpose of these requirements is to ensure the correct parameters are measured and to prevent devices being used for measurement that will not yield accurate and precise results.

Guidance on interpretation

There are too many requirements in this clause to give more than a cursory examination of the more significant ones.

Applicability

It is not intended that all these requirements be satisfied by one procedure. Several may be needed. Some of the requirements relate to the process where parameters to be measured are identified. This may be during design, development or planning rather than in the calibration process which deals with particular measuring devices. Certainly, in meeting the requirements in clause 4.10.1 the supplier will implement the first two requirements of this clause.

Accuracy and precision

Accuracy and precision are often perceived as synonyms but they are quite different concepts. Accuracy is the difference between the average of a series of measurements and the true value. Precision is the amount of variation around the average.

Devices affecting quality

The register or listing should include the following details as appropriate:

- Name of device, type designation and serial number in order to distinguish it from others
- Specification or drawing defining the device, together with its date and issue status as a record of the acceptance criteria
- Date of manufacture or purchase to determine its age and origin
- Name of custodian and the location of the device in order to trace and resolve problems
- Date when proven against specification and first off in order to determine when it was first deemed serviceable
- Date when re-verification is required
- Details of any modifications and repairs
- Details of any limitations of use
- Details of application if restricted to particular processes, products, ranges etc.

Calibration standards

The calibration standards should be calibrated periodically against national standards held by your national measurement laboratory. This unbroken chain ensures that there is compatibility between measurements made in different locations using different measuring devices.

Calibration records

Calibration records are records of the calibration activities that have taken place. These records should include, where appropriate:

- The precise identity of the device being calibrated (type, name, serial number, configuration if it provides for various optional features)

- The name and location of the owner or custodian

- The date calibration was performed

- Reference to the calibration procedure, its number and issue status

- The condition of the device on receipt

- The results of the calibration in terms of readings before adjustment and readings after adjustment for each designated parameter

- The date fixed for the next calibration

- The permissible limits of error

- The serial numbers of the standards used to calibrate the device

- The environmental conditions prevailing at the time of calibration

- A statement of measurement uncertainty (accuracy and precision)

- Details of any adjustments, servicing, repairs and modifications carried out

- The name of the person performing the calibration

- Details of any limitation on its use

Action on devices found out of calibration

The requirements apply not only to your working standards but also to your calibration standards. In order to reduce the effect of inaccurate equipment, you can select measuring devices that are several orders of magnitude more accurate than your needs so that when the devices drift outside the tolerances, they are still well within the accuracy you require. There still remains a risk that the device might be wildly inaccurate due to being damaged or a malfunction. In such cases you need to adopt the discipline of re-calibrating devices that have been dropped or are otherwise suspect before further use.

Consequences of failure

Failure to identify the measurements to be made may result in nonconforming product being released to customers. Failure to select and apply adequate measuring devices may result in inaccurate results even if the devices chosen are accurate in themselves. Failure to calibrate devices will over time result in inaccurate measurements being taken and failure to adequately protect these devices will result in damage or deterioration and, hence, invalidate the measurements taken.

Inconsistency of requirements

There is no requirement to document the calibration process, only to define it. As with other examples, clause 4.2.1 requires the system to be documented, so the calibration process needs to be documented as well as defined.

Tasks for developers

1 Fix labels to all devices that have been designated for inspection purposes and indicate their calibration status.

2 Calibrate personal tools if they are to be used for making acceptance decisions.

3 Vary the intervals of calibration with the proven stability of the device.

4 Require external calibration laboratories to provide calibration certificates and results.

5 Don't use calibration labels that will not retain their markings in the equipment's operating environment.

6 Provide set-up instructions and diagrams for making special measurements.

7 Calibrate working standards against calibration standards having at least an order of accuracy greater than the working standards.

8   Don't calibrate test devices in the same environment in which they will be used unless you compensate for the environmental effects on measurement accuracy.

9   Retain calibration records for periods which match the period from manufacture to end of warranty or longer.

10 Keep calibration records in secure areas.

11 Display notices on calibration rooms and test laboratories, etc. to warn unauthorized persons of prohibited access.

12 Don't leave the doors of calibration and test rooms open when vacated.

13 Don't purchase any second-hand measuring equipment without the original manual.

14 Don't permit measuring equipment to collect on the floor whilst awaiting calibration.

15 Provide recall notices to recall devices requiring calibration.

16 Provide defect reports for reporting details of unserviceable equipment.

17 Provide labels for fixing to devices in order to denote their calibration status.

18 Provide facilities for the storage of calibration records.

19 Prepare procedures for controlling the use of measuring devices.

20 Prepare procedures for controlling the calibration of measuring devices.

21 Provide a calibration laboratory or select an approved laboratory to calibrate your measurement devices.

22 Arrange for the calibration of your calibration standards.

23 Prepare calibration procedures or data sheets for each measuring device.

24 Process all measuring devices through your established calibration system.

25 Ensure your test and inspection procedures identify the measurements to be made and the accuracy required.

26 Provide containers for transportation of measuring devices.

27 Provide procedures for tracing product verified with equipment and standards found out of calibration.

28 Make provision for recording the identity of devices used in product/process verification.

29 Provide specification and drawings for all jigs, tools, gauges etc. used for measurement purposes.

30 Establish a register of all reference materials used to judge characteristics of samples.

31 Provide specifications and validation certificates for reference materials.

32 Provide secure storage for reference materials and avoid cross contamination and degradation.

Questions to stimulate policies

1 How do you determine the measurements to be made and the accuracy required to demonstrate conformance of product to specified requirements?

2 How do you ensure that appropriate inspection, measuring and test equipment is selected?

3 How do you ensure that inspection, measuring and test equipment is capable of the accuracy and precision necessary?

4 How do you ensure that all inspection, measuring and test equipment that can affect product quality is identified?

5 How do you ensure that all inspection, measuring and test equipment that can affect product quality is calibrated at prescribed intervals or prior to use?

6 How do you ensure that devices are adjusted when they have drifted outside the specified limits?

7 How do you ensure all calibrated inspection, measuring and test equipment has a known valid relationship to nationally recognized standards?

8 In which documents do you record the basis used for calibration where no nationally recognized standards exist?

9 In which documents is the process of calibration defined?

10 What action is taken with devices when calibration results are unsatisfactory?

11 What means do you use to identify the calibration status of inspection, measuring and test equipment?

12 What documents record the calibration of inspection, measuring and test equipment?

13 What action is taken with previous verification results when devices are found to be out of calibration?

14 How do you ensure that environmental conditions are suitable for the calibrations, inspections, measurements and tests being carried out?

15 How do you maintain the accuracy of inspection, measuring and test equipment during handling and storage?

16 How do you safeguard inspection, measuring and test equipment, test facilities and test software from adjustments that would invalidate the calibration setting?

Questions for auditors

Identifying measurements

1 Who determines the measurements to be made for judging the acceptability of products and processes?

2 When are these measurements identified?

3 In what documents are these measurement requirements defined?

4 Under what conditions are these measurements to be made?

Selecting devices

1 How is the appropriate measuring device selected?

2 How do you ensure that the selected devices are of the required accuracy and precision?

3 What happens if the specified device is unavailable?

4 In which documents is the environment specified for performing specific measurements?

5 What records are produced that identify the particular device selected?

Identifying devices

1 How do you distinguish between those devices that can affect quality and those that do not?

2 In which documents are the devices affecting quality identified?

3 What markings are applied to these devices to indicate that they affect quality?

Intervals of calibration

1 How do you determine the intervals of calibration?

2 Against which standards are workshop devices calibrated?

3 Against which standards are secondary standards calibrated?

4 Who calibrates the primary standards?

5 What provisions have been made to ensure that primary standards are traceable to national, or international, standards?

6 What records are maintained of the standards used to calibrate particular instruments?

7 What records are maintained of the condition of devices prior to making adjustment or performing maintenance?

8 What is the policy on adjustment of devices that are found to be within calibration on receipt?

Basis of calibration

1 What situations exist where there are no standards available for the calibration of devices?

2 In which documents is the basis for calibration in such situations defined?

3 How was the accuracy and precision of these standards determined?

4 What records are maintained that prove the validity of such standards?

Calibration procedures

1 What is the process by which a particular device is calibrated?

2 How do you know where particular devices are located?

3 What method is used to trace a device to the calibration records of that device?

4 In which documents are the calibration methods defined?

5 Who specifies the acceptance criteria?

6 Where is the acceptance criteria specified?

7 Where is the frequency of calibration defined?

8 What action is taken when a device fails to meet the acceptance criteria?

9 Where does it define the calibration records required for each device?

Identification of measuring devices

1 How do users establish that the device they are about to use is within calibration?

2 What methods are used to indicate the calibration status of devices?

3 When a device becomes unserviceable, what means are employed to prevent it from being used?

4 Where the item is too small to place a calibration label, what other method is used?

5 What provisions have been made to ensure that the calibration labels will survive the working environment?

Calibration records

1 What records are maintained of the calibrations carried out?

2 Where are these calibration records located?

3 What records are retained of calibrations performed by external laboratories?

4 What records are retained of employee-owned gauges?

5 What records are maintained of the condition of devices as received for calibration?

6 How do you know who calibrated what, when and with what standards?

7 How do you determine when a device reaches the end of its useful life?

Action on devices found out of calibration

1 What information on devices found to be out of calibration is conveyed to the personnel who were the previous users?

2 When and how is this information transmitted?

3 How do you know who to convey such information to?

4 What action is taken by these personnel on receipt of this information?

5 What examples can you provide that demonstrate that appropriate action was taken in such circumstances?

Environmental conditions

1 In which documents is the environment specified for the calibration laboratory?

2 How do you know that this environment is suitable for maintaining the accuracy of measurements?

3 In which document is the environment specified for production inspection and tests?

4 Which devices require special environmental conditions to provide the required accuracy of measurement?

5 How are these devices identified?

6 What provisions have been made to control the environment within the prescribed limits?

Protection of measuring devices

1 What provisions have been made to protect measuring devices from damage and deterioration during use, transportation and storage?

2 How are devices transported between locations?

3 When devices are not in use, what instructions have been provided to personnel to preserve their condition?

4 When devices are in use, what instructions have been provided to personnel to prevent damage and deterioration?

5 Where are devices stored when not in use?

Safeguarding measuring devices

1 What measures have been taken to safeguard devices from unauthorized adjustment?

2 What instructions have been provided to personnel to warn them of actions that may invalidate calibration settings?

3 What action are staff instructed to take should they discover that a seal has been broken?

4 What provisions have been made to prevent unauthorized changes to test software and other comparative references?

5 Who is authorized to enter calibration and test laboratories fitted with environmental controls?

40 Inspection and test status

Requirements of ISO 9001 clause 4.12

The supplier is required to:

1   Identify the inspection and test status of product by means that indicate conformance or nonconformance with inspections and test performed.

2   Maintain the inspection and test status as defined in the quality plan and/or documented procedures throughout production.

3   Maintain the inspection and test status as defined in the quality plan and/or documented procedures throughout installation.

4   Maintain the inspection and test status as defined in the quality plan and/or documented procedures throughout servicing.

5   Only dispatch, use or install product that has passed the required inspections and tests unless released under authorized concession.

Purpose of requirements

The purpose of these requirements is to prevent inadvertent use, dispatch or installation of product that has not been verified or that has failed to meet prescribed verification requirements.

Guidance on interpretation

Applicability

These requirements apply to any product or service that is subject to verification and could be termed 'verification status'. In the service sector, verification status applies to whether a service is operational or non-operational. Such status is often exhibited by notices such as the 'Out of

Order' notice on an automatic cash dispenser in a bank. Tailoring is necessary for specific industries.

Application

With inspection and test status there are only three conditions:

- Uninspected

- Inspected and found conforming (accept)

- Inspected and found nonconforming (reject)

There are no grey areas. Uninspected product is identified by not having an inspection label; inspected product is identified by having an inspection label of the appropriate type (accepted or rejected). If labels are not appropriate, location can be an indicator, providing there is no possibility of mixing conforming product with nonconforming product.

Consequences of failure

Failure to adequately identify the inspection status of product may result in either uninspected or nonconforming product being stored, processed, packed or dispatched.

Inconsistency of requirements

There is an implication that product which does not meet requirements can be released under an authorized concession but there is no requirement in clause 4.13.2 defining who should authorize the concession. The implication is that authorization by the customer is required but it can be anyone who has been authorized through meeting the requirements of clause 4.13.2. In some cases, suppliers may authorize concessions without referral to their customer. This is valid where the customer has not imposed any specific requirements and is purchasing product to the supplier's specification. The auditor needs to verify that such concessions do not conflict with the description of the product as advertised, otherwise there is a nonconformity.

Tasks for developers

1 Don't re-assign inspection stamps to another individual until a reasonable period of time has elapsed.

2 Secure stamps from unauthorized use.

3 Don't leave stamps unattended.

4 Don't lend your stamp to another person.

5 Don't stamp anything unless you have personally inspected the item.

6 Don't stamp any document unless there is a proper location to place the stamp – because it could mean anything; a stamp has to indicate that the specified requirements have been met.

7 Document the methods you employ to denote inspection and test status for hardware, software, documents and services.

8 Specify the status identification methods to be used in product drawings and specifications.

9 Maintain registers of inspection stamp holders.

Questions to stimulate policies

1 How do you identify product in a way that indicates its conformance or nonconformance with regard to inspections and tests performed?

2 How do you ensure the identification of inspection and test status is maintained throughout production and installation?

3 What procedures are employed to ensure that only product that has passed the required inspections and tests is dispatched, used or installed?

Questions for auditors

Identifying inspection status

1   How do you indicate that products have undergone inspection and test?

2   In what circumstances does the location of product indicate its inspection status?

3   How are nonconforming products identified?

4   When are nonconforming products identified as nonconforming?

5   In which documents is the location of the markings specified?

6   What special inspection status identification methods have been specified by your customer?

7   In which documents are these provisions defined?

Maintaining inspection status

1   What provisions have been made to prevent labels from becoming detached from products during production?

2   What happens to the labels removed from products installed in assemblies?

3   What action would be taken in the event that an inspection status label became parted from the product?

4   In which documents are these provisions defined?

41 Nonconforming product control procedures

Requirements of ISO 9001 clause 4.13.1

The supplier is required to:

1 Establish and maintain documented procedures to prevent unintended use of nonconforming product.

2 Provide for the identification of nonconforming product.

3 Provide for the documentation of nonconforming product.

4 Provide for the evaluation of nonconforming product.

5 Provide for the segregation of nonconforming product.

6 Provide for the disposition of nonconforming product.

7 Notify functions concerned of nonconforming product.

Purpose of requirements

The purpose of these requirements is to prevent the unintended use of product which does not conform to specified requirements.

Guidance on interpretation

Applicability

These requirements apply to any product or service which has been subject to verification and found not to conform to specified requirements. They only apply to the particular product or service found nonconforming and those exhibiting the same deficiency whether before or after delivery of product or service. They do not apply to processes or quality systems. In a continuous process where product is sampled and the mix adjusted until the correct consistency or proportions are achieved, nonconformities do not arise until completion of the process and at a stage where it is not possible for product to be re-processed. They do not apply to product that has been released to customers. This condition is addressed in clause 4.14.2. Tailoring is necessary for specific industries.

Application

ISO 9000 requires that you meet specified requirements, it does not require that you produce products which satisfy stated or implied needs, or satisfy intended usage requirements. In practice, however, you should produce products and services which:

- Satisfy the specified requirements

- Satisfy intended usage requirements

- Satisfy stated or implied needs

- Satisfy your own requirements

Documenting nonconforming product

There are several ways in which you can document the presence of a non-conformance. You can record the condition:

- On a label attached to the item

- On a form unique to the item, such as a nonconformance report

- Of functional failures on a failure report and physical errors on a defect report

- In a log book for the item, such as an inspection history record or snag sheet

- In a log book for the workshop or area, such as a process log.

Consequences of failure

Failure to control nonconforming product may result in unacceptable product being stored, used or delivered. By not identifying and segregating such product, staff may inadvertently use it. By not documenting the nonconformity errors may arise in communication and inadequate action result. By not providing for nonconforming product to be dispositioned under controlled conditions, unauthorized personnel may release unacceptable product into the delivery stream.

Inconsistency of requirements

- The standard does not indicate whether these requirements are to apply to product that is suspected of being nonconforming – which might be the case with a batch of product that has failed the sampling inspection. Only the samples checked are definitely nonconforming – the others in the batch are only suspected as being nonconforming. You should therefore look further than the product that has been found to be nonconforming and seek out other products which may possess the same characteristics as those found to be nonconforming.

- The requirement for the documented procedures to provide for the disposition of nonconforming product is incomplete. The supplier's procedures for the control of nonconforming product should cover the disposition process including the decisions, the execution of the decisions and their subsequent verification.

- The standard does not make it clear whether these requirements apply to nonconformities detected whilst the supplier is responsible for the product or after the supplier's responsibility ceases as is the case with nonconformity reports received from customers. Reports of nonconformities are also addressed under corrective action in clause 4.14 but it is assumed that in this case the standard is concerned with external reports of nonconformities.

- The limitation of the term to specified requirements causes problems when you have failed to meet your own requirements but still meet the specified customer requirements. What does one call such an error? There will be cases also where you fully satisfy the specified requirements but the product is unfit for use because of omissions in the specified requirements. ISO 8402 states that the nonfulfilment of intended usage requirement is a defect rather than a nonconformity. ISO 9000 does not address the subject of defects since it assumes that a product which meets the specified requirements must meet intended usage requirements. However, a product may fail to meet the specified requirements and still be fit for use.

Tasks for developers

1   Don't apply the nonconformance controls of the standard to anything other than products and services.

2   Specify the requirement as well as the actual condition on nonconformance reports.

3   Schedule verification activities so as to detect nonconformances, as early as possible.

4   Make nonconformance data available at final inspection.

5   Don't identify nonconformances in a manner that will leave a permanent mark on the article.

6   Remove nonconforming articles from the process as soon as the nonconformance has been confirmed.

7   Provide limited access to quarantine areas.

8   File nonconformance data where operators and inspectors can review it.

9   Decide on your own definition of what constitutes a nonconformance.

10 Decide on what products and processes will be governed by the nonconformance control procedures.

11 Develop a means of classifying nonconformances.

12 Decide on who the acceptance authority is to be for each product, project or contract for each class of nonconformance.

13 Provide forms or logs for recording details of nonconformances.

14 Provide reject labels for identifying nonconforming articles.

15 Provide serviceable and unserviceable labels for identifying operational equipment.

16 Provide a register of nonconformance reports.

17 Prepare procedures for processing nonconforming articles.

18 Provide quarantine areas in which to place articles pending disposition action.

19 Prepare procedures for controlling these quarantine areas.

20 Provide inspectors with the criteria for selecting the functions to be contacted when nonconformities are detected.

21 Provide inspectors with information necessary to contact the disposition authorities promptly and with escalation procedures in the event that initial contact fails.

Questions to stimulate policies

1 What procedures have been established and documented controlling nonconforming product?

2 How do you ensure that product which does not conform to specified requirements is prevented from inadvertent use or installation?

3 How do you ensure nonconforming product is identified?

4 How do you ensure nonconforming product is documented?

5 How do you ensure nonconforming product is evaluated?

6 How do you ensure nonconforming product is segregated?

7 How do you ensure nonconforming product is dispositioned and concerned functions notified?

Questions for auditors

Identifying nonconforming product

1 How is nonconforming product distinguished from conforming product?

2   Who is responsible for identifying nonconforming product?

3   What measures are taken to identify areas containing nonconforming product?

4   What information is provided on the labels attached to nonconforming product?

5   In which documents are these provisions defined?

Documenting nonconforming product

1   Who determines if a product is nonconforming?

2   What details are recorded of the nonconformity?

3   When are these documents created?

4   In which documents are these details specified?

5   What action would be taken if a nonconformity was only suspected?

Segregating nonconforming product

1   Where are nonconforming products located?

2   When segregation is not feasible, how is the nonconforming product prevented from re-entering the production flow?

3   What records are maintained of nonconforming items entering and leaving the segregated area?

4   What provisions have been made to prevent access to these areas?

5   In which documents are these provisions defined?

Notifying function concerned

1   Which functions are notified of the existence of nonconforming product?

2   How do the detectors of nonconforming product know who to notify?

3   How is this information conveyed to these functions?

4   What measures are in place to expedite dispositions from the functions that have been notified?

42 Nonconformity review and disposition

Requirements of ISO 9001 clause 4.13.2

The supplier is required to:

1   Define the responsibility for the review and authority for the disposition of nonconforming product.

2   Review nonconforming product in accordance with documented procedures.

3   Report proposed use of nonconforming product to customer when required.

4   Record the actual condition of accepted nonconformity and repairs.

5   Re-inspect repaired and/or reworked product in accordance with quality plan and/or documented procedures.

Purpose of requirements

The purpose of these requirements is to prevent unauthorized personnel disposing of nonconforming product and to prevent corrected nonconforming product from entering the conforming product stream until verified conforming.

Guidance on interpretation

Applicability

These requirements apply to the disposal of nonconforming product or service including any which is deemed useable without change.

Application

When product is found to be nonconforming there are three decisions you have to make:

- Can the product be made to conform?

- If not, is it fit for use?

- If not, can it be made fit for use?

If you choose to accept a nonconforming item without rework, repair etc. then you are, in effect, granting a *concession* for that particular item only. If the requirements cannot be achieved at all, this is not a situation for a concession but a case for a change in requirement. If you know in advance of producing the product or service that it will not conform with the requirements, you can request a deviation from the requirements (also called a *production permit*). Both requests should be made to the acceptance authority for the product.

Dispositions

To implement these requirements your nonconformance control procedures need to cover the following:

- Specify how product should be scrapped, or recycled, the forms to be used, the authorizations to be obtained.

- Specify the various repair procedures, how they should be produced, selected and implemented.

- Specify how modifications should be defined, identified and implemented.

- Specify how production permits (deviations) and concessions (waivers) should be requested, evaluated and approved or rejected.

- Specify how product should be returned to its supplier, the forms to be used and any identification requirements so that you can detect it on its return.

- Specify how regrading product is to be carried out, the product markings, prior authorization and acceptance criteria.

Remedial action

When making the disposition your remedial action needs to address:

- Action on the nonconforming item to remove the nonconformity

- A search for other similar items which may be nonconforming (i.e. *suspect* product)

- Action to recall product containing suspect, nonconforming product

Recall

If you need to recall product that is suspected as being defective you will need to devise a *recall plan*, specify responsibilities and time-scales and put the plan into effect. Product recall can be either a *remedial action* or a *preventive action*, depending on whether the failure has already occurred in the product being recalled. It is not a *corrective action*.

Consequences of failure

Failure to assign responsibility for the review and disposition on nonconformities may leave unauthorized staff to decide what to do and result in delivery of unacceptable and/or unsafe product and, hence, irate customers. It may also result in inconsistent decisions and a reputation for sloppy workmanship. Without proof of the actual condition accepted, you cannot hold those who made a decision accountable. Failure to re-inspect/retest product following remedial action has the same result as failing to inspect/test the product initially. During the rework/repair process previously acceptable features may have been affected and therefore the inspection should not be limited to the features that were nonconforming.

Inconsistency of requirements

- The requirement for responsibility for review and authority for the disposition of nonconforming product to be defined duplicates that given in clause 4.1.2.1. The requirement should have indicated that those performing the review and making the decision need to be qualified.

- The context in which the term *specified requirements* is used in clause 4.13.2 implies that they are customer requirements and not supplier requirements, otherwise there is no reason to report the nonconformance to the customer for concession.

- There is no requirement for the concession reported to the customer to be accepted by the customer. Clause 4.12 permits nonconforming product to be released under an authorized concession but does not specify that the customer should have authorized it. The contract will usually define the acceptance criteria and the arrangements for delivery of nonconforming product.

Tasks for developers

1   Consider the cost of replacement against the cost of rework or repair.

2   Check other articles if the nonconformance appears to be symptomatic of the producing process.

3   Don't change the design by means of a nonconformance report or concession.

4   Confirm the nonconformance before advocating remedial action.

5   Investigate the history of the nonconformance before specifying remedial action – the previous remedial action may not have been successful.

6   Record the remedial action required and the nature of re-verification.

7   Obtain agreement to any repair instructions prior to being implemented.

8   Don't limit the nonconformance review board to members of the quality department.

9   Subject reported subcontractor nonconformances to equal treatment.

10   Achieve unanimous agreement on the disposition of all nonconformances.

11   Keep the records of the nature of nonconformance, the disposition and the result of post remedial action verification together.

12   Decide on who is to evaluate nonconformances.

13   Set up a review board to disposition nonconformances and allocate responsibilities.

14   Set up a file for storing records of nonconformance dispositions.

15   Provide for product to re-enter the process for rework, repair or modification action.

16 Provide a means of controlling the return of reject articles to suppliers.

17 Provide a means for scrapping unusable articles under controlled conditions.

18 Provide forms for requesting deviations and waivers from your customer, when appropriate.

19 Provide a means for tracking remedial actions on nonconforming articles.

Questions to stimulate policies

1 In which documents do you define the responsibility for the review and the authority for the disposition of nonconforming product?

2 How do you ensure that dispositions on nonconforming product are implemented as specified?

3 How do you seek permission for the purchaser to use or repair product that does not conform to specified requirements?

4 In which document do you record the description of nonconformity or repairs that have been accepted?

5 How do you ensure that repairs and reworked product are re-inspected in accordance with documented procedures?

Questions for auditors

Evaluation of nonconforming product

1 Who is informed when a nonconformity is detected?

2 Who carries out the evaluation of the nonconforming product?

3 What factors are taken into account in performing the nonconformity evaluation?

4 How do you determine who should be involved in the review and disposition of the nonconformity?

5 How is information on the nonconformity conveyed to these personnel?

6 In which documents is the responsibility and authority of those carrying out nonconformity review and disposition defined?

7 What are the criteria used in the review and disposition of nonconforming product?

8 In which documents is the disposition action conveyed to those who are to carry it out?

Control of dispositioned product

1 What instructions are provided to personnel assigned to carry out the nonconformity disposition?

2 What measures are taken to seek out other products which may possess the same nonconformity?

3 What action is taken on product already delivered to customers?

4 What procedures are employed for returning nonconforming product to subcontractors?

Use of nonconforming product

1 When the disposition action is 'use-as-is', how is this conveyed to production?

2 Under what circumstances would a 'use-as-is' decision be made?

3 Under what circumstances would customer approval be sought for such decisions?

4 How is customer approval for a waiver obtained?

5 How do you identify product subject to waiver application?

6 Where are the waiver applications filed?

7 What record of the waiver approval is provided to customers in the shipping documentation?

Re-inspection and test

1 In what documents do you define the inspection and test requirements for rectified nonconforming product?

2 How does rectified nonconforming product enter the production flow?

3 At what stage is the nonconformity identification label removed?

43 Corrective action

Corrective action requirements of ISO 9001 clauses 4.14.1 & 4.14.2

The supplier is required to:

1 Establish and maintain documented procedures for implementing corrective actions.

2 Eliminate the causes of actual nonconformities to a degree appropriate to the magnitude of problems and commensurate with the risks encountered.

3 Implement any changes to the documented procedures resulting from corrective actions.

4 Record any changes to the documented procedures resulting from corrective actions.

5 Provide for the effective handling of customer complaints.

6 Provide for the effective handling of reports of product nonconformities.

7 Investigate the cause of nonconformities relating to products.

8 Investigate the cause of nonconformities relating to processes.

9 Investigate the cause of nonconformities relating to the quality system.

10 Record the result of investigations to determine the cause of nonconformities.

11 Determine the corrective actions needed to eliminate the cause of nonconformities.

12 Apply controls to ensure that corrective action is taken and is effective.

Purpose of requirements

The purpose of these requirements is to prevent the recurrence of identified nonconformities.

Guidance on interpretation

Applicability

The corrective action requirements apply to any product, service, process or quality system possessing nonconformities, not just products. The preventive action requirements apply to all products, services and operations affecting the quality of those products and services. Corrective actions can only be taken when there has been a nonconformity. No tailoring is needed for specific industries.

Application

Corrective action is the pattern of activities which traces the symptoms of a problem to its cause, produces solutions for preventing the recurrence of the problem, implements the changes and monitors that the change has been successful in eliminating the problem. *Corrective action* is not an action taken to remedy a nonconformity; this is *remedial action* and is addressed by element 4.13 of ISO 9001. A problem has to exist for you to take corrective action.

Corrective action procedures

As the sources of nonconformances are so variable it may not be practical to have a single corrective or preventive action procedure. It may be more practical to embody corrective action provisions in several different procedures (for example, Failure Investigation, Nonconforming Material Review, Customer Complaints etc.)

Deciding to take corrective action

The decision to act should be based on the magnitude of the problem and the risks encountered and, hence, you only need act on the vital few. To find the vital few you have to collect and analyse the data in the first place. Having made your proposals, you should then conduct a risk analysis as part of the solution. Before managers will take action, they need to know:

- What is the problem?

- Has the problem been confirmed?

- What are the consequences of doing nothing; that is, what effect is it having?

- What is the preferred solution?

- How much will the solution cost?

- How much will the solution save?

- What are the alternatives and their relative costs?

- If I have to act, how long have I got before the effects damage the business?

The process is running while you carry out your analysis, other nonconformities may be being generated and remedial action taken. Timing may be critical or of no consequence. The cost of the solution may outweigh the benefits.

Customer complaints

Customer complaints may be as a result of persistent nonconformities or as a result of a single nonconformity. If the latter, the action you take is initially a remedial action, followed by a corrective action to prevent a recurrence of the complaint.

Your customer complaints procedure should cover the following aspects to be effective:

- A definition of when a message from a customer can be classified as a complaint

- The method of capturing the customer complaints from all interface channels with the customer

- The registration of complaints so that you can account for them and monitor progress

- A form on which to record details of the complaint, the date, customer name etc.

- A process for acknowledging the complaint so that the customer knows you care

- A process for investigating the nature of the complaint

- A process for replacing product, repeating the service or compensating the customer

Reports of nonconformities

Assuming that the standard is only referring to external reports of non-conformities, your procedures should cover very similar processes as those for the handling of customer complaints:

- The method of receiving and identifying returned product

- The method of logging reports of nonconformities from customers

- The process of responding to customer requests for assistance

- The process of dispatching service personnel to the customer's premises

- A form on which to record details of the nonconformance, the date, customer name etc.

- A process for acknowledging the report so that the customer knows you care

- A process for investigating the nature of the nonconformance

- A process for replacing or repairing nonconforming product and restoring customer equipment into service

- A process for assessing all product in service which is nonconforming and determining and implementing recall action if necessary

Investigating nonconformities

In order to investigate the cause of nonconformances you will need to:

- Identify the requirements that have not been achieved.

- Collect data on nonconforming items, the quantity, frequency and distribution.

- Identify when, where and under what conditions the nonconformances occurred.

- Identify what operations were being carried out at the time and by whom.

Many organizations use a Nonconformity Report to deal with the remedial action and a Corrective Action Report or Request to prevent the recurrence of one or more nonconformities. In this way you are not committed to taking action on every incident but on a group of incidents when the action and its cost can be more easily justified.

There are many tools you can use to help you determine the root cause of problems. These are known as *Disciplined Problem Solving Methods*.

The seven quality tools in common use are as follows:

1 *Pareto diagrams*, used to classify problems according to cause and phenomenon.

2 *Cause and effect diagrams*, used to analyse the characteristics of a process or situation.

3 *Histograms*, used to reveal the variation of characteristics or frequency distribution obtained from measurement.

4 *Control charts*, used to detect abnormal trends around control limits.

5 *Scatter diagrams*, used to illustrate the association between two pieces of corresponding data.

6 *Graphs*, used to display data for comparative purposes.

7 *Check-sheets*, used to tabulate results through routine checks of a situation.

The further seven quality tools for use when not all data is available are:

1 *Relations diagram*, used to clarify interrelations in a complex situation.

2 *Affinity diagram*, used to pull ideas from a group of people and group them into natural relationships.

3 *Tree diagram*, used to show the interrelations among goals and measures.

4 *Matrix diagram*, used to clarify the relations between two different factors (e.g. QFD).

5 *Matrix data-analysis diagram*, used when the matrix chart does not provide sufficiently detailed information.

6 *Process decision program chart*, used in operations research.

7 *Arrow diagram*, used to show steps necessary to implement a plan (e.g. PERT).

Causes of nonconformity

The source of causes is not unlimited. Nonconformities are caused by one or more of the following:

- Deficiencies in communication
- Deficiencies in documentation
- Deficiencies in personnel training, attitude, behaviour and motivation
- Deficiencies in materials
- Deficiencies in tools and equipment
- Deficiencies in the operating environment

Corrective action plans

Your corrective action plan should address as appropriate:

- Immediate action to prevent recurrence, such as warning notices, alerts etc.
- Longer term action to prevent recurrence, such as changes to plans, procedures, specifications, training etc.

Consequences of failure

Failure to take corrective action may result in escalation in customer complaints, internal costs and generally deteriorating standards with disastrous consequences. You cannot go on indefinitely fixing problems – there comes a time when you have to stop them recurring.

Inconsistency of requirements

- The corrective action requirements fail to stipulate when corrective action should be taken except to say that they shall be to a degree appropriate to the risks encountered. There is no compulsion for the supplier to correct nonconformances before repeat production or shipment of subsequent product.

- There is no requirement for the corrective action procedures to require proposed corrective actions to be defined and documented. This is an oversight. The auditor needs to examine the procedures and establish whether, in the circumstances, the effectiveness of the quality system is impaired by not documenting the corrective actions.

- There is no requirement to record the corrective actions taken, only those which result in changing documented procedures. Again an oversight. Records will usually exist but as there is no reference to clause 4.16, they do not have to be maintained for a defined period.

- The requirement for the corrective action procedure to include the effective handling of reports of product nonconformities duplicates the requirement in clause 4.13.1 for documented procedures for nonconforming product unless the requirement of clause 4.14.2 is intended to apply only after delivery of product to customers.

- There is no requirement for the relevant information on corrective actions taken to be submitted for management review unlike the requirements of clause 4.14.3d for preventive action. This is an oversight. As the management review is required to be of the quality system, then all aspects of the system should be reviewed, not just those where indicated in the standard.

- There is no requirement for corrective actions to be initiated, unlike clause 4.14.3c for preventive actions. An oversight but not a serious one. Control cannot be applied to something that has not been initiated.

Tasks for developers

1 Don't take action before you have confirmed the presence of a problem.

2 Don't announce you have confirmed that a problem exists before you have assessed its significance.

3 Check that the agreed corrective actions are being taken.

4 Don't wait until the due date for the completion of the action to check if work has started.

5 Accept legitimate reasons for inaction and agree new target dates.

6 Enlist the support of the organization responsible for the problem to investigate the cause.

7 Don't impose corrective actions on other organizations without their agreement.

8 Don't persist with proposals for corrective action if management tells you they are not economic – find more economic solutions.

9 Capture your organization's recovery plans into the corrective action system.

10 Impress on management that corrective action procedures exist to save resources.

11 Tell your complaining customers the action you have taken to resolve their problem.

12 Don't limit your corrective action system to products – apply it to all operations including management decision making.

13 Use corrective action procedures to remove the flaws in the system, and do it continually.

14 Provide a means of collecting data from all verification operations.

15 Set up a procedure for recording customer complaints.

16 Provide a means for collecting design change and document change requests.

17 Provide in the relevant procedures requirements for recording and transmitting data pertinent to any subsequent corrective action analysis.

18 Provide, where relevant, a means of recording continuous processes to detect deviation from the agreed standard.

19 Establish performance indicators for each significant process.

20 Establish a method of recording the baseline performance for each of these processes.

21 Decide on who is to collect and analyse the data for determination of both corrective and preventive actions.

22 Decide on who is to investigate and propose corrective actions and preventive actions.

23 Prepare procedures for the analysis, investigation and determination of the causes of deviation, including the formation of diagnostic teams where necessary.

24 Provide tools and techniques to help investigators discover the causes of actual deviation and determine their significance.

25 Provide for solutions to prevent the recurrence of deviations to be proposed and agreed.

26 Provide forms for recording the agreed corrective and preventive action and target dates for completion.

27 Prepare procedures for reporting the results of the analyses to management.

28 Provide links between the corrective action reports and document, product, process and organization changes.

29 Provide procedures for product recall.

30 Provide an escalation procedure for use when corrective action target dates have been exceeded or where detected problems require management action.

31 Provide procedures for managing corrective action programmes where collective action is required.

32 Provide visual evidence of required performance against actual performance at work locations.

33 Provide procedures for verifying that corrective actions achieve their objectives.

Questions to stimulate policies

1 In which documents have you defined your corrective action procedures?

2 How do you ensure that the corrective taken is to a degree appropriate to the magnitude of the problem and commensurate to the risks encountered?

3 How do you implement and record changes resulting from corrective action?

4 How do you handle customer complaints?

5 How do you handle reports of product nonconformities?

6 How do you ensure the cause of nonconforming product is investigated?

7 How do you eliminate the cause of nonconformities?

8 How do you ensure that corrective actions are taken and are effective?

Questions for auditors

Procedures

1 What procedures do you employ for detecting and eliminating product nonconformities ?

2 In what documents are these procedures defined?

Deciding appropriate action

1 What criteria do you use to decide whether to take corrective action?

2 Who carries out the analysis for the decision makers?

3 Who decides whether action should be taken?

4 What records are kept of these decisions?

5 In which documents are these methods defined?

Implementing changes to procedures

1 When a change to the quality system procedures is necessary to prevent the recurrence of a nonconformity, what records are kept of this change?

2 In which documents are these methods defined?

Customer complaints

1 Who is responsible for co-ordinating the resolution of customer complaints?

2 What action do you take on receipt of a customer complaint?

3 What criteria do you employ to validate the complaint?

4 What action do you take should you find the complaint is unjustified?

5 How do you know that you have captured all customer complaints?

6 What instructions have been issued that will ensure all complaints are captured?

7 How soon after receipt of a complaint is the customer notified of the action you intend taking?

8 What records are kept of the complaint and the action taken?

9 In which documents are these methods defined?

10 What happens to the records once the complaint has been resolved?

11 Under what circumstances would the complaint be reported to top management?

Product nonconformities

1 Who is responsible for dealing with products returned from customers?

2 How do you deal with products returned from customers reported as being nonconforming with their requirements?

3 How are these items identified?

4 Who is responsible for resolving these issues?

5 In which documents are these methods defined?

6 How do you process repairs and replacements?

7 If the customer is unable to return the product, how is the nonconformity resolved?

8 What records are kept of reported nonconformities?

9 How soon after receipt of the nonconforming product is the customer notified of the action you intend taking?

Nonconformity investigations

1 What constitutes a product/process/system nonconformity?

2 What action is taken on detection of a product/process/system nonconformity?

3 What measures are employed to determine the root cause of product/process/system nonconformities?

4 How often are investigations into the cause of product/process/system nonconformity conducted?

5 Who conducts these investigations?

6 What techniques are employed to determine the cause?

7 What records are kept of the results of investigations into product/process/system nonconformity?

8 In which documents are these methods defined?

Preventing recurrence of nonconformities

1 Who determines the action to be taken to prevent a recurrence of the nonconformity?

2 In which documents are the proposed corrective actions defined?

3 If the action required will affect more than one department, how is this handled?

4 Whose approval is needed before a corrective action can be implemented?

5 Who checks whether the proposed action will, if implemented, resolve the problem?

6 What action is taken if the corrective action requires additional resources?

7 To what extent is the customer involved in agreeing the corrective action when the nonconformity resulted from a customer complaint or returned product?

8 What time-scales are given for the completion of corrective actions?

9 In which documents are these methods defined?

Corrective action controls

1 How do you ensure that the agreed corrective action is actually taken?

2 In which documents are the checks defined for evaluating the effectiveness of specific corrective actions?

3 Who carries out these checks?

4 How long after completion of the corrective action do the checks continue to be made?

5 What action do you take if the corrective action is found to be ineffective?

6 In which documents are these methods defined?

44   Preventive action

Requirements of ISO 9001 clauses 4.14.1 & 4.14.3

The supplier is required to:

1   Establish and maintain documented procedures for implementing preventive actions.

2   Eliminate the causes of potential nonconformities to a degree appropriate to the magnitude of problems and commensurate with the risks encountered.

3   Implement any changes to the documented procedures resulting from preventive actions.

4   Record any changes to the documented procedures resulting from preventive actions.

5   Use appropriate sources of information to detect, analyse and eliminate potential causes of nonconformities.

6   Determine the steps needed to deal with any problems requiring preventive action.

7   Initiate preventive action.

8   Apply controls to ensure that preventive action is effective.

9   Submit relevant information on preventive actions taken for management review.

Purpose of requirements

The purpose behind such requirements is twofold:

1   To provide a means of detecting any deterioration in standards

2   To provide a means for detecting any inherent design weakness in products and processes

Guidance on interpretation

Applicability

These requirements apply to the procedures employed to prevent the occurrence of nonconformity in products, services, processes and quality systems. Since nonconformity prevention is often achieved by careful planning these requirements are not a substitute for the quality planning requirements of clause 4.2.3. However, some of the techniques used for planning purposes can also be used to satisfy this requirement, such as fault tree analysis, failure modes and effects analysis, and quality costing.

Detecting deterioration in standards

What may appear trivial on a case by case basis may well be significant when taken over a longer period or a larger population. This detective work is another form of inspection although this time it focuses on processes and not on specific products. Managers have a habit of reacting to events. What we are all poor at is perceiving the underlying trends that occur daily and gradually eat away at our profits. There is a need to alert management to these trends so that they may consider the corrective action to take.

The steps you need to take to detect specific problems will vary depending on the nature of the problem. The part that can be proceduralized is the discovery process for detecting problems and isolating their cause. A typical process may be as follows:

- Establish a means of collecting relevant data and transmitting it to personnel for analysis.

- Analyse the data and search for trends and conditions which signal a deterioration in standards.

- Establish the concentration of the variance.

- Establish if the variance is significant, both statistically and economically.

- Determine the effects if the trends continue.

- Gain agreement on the problem – expending further effort may be uneconomic if no one agrees with your prognosis.

- Investigate the cause of the deterioration.

- Isolate the dominant cause.

Plan the data requirements carefully so that you:

- Only collect data on events that you intend to analyse.

- Only analyse data with the intention of discovering problems.

- Only provide solutions to real problems.

- Only implement solutions that will improve performance.

Detecting design weaknesses

Several techniques have evolved to identify potential sources of failure in designs and process. These techniques serve to prevent nonconformity and, hence, are preventive action measures. One such technique is *Failure Mode and Effects Analysis* (FMEA) – see *Glossary*.

The FMEA is presented as a table or spreadsheet and contains the following information:

- Function of the item or process

- Potential failure mode (the manner in which the item or process could potentially fail to meet the design intent)

- Potential effects of failure in terms of what the customer might notice or experience

- Severity in the range 1 to 10, 10 being hazardous without warning and 1 having no effect

- Classification in terms of critical, key, major, significant

- Potential cause(s)/mechanism(s) of failure

- Occurrence (the likelihood that a specific cause/mechanism will occur in the range 1 to 10 with 10 being almost inevitable and 1 being unlikely)

- Current design/process controls in terms of the prevention, verification or other activities to assure design/process adequacy

- Detection in the range 1 to 10 with 10 meaning that the control will not detect the potential failure and 1 meaning that the control will almost certainly detect the potential cause of failure

- Risk priority number – This is the product of the severity, occurrence and detection factors

- Recommended actions, prioritizing action on the highest ranked concerns

- Responsibility for actions

- Actions taken

- Resulting severity, occurrence, detection ranking and risk priority number

Dealing with problems requiring preventive action

This is probably one of the most powerful requirements in the standard and much under-used in ISO 9000 quality systems. If you examine the words closely you will find that it can be applied to any situation where measures can be taken to prevent problems. A common weakness in many organizations is the absence of planning. Planning is a preventive action. We plan to achieve an objective which we would fail to meet if we didn't make adequate provision for the resources and activities needed to meet our objective.

The steps you need to take to deal with specific problems will vary depending on the nature of the problem. The part that can be proceduralized is the planning process for determining the preventive action needed. A typical process may be as follows:

- Devise a strategy for eliminating the cause together with alternative strategies, their limitations and consequences.

- Gain agreement on the strategy and prepare an improvement plan which, if implemented, would eliminate the potential problem and not cause any others.

- Prepare a timetable and estimate resources for implementing the plan.

- Gain agreement of the improvement plan, timetable and resources before going ahead.

Mistake proofing

Mistake proofing is a means to prevent the manufacture or assembly of nonconforming product. Mistake proofing can be effected by product design features so that the possibility of incorrect assembly, operation or handling is avoided. Mistake proofing can also be effected by process design features such as sensors to check the set-up before processing and audible signals to remind operators to do various things.

Product recall

To prevent a nonconformity from occurring you may need to take action on product which is in service. Some products may not have failed simply because they may not have been used in the manner needed to cause failure (here there is need for preventive action). Others may have failed but the product has not been used in a manner to cause the failure to be detected (here there is need for remedial action). You need to decide whether to recall all product which has the defect, devise a recall plan and put it into effect.

Implementing improvement plans

In order to initiate improvement the improvement plan should have defined who is to take the preventive action and also the extent of the action to be taken (that is, only in the area where the trend was detected or over a much wider area). In initiating the action you need to carry it out in an organized manner as follows:

- Notify those who will be affected by the change.

- Take the action in accordance with the prescribed control procedures.

- Monitor the effects of the action and collect the data.

- Analyse the data to determine whether the potential problem has been averted.

- Audit the implementation of the preventive action to verify that the agreed plans have been followed and conditions stabilized.

Consequences of failure

A culture in which failure has to occur before any action is taken is a reactive culture. The result is panic, lawsuits and the eventual closure of operations. Waiting for something to happen when it can be prevented is gross incompetence. There will of course be instances when the potential failure cannot be avoided given the resources available but it is a matter of timing. Detect the problem early enough and the resources required to eliminate it may be far less than if you wait.

Inconsistency of requirements

- There is no requirement for the preventive action procedures to require proposed preventive actions to be defined and documented. This is an oversight. An action may be difficult to implement reliably and timely if not documented.

- There is no requirement to record the preventive action taken, only to record those which result in changing documented procedures. Again an oversight. Records will usually exist but as there is no reference to clause 4.16, they do not have to be maintained for a defined period. The auditor should sample the management review records to see whether the preventive actions have been recorded.

- The requirement to determine the steps needed to deal with any problems requiring preventive action extends the scope of the preventive action procedures beyond potential nonconformities and does not limit it to quality problems. Suppliers can only take action on matters within their control.

Tasks for developers

1 Don't display performance data unless the those affected agree to it being displayed.

2 Look for potential causes of deviation, don't wait until the alarm bells ring.

3 Concentrate on the few vital problems.

4 Monitor the trivial problems to detect a systematic deterioration in standards.

5 Don't confuse the small with the trivial.

6 Don't collect data for the sake of it – always have a purpose.

7 Classify the problems into groups that have a common cause and special cause.

8 Attract management's attention to special cause problems and obtain commitment to action.

9 Train your investigators in diagnostic techniques.

10 Provide procedures for managing preventive action programmes where collective action is required.

11 Provide procedures for verifying that preventive actions achieve their objectives.

12 Provide an escalation procedure for use when preventive action target dates have been exceeded or where potential problems require management action.

13 Provide links between the preventive action reports and document, product, process and organization changes.

14 Provide forms for recording the agreed preventive action and target dates for completion.

15 Provide tools and techniques to help investigators discover the causes of potential deviation and determine their significance.

16 Provide for solutions to prevent the occurrence of deviations to be proposed and agreed.

17 Prepare procedures for the analysis, investigation and determination of the causes of potential deviation including the formation of diagnostic teams, where necessary.

18 Decide on who is to collect and analyse the data for determination of preventive actions.

19 Decide on who is to investigate and propose preventive actions.

Questions to stimulate policies

1 In what documents have you defined your preventive action procedures?

2 How do you ensure that the preventive action taken is to a degree appropriate to the magnitude of the problem and commensurate to the risks encountered?

3 How do you implement and record changes resulting from preventive action?

4 What sources of information are used to detect, analyse and eliminate potential causes of nonconformity?

5 How are problems requiring preventive action dealt with?

6 How is preventive action initiated?

7 What controls ensure the effectiveness of preventive actions?

8 How do you ensure that information on preventive action is submitted for management review?

Questions for auditors

Procedures

1 What procedures do you employ for detecting and eliminating potential product nonconformities?

2 In what documents are these procedures defined?

Deciding appropriate action

1 What criteria do you use to decide whether to take preventive action?

2 Who carries out the analysis for the decision makers?

3 Who decides whether action should be taken?

4 What records are kept of these decisions?

5 In which documents are these methods defined?

Implementing changes to procedures

1 When a change to the quality system procedures is necessary to prevent the ocurrence of a nonconformity, what records are kept of this change?

2 How do you indicate that the change resulted from a potential nonconformity?

3 In which documents are these methods defined?

Detecting potential nonconformities

1 What types of information do you use to detect potential nonconformities in products, processes and the quality system?

2 What measures are employed to collect this information and ensure its accuracy?

3 What criteria is used to judge whether a potential nonconformity exists?

4 Who is responsible for identifying such situations?

5 How often is the analysis carried out?

6 In which document are the techniques defined?

Dealing with problems requiring preventive action

1 What techniques are employed to assist the elimination of potential nonconformities?

2 In which documents are these techniques defined?

3 How do you judge whether a situation demands preventive action?

4 What action is taken should a potential nonconformity be detected?

5 In which documents are the measures to be taken defined?

6 Who is responsible for preparing this document?

7 How is commitment to action secured from those concerned?

8 What action is taken if the preventive action requires additional resources?

Preventive action controls

1 How is the agreed preventive action plan put into action?

2 What measures are taken to verify that the agreed action is taken?

3 Who carries out these checks?

4 How long after completion of the preventive action do the checks continue to be made?

5 What action do you take if the preventive action is found to be ineffective?

6 In what documents are these methods defined?

Inputs to management review

1 What information relating to preventive action is submitted for management review?

2 In what form is the data presented?

3 Who submits this information?

45 Handling

Requirements of ISO 9001 clauses 4.15.1 & 4.15.2

The supplier is required to:

1 Establish and maintain documented procedures for handling of product.

2 Provide methods of handling product that prevent damage and deterioration.

Purpose of requirements

The purpose of these requirements is to prevent damage or deterioration to conforming product when handling the product.

Guidance on interpretation

Applicability

This requirement applies to handling of product at any stage in its life cycle whilst it is under the supplier's control and not just the finished product.

Application

The identification of special handling provisions usually occurs in the design stage, or the manufacturing or service planning phase, by assessing the risks to product quality during its manufacture, storage, movement, transportation and installation. Handling provisions should include handling by machines and handling by personnel.

Handling provisions serve two purposes, both related to safety: protection of the product from the individual and protection of the individual handling the product.

There follows a short list of handling provisions which your procedures may need to address:

- Lifting equipment

- Pallets and containers

- Conveyors and stackers

- Design features for enabling handling of product

- Handling of electrostatic sensitive devices

- Handling hazardous materials

- Handling fragile materials

Consequences of failure

Failure to adequately provide for handling the product may result in damage or deterioration to the product and injury to personnel.

Inconsistency of requirements

Preservation and segregation is required only when the product is under the supplier's control but this is also true of handling. This is an oversight and should have appeared in clause 4.15.1.

Tasks for developers

1   Identify items with special handling requirements.

2   Produce procedures for developing handling instructions.

3   Identify handling requirements for bulky, fragile, sensitive and hazardous items.

Questions to stimulate policies

1 What procedures have been established and documented for handling product?

2 How do you prevent damage or deterioration of product in handling?

Questions for auditors

Procedures

1 How do you determine the controls needed to protect conforming product during handling?

2 Who determines the controls needed?

3 In which documents are these controls defined?

Handling

1 How do you determine whether product is at risk due to handling from receipt through to delivery?

2 Who determines the handling provisions that are required?

3 What handling instructions have been provided?

4 What types of equipment and tools are used to handle product?

5 Who is responsible for supplying these tools and equipment?

6 What checks are carried out before such tools and equipment enter service?

7 What instructions are provided for using such tools and equipment?

8 How are staff made aware of the handling provisions that should be applied?

9 What training is provided for staff using handling equipment?

46 Storage

Requirements of ISO 9001 clauses 4.15.1 & 4.15.3

The supplier is required to:

1 Establish and maintain documented procedures for storage of product.

2 Use designated storage areas or stock rooms to prevent damage and deterioration of product, pending use or delivery.

3 Stipulate appropriate methods for authorizing receipt into storage areas.

4 Stipulate appropriate methods for authorizing dispatch from storage areas.

5 Assess the condition of product in stock at appropriate intervals.

Purpose of requirements

The purpose of these requirements is to prevent damage or deterioration to conforming product when it is in storage.

Guidance on interpretation

Applicability

These requirements apply to any area in which product is stored, whether awaiting receipt inspection, processing or delivery. Such areas need to be designated as storage areas so that adequate controls are employed.

Application

In order to preserve the quality of items that have passed receipt inspection, they should be transferred to stores in which they are secure from damage and deterioration. You need secure storage areas for several reasons:

- For preventing personnel from entering the stores and removing items without authorization.

- For preventing items from losing their identity. Once identity is lost it is often difficult, if not impossible, to restore complete identification without testing material or other properties.

- For preventing vermin damage to the stock.

- For preventing climatic elements causing stock to deteriorate.

The requirement is for you to designate storage areas. This means that any area where product is stored should have been designated for that purpose so that the necessary controls can be employed. If you store product in undesignated areas then there is a chance that the necessary controls will not be applied.

Consequences of failure

Failure to provide adequate storage areas may result in its unauthorized movement or product being stolen, lost, misused, damaged or contaminated.

Inconsistency of requirements

- The standard does not require the use of designated storage areas or stock rooms to prevent loss of product, unlike clause 4.16 which requires quality records to be stored in facilities that prevent loss. The auditor should establish what the stores are used for and, if containing finished product or customer supplied product, then provision needs to be made to prevent loss, otherwise contract deliveries will be jeopardized and clause 4.3.2 requirements will not be met.

- Preservation and segregation is required only when the product is under the supplier's control but this is true also of storage. This is an oversight and should have appeared in clause 4.15.1.

Tasks for developers

1 Don't allow items into stores without being subject to satisfactory inspection.

2 Don't allow unauthorized access to stores.

3 Don't store items that have lost their identity with items that haven't.

4 Identify items with special storage requirements.

5 Identify remnant material.

6 Remove life-expired items from the serviceable items store.

7 Instruct stores staff on the effects of lost identity, mixing product, handling and packaging methods.

8 Maintain good housekeeping practices in stores areas.

9 Issue articles on a first in, first out basis.

10 Don't permit unauthorized disposal of items suspected as being damaged.

11 Don't replenish stock other than with articles of the same specification.

12 Produce procedures for developing storage instructions.

13 Identify storage conditions for hazardous and environmentally sensitive items.

14 Provide storage areas or rooms for items pending use.

15 Provide separate storage areas or rooms for items awaiting disposal, remedial action or further processing.

16 Assess conditions of stock and storage areas, rooms and buildings periodically.

Questions to stimulate policies

1 What procedures have been established and documented for storage of product?

2 How do you prevent damage, or deterioration, of product in storage?

3 Which areas have you designated for the storage of product pending use or delivery?

4 How do you authorize receipt into storage areas or stock rooms?

5 How do you authorize dispatch from storage areas or stock rooms?

6 How do you detect deterioration in the condition of product in stock?

Questions for auditors

Procedures

1 How do you determine the controls needed to protect conforming product during its storage?

2 Who determines the controls needed?

3 In which documents are these controls defined?

Designated storage areas

1 What areas have been designated for the storage of product?

2 In which document are these designated areas identified?

3 Who is responsible for maintaining each of these storage areas?

4 What areas are provided for holding product waiting inspection?

5 What areas are provided for holding product waiting further processing?

6 What areas are provided for holding nonconforming product pending disposition?

7 What areas are provided for holding product waiting delivery?

8 What storage conditions have been specified for each of the storage areas?

9 What limitations are there concerning the storage of items in each of these areas?

10 What provisions have been made to prevent loss or damage to product held in stock rooms?

Authorizing receipt and dispatch

1 What authorization is required to move product into stock rooms?

2 How are products received into storage areas?

3 How are staff made aware of the storage area into which a particular product should be moved?

4 What authorization is required to release product from stock rooms?

5 How are products released from stock rooms?

6 In what documents are these provisions defined?

Stock condition assessment

1 How often are the storage conditions checked?

2 Who carries out these checks?

3 What information is recorded following these checks?

4 When was the last storage condition check carried out?

5 What were the results of the checks?

6 What action was taken on the results?

7 In which documents are these procedures defined?

47   Packaging

Requirements of ISO 9001 clauses 4.15.1 & 4.15.4

The supplier is required to:

1   Establish and maintain documented procedures for packaging of product.

2   Control packing processes to the extent necessary to ensure conformance to specified requirements.

3   Control packaging processes to the extent necessary to ensure conformance to specified requirements.

4   Control marking processes to the extent necessary to ensure conformance to specified requirements.

5   Control the material used in packing processes to the extent necessary to ensure conformance to specified requirements.

Purpose of requirements

The purpose of these requirements is to prevent damage or deterioration to conforming product occurring due to inadequate packaging.

Guidance on interpretation

Applicability

These requirements apply to any packaging applied to product on receipt, prior to, or after processing or for transportation to customers. They also apply to any marking processes, whether applied to the packaging or the product.

Application

Packing is an activity and *packaging* a material in this context. A packing specification defines how an item should be packed, whereas a Packaging specification details the nature of the package.

Control of packing and marking processes commences during the design phase or the manufacturing or service planning phase. Packaging design should be governed by the requirements of clause 4.4 although if you only select existing designs of packaging these requirements would not be applicable.

Markings should be applied both to primary and secondary packaging as well as to the product itself. Markings should also be made with materials that will survive the conditions of storage and transportation.

Packing instructions should provide not only for protecting the product but for including any documentation that should accompany the product, such as:

- Assembly and installation instructions

- Licence and copyright notices

- Certificates of conformity

- Packing list identifying the contents of the container

- Export documents

- Warranty cards

Consequences of failure

Failure to provide adequate packaging of product at any stage from receipt by supplier through to receipt by customer may result in damage and the cost and inconvenience of replacement.

Inconsistency of requirements

- Packing, packaging and marking processes are required to be controlled only to ensure conformance to specified requirements and not to provide protection to, and identity of, the packaged product. The purpose of packaging is to protect the product so that if it appears inadequate even though meeting the specified requirements there is a nonconformity with clause 4.15.6.

• Preservation and segregation is required only when the product is under the supplier's control but this is true also of packaging. This is an oversight and should have appeared in clause 4.15.1.

Tasks for developers

1 Don't allow packaging seals to be broken other than by authorized personnel.

2 Identify contents of containers on the outside.

3 Provide check lists for packaging operations.

4 Identify items with special packaging requirements.

5 Maintain good housekeeping practices in packaging areas.

6 Don't permit unauthorized disposal of items suspected as being damaged.

7 Produce procedures for developing packing instructions.

8 Identify packaging requirements for all types of items.

9 Provide packing instructions for packing certain types of product.

10 Identify marking requirements for items, secondary and primary packaging

Questions to stimulate policies

1 What procedures have been established and documented for packaging product?

2 How do you control packing and packaging processes, including the materials used?

Questions for auditors

1   How do you determine the controls needed over packaging operations?

2   Who determines the controls needed?

3   In which documents are these controls defined?

4   Who determines the packing, packaging and marking requirements?

5   How do you determine these requirements?

6   How are these requirements conveyed to the packers?

7   Who is responsible for packing product?

8   What packing instructions have been provided?

9   What marking instructions are provided?

10 What document specifies the required contents of each package?

11 What types of equipment and tools are used to pack product?

12 What checks are carried out before such tools and equipment enter service?

13 What instructions are provided for using such tools and equipment?

14 What packaging materials are used?

15 In which documents are the packaging materials specified?

16 Where are the packaging materials stored?

48   Preservation

Requirements of ISO 9001 clauses 4.15.1 & 4.15.5

The supplier is required to:

1   Establish and maintain documented procedures for preservation of product.

2   Apply appropriate methods of preservation of product when the product is under the supplier's control.

3   Apply appropriate methods of segregation of product when the product is under the supplier's control.

Purpose of requirements

The purpose of these requirements is to prevent damage or deterioration to conforming product due to contact with other products or the environment in which it is stored or used.

Guidance on interpretation

Applicability

These requirements apply to preservation methods employed when product is in storage, in-process or in transit.

Application

Preserving product whilst the product is under your control may be addressed by your handling and packaging provisions but in-process preservation may also be necessary to protect finishes from deterioration during further processing. The preservation processes should be designed to prolong the life of the product by inhibiting the effect of natural elements.

Segregation is a means of preserving product from contamination and damage. Examples where segregation makes sense are:

- Toxic and non-toxic materials

- Flammable and non-flammable materials

- Limited life items

- Explosives

- Dry and wet ingredients

- Meat and vegetables and many more

Segregation is not limited to the product only but also to the containers and tools used with the product. Particles left in containers and on tools, no matter how small, can taint food and drink, cause blemishes in paint and other finishes as well as violate health and safety regulations. Segregation may also be necessary in the packaging of products not only to prevent visible damage but also electrical damage, as with electrostatic sensitive devices.

Consequences of failure

Failure to preserve and segregate product may result in contaminated, damaged or degraded product.

Inconsistency of requirements

Preservation and segregation is required only when the product is under the supplier's control but this is true also of storage, handling and packaging. This is an oversight and should have appeared in clause 4.15.1.

Tasks for developers

1   Segregate serviceable items from unserviceable items.

2   Segregate limited life items.

3   Inspect items for identity, damage and deterioration prior to issue.

4   Produce procedures for developing preservation instructions.

5   Identify preservation requirements for all types of items.

6   Specify segregation rules for keeping items and materials apart.

7   Provide procedures for controlling limited life items.

8   Establish re-test conditions for items that may deteriorate when dormant.

Questions to stimulate policies

1   What procedures have been established and documented for the preservation of product?

2   How do you control preservation processes, including the materials used?

3   How do you control marking processes, including the materials used?

4   How do you preserve product when such product is under your control?

5   How do you segregate product when such product is under your control?

Questions for auditors

Procedures

1   How do you determine the controls needed to preserve conforming product whilst the product is under your control?

2   Who determines the controls needed?

3   In which documents are these controls defined?

Preserving product

1 Who is responsible for determining product preservation requirements?

2 How are preservation requirements determined?

3 In which document are these requirements specified?

4 How are preservation requirements conveyed to those handling product?

5 How do you ensure that personnel outside the production environment who may come into contact with the product know of the preservation requirements?

Segregating product

1 Who determines the product segregation requirements?

2 In which documents are the segregation requirements defined?

3 How do you prevent cross-contamination of chemicals and paints used in the manufacturing processes?

4 How are segregation requirements conveyed to personnel handling product?

49 Delivery

Requirements of ISO 9001 clauses 4.15.1 & 4.15.6

The supplier is required to:

1   Establish and maintain documented procedures for delivery of product.

2   Arrange for the protection of product after final inspection and test and up to delivery, when required.

Purpose of requirements

The purpose of these requirements is to prevent damage or deterioration to conforming product after final inspection up to when product is received by the customer.

Guidance on interpretation

Applicability

These requirements only apply to protection of product after final inspection rather than the delivery process as a whole. Delivery may take place between locations under the supplier's control as well as to locations designated by the customer.

Application

Delivery procedures would include the handling, packing and transportation of product to destination. Handling and packing has been dealt with in previous chapters. Transportation can take many forms and, in designing or selecting the packaging, the designated mode of transportation should be taken into account. Sometimes delivery is made electronically using a modem and telephone line. The product may be a software package, a document stored in electronic form or a facsimile. Protection of the product is still required but takes a different form. You have to protect the product against loss and corruption during transmission.

Consequences of failure

Failure to prevent damage or deterioration during delivery may result in product arriving at its destination in an unacceptable condition, thus causing customer complaints.

Inconsistency of requirements

Procedures are required for delivery of product in clause 4.15.1 but the specific requirement in clause 4.15.6 only addresses protection of product (that is, the right condition). There is, therefore, an ambiguity as the requirement does not specifically address the provisions required for ensuring the right product with the right paperwork is dispatched to the customer. After final inspection product would normally be stored and the storage area dispatch procedures required by clause 4.15.3 would take care of such cases. Where product is not stored subsequent to final inspection, the general requirement of clause 4.2.1 for the system to ensure product meets specified requirements and that the system is to be documented provides the argument for delivery procedures to cover more than product protection.

Tasks for developers

1   Produce procedures for developing delivery instructions.

Questions to stimulate policies

1   What procedures have been established and documented for delivery of product?

2   How do you prevent damage or deterioration of product during delivery?

3 How do you ensure that the quality of product after final inspection and test is protected up to its destination?

Questions for auditors

1 How do you determine the controls needed to protect conforming product during delivery?

2 Who determines the controls needed?

3 In which documents are these controls defined?

4 Who is responsible for determining the delivery methods?

5 What factors are taken into account when deciding the delivery method?

6 What delivery requirements have been specified by the customer?

7 In which documents are delivery requirements defined?

8 How are these requirements conveyed to the personnel responsible for delivery?

9 What checks are performed to verify condition and completeness of consignments, prior to delivery?

10 Who transports product to customers?

50   Control of quality records

Requirements of ISO 9001 clause 4.16

The supplier is required to:

1 Establish and maintain documented procedures for the identification of quality records.

2 Establish and maintain documented procedures for the collection of quality records.

3 Establish and maintain documented procedures for the indexing of quality records.

4 Establish and maintain documented procedures for the access of quality records.

5 Establish and maintain documented procedures for the filing of quality records.

6 Establish and maintain documented procedures for the storage of quality records.

7 Establish and maintain documented procedures for the maintenance of quality records.

8 Establish and maintain documented procedures for the disposition of quality records.

9 Maintain quality records to demonstrate conformance to specified requirements.

10 Maintain quality records to demonstrate the effective operation of the quality system.

11 Maintain subcontractor quality records.

12 Ensure that quality records are legible.

13 Store quality records in such a way as to prevent damage, deterioration and loss.

14 Retain quality records in such a way that they are readily retrievable.

15 Establish and record retention times for quality records.

16 Cause quality records to be available for evaluation by the customer for an agreed period, when required.

Purpose of requirements

The purpose of these requirements is to prevent documentary evidence of conformity with specified requirements from being irretrievable. Throughout the standard various clauses reference the clause on quality records and, so as to avoid repetition, the common requirements for quality records are assembled under one heading.

Guidance on interpretation

Applicability

These requirements apply to all records classified as quality records. Records are historical documents – they record events and achievements that have taken place. Quality records are the results of formal product, service, process and system verification activities. They provide objective evidence of the achieved characteristics of products and services and the results of system or supplier assessments, audits, examination etc. Not every record is a quality record – only those identified in ISO 9001 by a cross-reference to clause 4.16 of the standard. No tailoring is needed for specific industries.

Some auditors believe that any document generated or used by the quality system is a quality record and will attempt to apply the requirements of clause 4.16. Whilst it can be argued that any documented output is a record of an activity, not every record is a record of achievement. For example, a completed exam paper may be an output of an activity but the record of achievement is not the exam paper but the certificate awarded after the paper has been marked.

Application

If we put all the references to clause 4.16 together we get a list of 21 quality records:

- Management review records (clause 4.1.3)
- Contract review records (clause 4.3)
- Design review records (clause 4.4.5)
- Design verification measures (clause 4.4.7)
- Records of acceptable subcontractors (clause 4.6.2)
- Records of unsuitable customer supplied product (clause 4.7)
- Product identification records (clause 4.8)
- Qualified process records (clause 4.9)
- Qualified equipment records (clause 4.9)
- Qualified personnel records (clause 4.9)
- Positive recall records (clause 4.10.2.3)
- Inspection and test records (clause 4.10.5)
- Verification records for test hardware and test software (clause 4.11.1)
- Calibration records (clause 4.4.11.2)
- Nonconformance records (clause 4.13.2)
- Nonconformance investigation records (clause 4.14.2)
- Subcontract quality records (clause 4.16)
- Internal audit result records (clause 4.17)
- Follow-up audit records (clause 4.17)
- Training records (clause 4.18)

These are the minimum number of records to be created and maintained. There are a further three records which a scan of the standard will reveal although there is no cross-reference to clause 4.16:

- Calibration status identification record (clause 4.11.2)

- Procedure change records (clause 4.14.1) – these are not quality records (see above)

- Subcontractor surveillance records (clause 4.6.2)

It is advisable to identify all your quality records within your procedures. This will then avoid arguments on what is or is not a quality record.

Identification

Whatever the records they should carry some identification so that you can determine what they are, what kind of information they record and what they relate to. A simple way of doing this is to give each record a reference number and a name or title.

Collection

In order to demonstrate the achievement of quality and the effectiveness of the quality system, records will need to be gathered in from the locations where they were produced. This is more than a convenience because you will be unable to analyse all the data efficiently unless you have it in front of you.

Indexing

A simple means of indexing quality records is to create and maintain registers listing the records in numerical order as reference or serial numbers are allocated.

Access

Access has two meanings: one allowing access and the other prohibiting access. You need to ensure that the current records are accessible as well as those in the archive. If your records are held on a computer database, password protection may be necessary. Your procedures should define how you provide and prohibit access to the records.

Filing

You should know where to find your quality records so that you can retrieve them when needed. One method is to create a filing system which allocates file locations to certain types of documents.

Storage

Record storage provisions need to prevent loss by fire, theft and unauthorized removal, as well as damage and deterioration. If using computers you will also need to consider loss through computer viruses and unauthorized access, deletion or the corruption of files.

Maintenance

There are three types of maintenance regarding quality records:

- Keeping records up to date
- Keeping the information in the records up to date
- Keeping the records in good condition

Retention

There are several factors to consider when determining the retention time for quality records:

- The duration of the contract
- The life of the product
- The period between quality system assessments

You will also need to take account of the subcontractor records and ensure adequate retention times are invoked in the contract.

Specify the retention times in the procedures which describes the records. In this way you can be more selective than by having a general policy containing a retention duration.

Consequences of failure

Failure to control quality records can cause several problems:

- Inability to locate records containing data needed to resolve a problem
- Inability to defend a customer complaint or product liability lawsuit
- Inability to demonstrate to a third party that your system is effective

- Inability to determine the achieved characteristics of a product and, hence, its fitness for use

- Inability to report on actual quality performance to executive management

Inconsistency of requirements

- The requirement for quality records to be maintained to demonstrate conformance to specified requirements conflicts with the cross-references to clause 4.16 within the standard. All the cross references relate to where records are required to be maintained. This requirement, however, implies that whatever the specified requirement, quality records have to be maintained to demonstrate conformance even with aspects which do not affect product or service quality if specified in a contract, order or documented procedure. Auditors should be aware that ISO 9001 addresses quality assurance requirements and not quality management requirements. The requirements, if met, are intended to give assurance to customers that products supplied *will* meet their requirements. If conformance with a requirement cannot be demonstrated by the supplier it does not follow that the supplier is noncompliant. The auditor has to establish that operations are under control and this can be done without there being records – there are forms of objective evidence other than quality records.

- The requirement for pertinent quality records from the subcontractor to be an element of the supplier's quality records applies only where such records have been supplied; therefore, the term 'where appropriate' should have been used. Suppliers cannot be expected to include records that they do not possess. Typical records that may well be supplied are certificates of conformity and inspection and test results (but only if required to do so by the supplier).

- The requirements for the storage of quality records are more onerous than for the storage of product since such areas are required to prevent loss. Products can be replaced, whereas records cannot. Records are results of an event that has taken place. Unless one can repeat the event, lost records are lost for good.

Tasks for developers

1   Don't retain boxes on forms that serve no purpose.

2   Don't permit unauthorized deletions on certified records.

3   Don't permit the unauthorized design of record blanks.

4   Don't change record blanks without authorized changes to the related procedure.

5   Don't leave records lying about.

6   Don't archive uncompleted records.

7   Don't lose track of where records are stored.

8   Don't forget to transfer records to their new owners.

9   Ensure someone is made responsible for maintaining each type of record.

10 Record all product and process acceptance decisions.

11 Record all changes to the quality system.

12 Record all changes to design, products, processes and measuring devices.

13 Ensure all records are dated.

14 Record the date on which new documents and changes become effective.

15 Test new records for their fitness for use before general release.

16 Denote the issue status on record blanks.

17 Identify all the records which demonstrate the achievement of quality.

18 Identify all the records which demonstrate the effectiveness of the quality system.

19 Give each record a name and a reference number and completed forms a serial number.

20 Create and maintain registers for allocation of reference numbers and serial numbers.

21 Quote the product/service identification number on all related records.

22 Include record collection or submission provisions in your procedures.

23 Introduce file references for containing records.

24 Take 'insurance copies' of all important records.

25 Introduce computer virus controls.

26 Provide means by which authorized staff can access records outside normal working hours.

27 Restrict access to records held on computer disk or tape.

28 Introduce a booking in and out system for files and records in storage.

29 Control storage conditions of paper, microfilm and computerized records.

30 Introduce filing disciplines, clean desk policies, etc.

31 Provide plastic wallets for records which may become soiled in use.

32 Introduce a disposal procedure for documentation.

33 Introduce standard clauses for insertion into subcontracts on quality records.

34 Specify retention times for quality records in the related procedures.

35 Store records by disposal date.

36 Provide a means of varying the retention times for specific customers.

Questions to stimulate policies

1 What procedures have been established and documented for controlling quality records?

2 In which document do you identify the records that demonstrate conformance to specified requirements?

3 In which documents do you identify the records that demonstrate the effective operation of the quality system?

4 How do you identify your quality records?

5   How do you collect and index your quality records?

6   How do you provide and prevent access to quality records?

7   How do you file and store your quality records?

8   How do you maintain your quality records?

9   How do you dispose of your quality records?

10 How do you ensure that pertinent subcontractor quality records are maintained?

11 How do you ensure that all quality records remain legible?

12 How do you ensure that quality records are readily retrievable?

13 What facilities have been provided to minimize deterioration and damage, and prevent loss of quality records?

14 In which documents do you record the retention times of quality records?

Questions for auditors

Procedures

1   Who is responsible for the control of quality records?

2   How are your quality records identified?

3   What provisions have you made for the collection of records from the place where they were generated?

4   Which procedure requires the completion of this form?

5   When complete, what happens to the original and any copies?

6   In what documents are these provisions defined?

Indexing and access

1   How do you distinguish between similar records produced for the same activity?

2   How do you determine whether any of these records are missing?

3 What happens if an allocated record is destroyed whilst being prepared?

4 What happens if the results change following preparation of a record?

5 Where are the quality records for this activity located?

6 What restrictions are there concerning access to these records?

7 What provisions are employed to prevent inadvertent change to records held on computer?

8 In which documents are these provisions defined?

Filing and storage

1 Where are these records filed when completed?

2 Who has access to the files?

3 What method is employed to facilitate retrieval of records?

4 What happens to old records?

5 What provision have been made to prevent misfiling of records?

6 In which documents are these provisions defined?

Maintenance and disposition

1 Who is responsible for maintaining the quality record files in this area?

2 What instruction has this person been given on maintenance of records?

3 What happens to records that have reached the end of their retention period?

4 What action would be taken should a record deteriorate in use or in storage?

5 How do you detect whether any completed records have been removed?

6 How do you dispose of old records?

7 Whose authorization is needed before any records are destroyed?

8 In which documents are these provisions defined?

Records for demonstrating conformance

1   What records are retained for products and services you provide to customers?

2   How do you determine that these records will collectively demonstrate compliance with customer requirements?

3   Can you show me the records that demonstrate compliance with this particular customer requirement for this range of products?

Records for demonstrating effective system

1   What records are held concerning the operation of the quality system itself?

2   How do you determine the effectiveness of this quality system?

3   What data is used in this assessment?

4   What records are kept that will demonstrate current performance of the system?

5   Who is responsible for maintaining these records?

Subcontractor records

1   Where do you hold your subcontractor records?

2   What subcontractor records are kept?

3   What are the requirements placed on subcontractors for the supply of quality records?

4   What do you do with the records of product that is returned to the subcontractor?

5   Who is responsible for maintaining these records?

6   In which documents are these provisions defined?

Legibility and storage

1   Where are the quality records stored?

2   Who is responsible for the security of these records?

3 How do you ensure that these records remain in their original condition?

4 Which records are produced using a fax machine?

5 How long are these faxed records stored?

6 What instructions have been issued regarding the completion of records by hand?

7 What measures are taken to prevent records becoming soiled during use?

8 What provision has been made for preventing loss through theft, fire or computer virus?

Record retention

1 In which documents are the retention times defined for these records?

2 Can you retrieve the records produced for this product that was shipped last year?

3 What happens to records that reach the end of their retention period?

4 Can you retrieve the records of the internal audit performed 30 months ago?

Availability of records

1 Can you provide the inspection and test records for the products shipped last December?

51   Internal quality audits

Requirements of ISO 9001 clause 4.17

The supplier is required to:

1   Establish and maintain documented procedures for planning internal quality audits.

2   Establish and maintain documented procedures for implementing internal quality audits.

3   Verify that quality activities and related results comply with planned arrangements by conducting internal quality audits.

4   Determine the effectiveness of the quality system by conducting internal quality audits.

5   Schedule internal quality audits on the basis of the status and importance of the activity to be audited.

6   Carry out internal quality audits using personnel who are independent of those having a direct responsibility for the activity being audited.

7   Record the results of internal quality audits.

8   Bring the results of internal quality audits to the attention of the personnel having responsibility in the area audited.

9   Take timely corrective action on deficiencies found during audits.

10 Verify the implementation of corrective actions by follow-up audits.

11 Verify the effectiveness of corrective actions by follow-up audits.

Purpose of requirements

The purpose of these requirements is to prevent a deterioration in agreed standards.

Guidance on interpretation

Applicability

These requirements apply to all operations of the organization governed by the quality system. They do not apply to external audits whether second- or third-party audits. They apply also to product audits, process audits and service audits as well as quality system audits, as evident from the definition given in ISO 8402. No tailoring is needed for specific industries.

Audit procedures

The standard requires procedures for both planning and implementing audits and these should cover the following:

- Preparing the annual audit programme
- The selection of auditors and team leader if necessary
- Planning (type) audits
- Conducting the audit
- Recording observations
- Determining corrective actions
- Reporting audit findings
- Implementing corrective actions
- Confirming the effectiveness of corrective actions
- The forms on which you plan the audit
- The forms on which you record the observations and corrective actions
- Any warning notices you send out of impending audits, overdue corrective actions, escalation actions

Determining the effectiveness of the system

You do not know anything about your quality system unless you measure it.

You need to know whether the formal quality system causes the business results you observe and whether you have eliminated the informal systems.

Informal systems are unpredictable and to sustain high performance you need predictable processes.

The quality system is effective if it fulfils its purpose and achieves its objectives. In measuring system effectiveness you therefore need to:

- Identify indicators of how well the system fulfils its purpose.

- Identify indicators of how well the system achieves its objectives.

The quality system is an interconnection of processes; therefore, in measuring the effectiveness of the quality system you need to measure the performance of individual processes. The performance of a process is measured by the amount of variation in the process parameters. If the variation in these parameters over time is within the defined limits, our processes are capable and the quality system is effective.

We can place the performance of a process into one of three categories.

Out of control

A process is *out of control* when the average spread of variation for a parameter does not coincide with the target value. This is due to the presence of a source of variation that causes the location, spread and shape of the distribution to change. This we call *special cause variation*.

In control

A process is *in control* when the average spread of variation coincides with the target value for a parameter. The range of variation may extend outside the upper and lower limits but the proportion of applications within the limits can be predicted. The source of variation due to special causes has been eliminated but that due to common cause remains excessive. Common cause variation is a source of variation which affects all the individual values of the process output and appears random.

Capable

A process is *capable* when the average spread of variation coincides with the target value for a parameter and the range of variation does not exceed the upper and lower limits. The source of variation due to common causes has been reduced.

For internal audits to determine whether the quality system is effective, they should therefore establish whether the processes are out of control, in control or capable. Only when all processes are capable is the system effective.

Effectiveness of audits

Audits should be providing management with knowledge they don't possess, not telling them what they already know as a fact. The audit and not the customer should be the first to reveal problems. If audits only report historical facts they are ineffective. If having conducted an audit, problems are later revealed which were clearly present when the audit was conducted, the audit has not been effective or if subsequent audits reveal facts that should have been detected during previous audits, measures should be taken to adjust the auditing method or the audit plan.

Status and importance

Status has three meanings in this context: the first to do with the relative position of the activity in the scheme of things, the second to do with the maturity of the activity and the third to do with the performance of activity. There is little point in conducting in-depth audits on activities which add least value. There is also little point auditing activities which have only just commenced. On the importance of the activity, you have to establish to whom is it important: to the customer, the managing director, the public, your immediate superior?

Independence of auditors

To ensure their independence, auditors need not be placed in separate organizations. Although it is quite common for quality auditors to reside in a quality department it is by no means essential. There are several solutions:

- Auditors can be from the same department as the activities being audited, provided they are not responsible for the activities being audited.

- Separate independent quality audit departments could be set up, staffed with trained auditors.

- Implementation audits could be carried out by trained line personnel supervised by an experienced quality auditor.

Audit reports

The audit report should state the results of the audit, what was found compliant as well as what was found noncompliant. Good points, nonconformities and opportunities for preventing nonconformity should all be recorded.

Taking timely action

Unless the auditee is someone with responsibility for taking the corrective action the auditee's manager should determine the remedial and corrective actions required. If the action required is outside that manager's responsibility, the manager and not the auditor should seek out the appropriate authority and secure a remedial and corrective action proposal. Your policy manual should stipulate management's responsibility for taking timely action and define what timely means.

Follow-up

Follow-up audits should verify that the agreed action has been taken and verify that the original nonconformity has been eliminated. (Simply verifying that the action has been taken will not prove the problem has been resolved.)

Consequences of failure

Without checks of performance, standards will ultimately deteriorate. Also, the effort invested in planning, training and other preventive measures will be wasted. Without internal audits there will be no alarm mechanism in place to provide advanced warning. When the accountants notice the decline it is already too late.

Inconsistency of requirements

- The requirement for quality activities and related results to comply with planned arrangements is inconsistent with other requirements of the standard which require activities to be carried out in accordance with documented procedures and results to comply with specified requirements. The term 'planned arrangements' is shorthand for policies, procedures, specifications, contracts, instructions etc. The term 'specified requirements' could have been used but this term seems to be used only when related to the product being supplied and not to activities being performed.

- There is no requirement for the audit schedule to be defined and documented. The quality system has to be documented and as the audit schedule is part of the system, it too must be documented as required by clause 4.2.1.

● There is no requirement for corrective actions resulting from deficiencies found during the audit to be defined and documented. This omission is similar to that in clause 4.14.2. Auditors can obtain evidence that corrective actions have achieved their objectives by examination of the follow-up audit records.

● There is a requirement for management personnel to take timely corrective action but not remedial action. As ISO 8402 defines corrective action as action taken to prevent the recurrence of a nonconformity, the action excludes remedial action or action taken on the nonconforming item. This is either an omission or an inconsistent use of the term 'corrective action'.

Tasks for developers

1 Don't limit the scope of your audit programme to the procedures.

2 Select your auditors carefully.

3 Don't use aggressive staff for auditing.

4 Don't persist in enforcing compliance with trivia.

5 Adjust the audit programme to cover aspects which have attracted management attention.

6 Don't audit for the sake of it – define your objective and make it important enough for management to take notice of the results.

7 Keep a log of audits and a log of corrective action reports.

8 Don't go into an area unannounced – always give advanced warning.

9 Explain the purpose and objectives of the audit to the manager before you commence.

10 Review the relevant documents before you audit operations.

11 Follow trails to discover facts and don't break the trail until you have uncovered the facts.

12 Check downstream of the operation being audited to gather facts on its effectiveness.

13 Be helpful to the auditee, don't argue but don't accept everything at face value.

14 Don't be critical of anyone's work or how they operate.

15 Listen to what the auditee and his or her manager says.

16 Don't leave the scene of the audit without obtaining agreement to corrective actions and either setting a target date for their completion or agreeing a date by which the target date will be set.

17 Act professionally: be courteous, tactful and diplomatic and avoid nit picking.

18 Establish whether your audit objective has been achieved before completing the audit.

19 Reduce the frequency of audits if you have confidence in a particular area.

20 Don't copy the audit report to anyone other than the auditee's manager without the manager's consent.

21 Decide on the scope of the audit programme.

22 Produce an annual audit programme.

23 Devise a method of determining when parts of the system were last audited.

24 Decide on the types of audits to be conducted and the level of staff to conduct them.

25 Determine the standards against which the organization is to be audited.

26 Train your quality auditors to a defined standard and train sufficient auditors to enable your programme to be met.

27 Use auditing as a means of familiarizing staff with the operations of the organization.

28 Allocate trained auditors to the programme.

29 Plan individual audits.

30 Produce audit procedures that cover products, processes and organizations.

31 Provide forms for recording observations, recommendations and corrective actions.

32 Conduct the audits to the defined plan and procedure with a clear objective.

33 Record the results of audits, both noncompliances and compliances.

34 Devise a means of tracking the status of corrective actions.

35 Provide a means for linking the corrective actions arising from audits to documentation changes, organization changes, process changes, design changes etc.

36 Assess audit data periodically and determine the effectiveness of auditing.

37 Provide for changing audit methods and training should auditing be not as effective as expected.

38 Create check-lists for assisting in following an audit trail through a department or process.

29 Audit your procedures immediately following their issue as a means of testing their auditability.

30 Conduct a system audit at least once a year to verify that the system is still intact and compliant with the standard.

Questions to stimulate policies

1 What procedures have been established and documented for planning and implementing internal quality audits?

2 How do you verify whether quality activities and related results comply with planned arrangements?

3 How do you determine the effectiveness of the quality system using quality audits?

4 Which documents constitute the internal quality audit plans?

5 How do you ensure that audits are scheduled on the basis of the status and importance of the activity to be audited?

6 How do you ensure that all audits are carried out by personnel independent of those having responsibility for the activities audited?

7 In which documents are the results of quality audits recorded?

8 How do you ensure that the results of audits are brought to the attention of the personnel having responsibility in the area being audited?

9 How do you ensure that management personnel responsible for the area audited take timely corrective action on deficiencies found by the audit?

10 How do you verify the effectiveness of any corrective actions taken?

Questions for auditors

Audit planning

1 Who is responsible for internal quality audits?

2 How do you plan your internal quality audit program?

3 In what document is the plan defined?

4 Who is responsible for planning internal audits?

5 What type of audits are carried out?

6 What standards do you audit against?

7 What areas of the business are covered by the audit program?

8 To what extent are previous audit results taken into account when planning an audit?

9 What techniques do you employ to ensure adequate coverage and depth in an audit?

10 How do you determine the frequency of internal audits?

11 What would cause you to change the frequency of audits?

12 Under what circumstances would you conduct an unannounced audit?

13 In what documents are audit planning provisions defined?

Auditor selection

1 Who is responsible for selecting the auditors?

2 What is the selection criteria for auditors?

3 What are these auditors' primary responsibilities?

4 How many auditors do you have?

5 What training have they been given?

6 What training have your auditors had in environmental, health and safety issues?

7 Can you show me the list of authorized auditors?

Audit conduct

1 What checks do auditors make when conducting audits?

2 How do you ensure that all provisions of the quality system are checked?

3 To what extent do your auditors check the content of technical documents?

4 To what extent do your auditors check the quality of products and services being produced?

5 What evidence can you show me of recent audits addressing the health, safety and environmental aspects of your operations?

Determining system effectiveness

1 How do you determine the effectiveness of your quality system?

2 What evidence can you provide to confirm that the current system is effective?

3 To what extent are the downstream effects of processes taken into account in your analysis?

Audit reporting

1 How many nonconformities were detected during this audit?

2 And how many during this audit? ... and this audit?

3 Who carried out these recent audits?

4 This auditor works in the same department that is being audited. Can you show me how you have ensured the auditor's independence in this case?

5 What information is required to be recorded during an internal audit?

6 What information is required to be recorded following an internal audit?

7 Where are the corrective actions taken recorded?

8 Who records the actions taken?

9 Where are the conclusions and recommendations recorded?

10 Where do you record the name of the manager responsible for the corrective action?

Audit follow-up

1 Where are the due dates recorded for each of the corrective actions?

2 When were these actions carried out?

3 What was the reason for these actions not being carried out by the due date?

4 How do you know how many corrective actions are outstanding?

5 What action is taken to expedite closure of these outstanding actions?

6 What checks do you carry out to verify the corrective actions?

7 How long do you wait before carrying out the follow-up audit?

8 Who is assigned to the follow-up audit?

9 Under what circumstances would a follow-up audit not be carried out?

10 What evidence do auditors look for when verifying the effectiveness of corrective actions?

11 Where are the follow-up audit results recorded?

12 What action would the auditor take in the event that the corrective action taken was found to be ineffective?

52 Training

Requirements of ISO 9001 clause 4.18

The supplier is required to:

1 Establish and maintain documented procedures for identifying training needs.

2 Provide for the training of all personnel performing specific assigned activities affecting quality.

3 Qualify personnel performing specific assigned tasks on the basis of appropriate education, training and/or experience, as required.

4 Maintain appropriate records of training.

Purpose of requirements

The purpose of these requirements is to prevent unqualified personnel from performing activities that affect quality.

Guidance on interpretation

Applicability

These requirements apply to all personnel who execute activities governed by the quality system. They do not apply to the training of customers or suppliers except where such personnel are working under the organization's quality system. No tailoring is needed for specific industries. They apply whether the training is performed internally or externally and whether the training is sponsored by the company, the individual or by government.

Application

Academic qualifications are often prerequisites for certain jobs but without training in the particular jobs in which they are engaged, personnel will not yield their full potential. Education imparts knowledge whereas training imparts skills. However, without the right motivation, any amount of qualifications and training will be wasted. Motivation is addressed in ISO 9004.

Strategic or tactical training

As a strategic issue, training would feature in the business plan as a means to move the company forward towards new goals. As a tactical issue, training features in staff appraisals to correct weaknesses or improve skills and not to move the company forward. It is futile to set either business goals or personal goals that are tougher than last year without considering what has to be changed to meet them.

Training needs

Training needs can be identified in two ways: as requirements for training and as a plan for providing the required training. Requirements for training arise in several ways:

- In job specifications

- In process specifications, maintenance specifications, operating instructions etc.

- In development plans for introducing new technologies

- In project plans for introducing new equipment, services, operations etc.

- In marketing plans for launching into new markets, new countries, new products and services

- In contracts where the customer will only permit trained personnel to operate customer-owned equipment

- In corporate plans covering new legislation, sales, marketing, quality management etc.

- From an analysis of nonconformances, customer complaints and other problems

- In developing design skills (4.4.2), problem solving skills (4.14.1), statistical skills (4.20.2)

- From introducing a quality system, thus requiring awareness of ISO 9000, the quality policies and objectives and training in the implementation of quality system procedures, standards, guides etc.

Training plans

Once the training requirements have been specified, managers should plan the training needed by their staff. This requires a *training plan*. Although the standard doesn't specifically require a training plan, without one you may have difficulty demonstrating that you have identified the training needs. The training plans should identify the person responsible for coordinating the training, the type of training, the organization that will deliver the training, the course material to be provided, examination and certification arrangements, the venue, the dates of the courses and the attendees.

Qualifications

Where personnel make judgements upon which the determination of quality depends, they should be qualified to make such judgements. To be qualified, a person should be able and competent to perform the required tasks.

For each position in the organization (not the individuals, but the position they occupy) you should produce a job specification which specifies the requirements an individual must meet to occupy this position. It should include academic qualifications, training and experience requirements, as well as personal characteristics, so that in recruiting for the position, one has a specification with which to compare candidates.

Effectiveness of training

The standard does not specifically require the effectiveness of training to be evaluated. However, it does require staff to be qualified on the basis of appropriate education, training and/or experience. If the education, training and/or experience has not been effective, the person concerned could be considered to be unqualified. Therefore, in order to ensure that staff are suitably qualified, the effectiveness of the education, training and/or experience received should be evaluated. There are three parts to the evaluation.

- An evaluation of the training course or training activity immediately on completion

- An evaluation of the training received weeks after the training

- An evaluation of the skills developed months after the training

Training records

Records of training should include records of formal training, where the individual attends a training course, and on-the-job training where the individual is given instruction whilst performing the job. The records should indicate whether the prescribed level of competence has been attained. Training records should contain evidence that the effectiveness of training given has been evaluated and this may be accomplished by a signature and date from the supervisor.

You will need two types of training records: those records relating to a particular individual and those relating to particular activities. The former are used to identify an individual's competence and the latter to select trained competent people or to check the competence of those who have performed particular activities.

Consequences of failure

Failure to train personnel may result in mistakes, poor decisions and poor workmanship at all levels in the organization. You cannot expect staff to be able to achieve the standards you set unless they are properly trained.

Inconsistency of requirements

- There is no requirement for documented procedures for the provision and control of training and for evaluating its effectiveness, only for identifying training needs. If the auditor can show that the effectiveness of the system is impaired by a lack of training procedures then a nonconformity could be stated against clause 4.2.1 to the effect that the system for training has not been documented.

- There is no requirement for suppliers to define and document the qualifications required of personnel performing specific, assigned tasks. The supplier needs to specify the qualifications required for staff to perform their assigned tasks. The system has to be documented so that a policy stating how the qualifications for various jobs are established may suffice. The auditor cannot insist on there being job specifications.

- If suppliers believe it is not appropriate to maintain training records for certain types of training then the standard gives them this right. Appropriate records of training does not mean appropriate training records. Appropriate records of training means that records of training have to be maintained but their content and format should be appropriate to the circumstances. In some cases, these records may be no more than a list of personnel undertaking a training course. In other cases it may need to contain levels of competency. As personnel can be qualified on the basis of education, training and experience then, in some cases, there may be no training records for an individual.

Tasks for developers

1 Don't specify that training is required if it cannot be provided.

2 Don't assign personnel to tasks for which you have specified training requirements unless the personnel are appropriately trained.

3 Don't rely on a person's own training records.

4 Keep central records of staff training.

5 Provide managers with ready access to staff training records.

6 Provide a certificate to every person that has received specific training.

7 Ensure that any training equipment is of a representative standard before training commences.

8 Don't use training equipment for operational purposes unless it is certified to current design standards before operational use.

9 Identify jobs which require particular skills.

10 Document the training requirements for specific jobs.

11 Produce and maintain training plans to implement the training requirements.

12 Implement only that training defined in the training plans.

13 Monitor the effectiveness of training.

14 Maintain personal records of training.

15 Maintain skill- or activity-based records of training.

16 Review training records periodically to identify re-training.

17 Make skill records available to managers on site.

18 Identify equipment used for training purposes.

19 Provide procedures for controlling the standard of training equipment.

Questions to stimulate policies

1 What procedures have been established and documented for identifying training needs?

2 How do you identify training needs?

3 How do you ensure that personnel performing specific assigned tasks are qualified on the basis of appropriate education, training and/or experience?

4 How do you ensure that training is provided for all personnel performing work affecting quality?

5 In which documents do you record the training provided?

Questions for auditors

Training needs

1 Who is responsible for training?

2 How do you determine training needs?

3 Who decides what training is needed?

4 How is training need recognition built into product development programmes?

5 How is training need recognition built into staff development programmes?

6 How is training need recognition built into the quality system development programme?

7 In which documents are these provisions defined?

Provision of training

1 What training plans have been agreed for the next 12 months?

2 How is training commissioned?

3 Who commissions the training ?

4 What are the selection criteria for external training courses?

5 Who carries out the training?

6 How are trainees selected?

7 How do you determine when to run training courses?

8 What qualifications are required of the instructors?

Personnel qualifications

1 What training and education is provided for you to learn to do your job more effectively?

2 What instruction have you received to familiarize you with the quality system?

3 What would be the minimum qualifications for a person doing this job?

4 In which documents are these requirements defined?

5 How did you learn to do this job?

6 What previous experience and qualification did you have?

Training records

1 What records of training are maintained?

2   Where are the records located?

3   What details are required to be recorded?

4   For which groups of people are training records created?

5   To whom are these records made available?

6   What forms of training do not warrant the creation of training records?

7   What happens to the training certificates issued by the course provider?

8   What happens to these records when an employee leaves the company?

53 Servicing

Requirements of ISO 9001 clause 4.19

The supplier is required to:

1 Establish and maintain documented procedures for performing servicing.

2 Establish and maintain documented procedures for verifying that servicing meets specified requirements.

3 Establish and maintain documented procedures for reporting that servicing meets specified requirements.

Purpose of requirements

The purpose of these requirements is to prevent servicing being carried out under uncontrolled conditions.

Guidance on interpretation

Applicability

These requirements only apply when the customer-supplier agreement includes post-delivery support, whether for products or services. (Note that 'Servicing' is not the same as 'Services'. *Servicing* is what is done to something. *Services* are what is provided.) In such cases, they apply to the servicing of products or services designed, produced or delivered by suppliers. They relate to the services carried out after delivery of the product or service, such as warranty repairs, maintenance, technical support etc. In a bank, customer-care programmes keeping customers appraised of latest interest rates etc. is servicing. In a hospital, post-operative care is servicing.

If the contract does not require you to service your products, or support the servicing of your products by others, then element 4.19 does not apply.

On the other hand, if your core process is servicing and your contract is for servicing only then you cannot ignore the other elements of the standard; you have to apply those that are relevant, but the core of your business is covered by 4.9 on process control. Tailoring is therefore necessary for specific industries.

Application

Maintenance

To provide adequate procedures for product maintenance you will need to:

- Define maintenance requirements covering what is to be maintained, by whom and to what depth.

- Define service restoration instructions covering the actions required to restore equipment, or facilities, into service including restoration and response times. This is usually first-line maintenance and may not require any repair action.

- Define maintenance instructions stating the performance parameters to be maintained, the frequency of maintenance, how it is to be conducted, the action to be taken in the event of failure, the procedures to be followed in carrying out repairs and the training required of those performing the maintenance tasks.

- Define spares schedules listing the spares by item identification number, manufacturer and quantity required on-site to maintain the specified service availability.

- Produce or acquire handbooks which detail the equipment to be maintained and procedures on fault finding, repair and verification after repair.

Technical support

If your operation is such that your after-sales service consists of technical assistance, to provide adequate procedures for technical assistance you will need to:

- Specify the service in terms of its scope, what is included, what is excluded, response times, the action in the event of a complaint, etc.

- Define operating procedures covering the receipt and recording of calls or letters, their acknowledgment and who to route them to for action.

- Provide technical support covering problem logs, actions taken, advice given, promises made, and details of follow-up on the product or service.

- Establish a complaints procedure covering the recording, investigation and resolution of complaints.

Servicing reports

Servicing reports should specify the following, as applicable:

- The identity of the product subject to the service activity

- The date on which the service took place

- The organization responsible for performing the servicing

- The condition of the product prior to servicing and any running time, mileage or other indication of life expired

- The specification defining the service or maintenance carried out, quoting the relevant part if not all requirements were verified

- The items exchanged, consummables used, item repaired, adjusted etc.

- The duration of the activity and the name of who performed it

- Details of any inspections and tests carried out to verify serviceability of the item

Consequences of failure

Failure to control the servicing operations may jeopardize long term relationships with clients. Servicing often brings the customer into direct contact with technical staff rather than sales staff and thus can change perceptions of the organization. Failure to honour one's servicing agreements causes customers to go elsewhere, sometimes to law for compensation.

Inconsistency of requirements

There is no requirement for records to be maintained of servicing activities, only reports that servicing meets specified requirements. Servicing should be treated as a group of processes that are governed by the requirements of clause 4.9. Although there are few requirements in clause 4.9 for quality records, the associated inspection, test, nonconforming product controls etc. should produce sufficient records to demonstrate that servicing operations are under control.

Tasks for developers

1 Don't specify levels of service beyond your capability.

2 Allocate adequate resources to provide the specified services.

3 Provide staff with adequate instructions on how to carry out the servicing.

4 Collect data on your servicing performance.

5 Create a means whereby servicing staff can keep abreast of changes in the quality system.

6 Institute a means of controlling servicing documentation and equipment.

7 Define the servicing levels that you intend to provide up to, and after, warranty expires.

8 Define the measures you need to take to honour your obligations to service products supplied to your customers.

9 Provide servicing staff with current instruction manuals for the equipment they are servicing.

10 Create forms for reporting servicing calls, time spent, components changed etc.

11 Set up a mechanism for analysing service reports so as to determine response times, time to repair and total down time.

12 Provide a means whereby servicing staff can use the in-house calibration service for their equipment.

13 Train servicing staff in the operation and maintenance of the equipment.

14 Prepare procedures for the receipt, repair and return into service (or disposal) of components removed by servicing staff.

Questions to stimulate policies

This questionnaire is somewhat limited as there are only three specific servicing requirements in the standard. As other parts of the standard apply to servicing, you should consult the relevant questionnaires to help establish your policies in this area.

1 What procedures have been established and documented for performing, verifying and reporting servicing activities?

2 How do you ensure that servicing is performed in a way that meets the specified requirements?

3 How do you report servicing activities?

4 How do you ensure that servicing is verified in a way that meets the specified requirements?

Questions for auditors

Planning

1 At what stage are servicing requirements determined?

2 Who is responsible for defining servicing requirements?

3 In which documents are the servicing requirement defined?

4 How are the provisions for meeting the servicing requirements determined?

5 How are servicing resources determined and secured?

6   What help line facilities are provided for customers?

7   How are servicing contracts secured?

8   In which documents are the servicing planning processes defined?

Servicing operations

1   Who is responsible for carrying out servicing operations?

2   How does product enter the servicing process?

3   What identity is given to the product to preclude inadvertent loss or delay?

4   What records are maintained of product awaiting servicing?

5   Where is product stored awaiting servicing?

6   How is product prepared for servicing?

7   What provisions are made for obtaining customer approval prior to commencing servicing operations?

8   In which documents are the servicing procedures defined?

9   What action is taken should the work required be greater than that approved by the customer?

10 How are spare parts requisitioned?

Reporting

1   What records are maintained of servicing activities performed?

2   What information is provided to the customer, specifying the servicing carried out?

Verification

1   What records are maintained to demonstrate that servicing operations were performed as specified in the servicing procedures?

2   What checks are performed to verify completion of servicing operations?

3   What action is taken should the customer not accept delivery of the product?

54 Identifying the need for statistical techniques

Requirements of ISO 9001 clause 4.20.1

The supplier is required to:

1 Identify the need for statistical techniques required for establishing process capability.

2 Identify the need for statistical techniques required for controlling process capability.

3 Identify the need for statistical techniques required for verifying process capability.

4 Identify the need for statistical techniques required for establishing product characteristics.

5 Identify the need for statistical techniques required for controlling product characteristics.

6 Identify the need for statistical techniques required for verifying product characteristics.

Purpose of requirements

The purpose of these requirements is to prevent decisions being made that affect process capability and product characteristics without the necessary tools being available required.

Guidance on interpretation

Applicability

These requirements apply to product and process acceptance decisions taken on the basis of data generated by statistical means. They do not apply to the manipulation of data by methods which do not rely on probability theory. No tailoring is necessary for specific industries.

These requirements also apply to the process used to identify whether statistical techniques are needed to accept products and the processes which produce the product.

Application

The standard does not require you to use statistical techniques but identify the need for them. Within your procedures you will therefore need a means of determining when statistical techniques will be needed to determine product characteristics and process capability. One way of doing this is to use check lists. These check lists need to prompt the user to state whether the product characteristics, or process capability, will be determined using statistical techniques and, if so, which techniques are to be used.

Some of the statistical techniques used in establishing and controlling product characteristics are:

- Sampling inspection
- Statistical process control
- Reliability prediction
- Market surveys

  Design by experiment

Consequences of failure

Failure to identify statistical techniques may result in an inconsistency and unpredictability in product acceptance and process capability decisions, thus causing unnecessary variation in the quality of product produced and delivered.

Inconsistency of requirements

There is no requirement for documented procedures which enable the need for statistical techniques to be identified or for such needs to be documented. It would be logical for the need for statistical techniques to be identified within the relevant control procedures – such as design, purchasing, production, installation and servicing procedures – but other means are equally valid.

Tasks for developers

1 Don't rely on statistical techniques unless you have evidence they are valid.

2 Don't claim emphatically that all products meet the specification if conformance is determined by statistical techniques.

3 Don't derive your sampling plans from unproven statistical methods.

4 Identify product and process acceptance decisions that are based or statistical techniques.

5 Determine and document the statistical theory or national standards used.

Questions to stimulate policies

1 How do you identify the need for statistical techniques required fo establishing process capability?

2 How do you identify the need for statistical techniques required fo controlling and verifying process capability?

3 How do you identify the need for statistical techniques required fo establishing product characteristics?

4 How do you identify the need for statistical techniques required fo controlling and verifying product characteristics?

Questions for auditors

1   Who is responsible for identifying the need for statistical techniques?

2   How is the need for statistical techniques identified?

3   When are these techniques identified?

4   In which document is this process defined?

5   What types of statistical techniques are used for establishing product characteristics?

6   What types of statistical techniques are used for establishing process capability?

7   What types of statistical techniques are used for controlling product characteristics?

8   What types of statistical techniques are used for controlling process capability?

9   What types of statistical techniques are used for verifying product characteristics?

10 What types of statistical techniques are used for verifying process capability?

55 Procedures for applying statistical techniques

Requirements of ISO 9001 clause 4.20.2

The supplier is required to:

1 Establish and maintain documented procedures to implement the application of the identified statistical techniques.

2 Establish and maintain documented procedures to control the application of the identified statistical techniques.

Purpose of requirements

The purpose of these requirements is to prevent invalid techniques being used to establish, control or verify product or process capability.

Guidance on interpretation

Applicability

These requirements only apply to the statistical techniques identified when meeting clause 4.20.1. Procedures are not necessary for other uses of statistics.

Application

Where statistical techniques are used for establishing, controlling and verifying process capability and product characteristics, procedures need to be produced for each application such that you would have a Process Control Procedure, Process Capability Analysis Procedure, Receipt Inspection Procedure, Reliability Prediction Procedure and Market Analysis

Procedure, etc. Where computer programs are employed, they will need to be validated to demonstrate that the results being plotted are accurate, since you may be relying on what the computer tells you rather than on any direct measurement of the product.

Consequences of failure

Failure to provide documented methods of using statistical techniques may result in uncontrollable variation in the results of measurement. Everyone may use a different formula, make different assumptions and hence generate unpredictable results.

Inconsistency of requirements

No inconsistencies within these requirements have been identified.

Tasks for developers

1   Record the basis on which decisions are made if using statistical techniques.

2   Don't flinch results if on the borderline – take more samples.

3   Locate control charts where they can be used as a nonconformance prevention tool.

4   Provide instructions, charts and other data to enable staff to use the techniques properly.

5   Review the techniques periodically and revise them, if necessary, to take advantage of new developments in the field.

6   Monitor the effectiveness of the decisions and adjust your rules accordingly.

7   Perform studies in the pre-production period to determine the capability of the manufacturing processes.

8   Perform studies to show that the combination of measurement equipment tolerances or variations and the design tolerances cannot result in nonconforming product.

9   Perform studies to prove the soundness of acceptable quality levels.

Questions to stimulate policies

1   What procedures have been established and documented for controlling the application of statistical techniques?

2   How do you control the application of identified statistical techniques?

3   What documented procedures exist for implementing the identified statistical techniques?

Questions for auditors

1   How do you ensure that all staff concerned have a knowledge of basic statistical concepts?

2   What training and information is provided to such staff to help them acquire proficiency in the use of statistical techniques?

3   In which documents are the required statistical techniques specified?

4   How do staff know when to apply a given technique?

5   What instructions are provided for the application of these techniques?

6   What checks are carried out to verify that the techniques have been properly applied?

7   What action is taken when it is found that the techniques have not been properly applied?

Part 4

Quality system audits

Contents

1 Principles of auditing

Purpose of audits

- All audits are performed to establish facts rather than faults.

- Audits aim to establish, by an unbiased means, factual information on some aspect of performance.

- The performance of any organization will degrade unless some checks are carried out.

- Audits are performed as a safeguard against a deterioration in standards.

- Audits will detect variation from pre-defined standards.

Audit objectives

All audits aim to provide assurance to those who commissioned them and establish:

- Whether certain agreed provisions, if implemented, will yield the required results.

- Whether only the agreed provisions are being implemented.

- Whether the provisions have yielded results that are fit for their purpose and meet the needs of those who require them.

Characteristics of audits

- Audits should not change the performance of what is being measured, otherwise the facts gathered will not be representative of the true performance of the audit subject.

- Audits should always be performed by someone who has no responsibility for what is being measured, otherwise they may bias the results.

- Audits should not be performed to find faults or to apportion blame.

- Audits are performed to obtain a level of confidence rather than 100% certainty.

- Audits need to be carried out by personnel who have the capability to investigate aspects of performance pertinent to the decision to be taken and hence auditors need to have sufficient knowledge of the subject they are auditing.

- Audits can be undertaken at any level in the organization.

- Audits must be against standards that have been accepted by the organization being audited.

- Audits comprise three elements: an examination of intention, the examination of actions and the evaluation of the evidence to determine whether actions match intentions.

The benefits of audits

Audits provide:

- Facts for decision making and thus remove subjectivity

- Opportunities for improvement

- Safeguards against a deterioration in standards

- Early warning of impending situations that could jeopardize the business

- Objective evidence to demonstrate whether policies match the needs of customer and society

- Objective evidence to demonstrate whether practices implement policies

- Objective evidence to demonstrate whether we do what we say we do

- Objective evidence that our policies and practices will enable us to meet our objectives

- Information to tell us whether our practices are consistent across all areas

- Information to tell us whether managers are acting consistently with our policies

- The impetus to keep us on course towards our objectives

Types of audit

Whilst the aim is common to all audits, there are several types of quality audit. In each case, the auditor uses a different method and involves different people in the organization.

Management audits

These audits include such elements as:

- The *Strategic Quality Audit* – to verify that the strategic plans of the organization address current and future legal, environmental, safety and market quality requirements.

- The *Policy Audit* – to verify that the documented policies promulgate the requirements of the market and the objectives of the business.

- The *Organization Audit* – to verify that the organization is structured and resourced to implement the policies and to achieve the stated objectives efficiently and effectively.

Product/service audits

These audits include such elements as:

- The *Planning Audit* – to verify that the organization's plans or proposals for supplying a product or service will, if properly implemented, result in product or service that complies with specified requirements.

- The *Conformance Audit* – to verify that the product being produced, or service being delivered, conforms to specified requirements.

Process audits

These audits include such elements as:

- The *Planning Audit* – to verify that the plans for operating a result-producing process will, if properly implemented, yield product which consistently meets the agreed specifications.

- The *Capability Audit* – to verify that a process has the capability to consistently yield product which meets agreed requirements.

Procedure audits

Procedure audits include such elements as:

- The *Documentation Audit* – to verify that the documented practices implement the approved policies and the relevant requirements of the standard and will, if properly implemented, provide an adequate degree of control over the organization's operations.

- The *Implementation Audit* – to verify that the activities and related results implement the approved documented practices.

System audits

These audits include such elements as:

- The *Documentation Audit* – to verify that the documented system complies with the relevant requirements of the governing standards.

- The *Implementation Audit* – to verify that the activities and related results comply with the documented requirements and that the system is effective in providing an adequate degree of control over the organization's operations.

- The *System Surveillance* – to verify that the organization has maintained its quality system and it continues to be suitable for achieving its stated objectives and is effective in providing an adequate degree of control over the organization's operations.

Categories of audits

There are several categories of audits which can be applied whatever the audit objective:

- *First-party audits* are audits of a company or parts thereof by personnel employed by the company (also called *internal audits*).

- *Second-party audits* are audits carried out by customers upon their suppliers. These audits are *external audits* and are also called *Vendor Audits*. When second parties audit a supplier's quality system such audits are referred to as *Supplier Approval Audits* or *Quality System Assessments*.

- *Third-party audits* are audits carried out by personnel who are neither employees of the customer nor the supplier and are usually employees of certification bodies. These audits are also external audits and can be referred to as *Certification Audits*, *Compliance Audits* and *Quality System Assessments*.

The audit process

A model of the generic quality system audit process is illustrated in Part 5, Figure 38. The steps involved at each stage may differ depending on the type of audit and the audit objectives. The principles involved at each stage are described below. These principles apply only to management audits, quality system audits and procedure audits, and not to product and process audits.

The audit programme

- Internal audit programmes address certain parts of the business, by function, procedure, product or process, whereas external audit programmes address organizations, contracts or projects.

- Audit programmes define the subject, location and date of the audit and may identify the name of the auditor or lead auditor.

- Audit programmes are duration-limited either annually or contract/project duration.

- Audit programmes are prepared by the audit organization rather than the auditor unless they are one and the same.

Planning and organizing the audit

- Each audit in the audit programme should be defined by an audit brief prepared by the audit organization.

- The auditor is appointed by the audit organization and given the audit brief.

- The auditor is responsible for planning and organizing the audit.

- Contact with the auditee is through the lead auditor if a team of auditors is to be deployed.

- The audit team should be selected on ability and expertise in particular business sector/technology/process depending whether internal or external audit.

- For external audits, pre-audit visits are needed to gather information for audit planning purposes.

- For external audits, preliminary assessments are carried out to determine the readiness of the organization for a formal assessment.

- Examination of quality system documentation is needed for audit planning purposes as well as for verifying compliance with standards.

- If the documentation audit is performed several months before the implementation audit, then the company may be requested to correct the documentation prior to the implementation audit.

- Audit schedules define which areas of the business will be audited by which auditors at what times.

- Audit check lists indicate what auditors will do when in each area and are guides to help auditors cover the scope and depth required.

- Auditors should be briefed by the lead auditor before they proceed to the area concerned.

Conducting the audit

- The quality system documentation is submitted and examined before proceeding with the implementation audit and can be carried out off-site or on-site.

- The implementation audit commences with an opening meeting between the auditors and the management to agree the purpose, scope and conduct of the audit.

- The implementation audit takes place through interviews with staff performing activities which affect quality.

- Objective evidence is gathered on representative samples of activities being carried out and the documentation used both to perform the activities and to record the results of the activities.

- Objective evidence is confirmed with the organization's representatives during the audit.

- The objective evidence is analysed, and decisions made, as to whether the sampled documentation and/or activities conform to the specified requirements.

- Deviations from requirements are assessed to determine their effect on quality and the effectiveness of the quality system and conclusions made as to whether the audit objectives have been achieved.

Reporting the audit

- The findings of the auditor are reported verbally during the audit.

- The results of the audit are documented in the form of a report detailing the conformities and nonconformities with the prescribed standard, together with other observations which signify opportunities for improvement.

- The results and conclusions of the audit are reported at a closing meeting between the auditors and the management.

- Corrective action proposals offered by the organization are agreed and a schedule established for evaluating their effectiveness.

Following up the audit

- Corrective action proposals are submitted to the auditor for evaluation and acceptance.

- The auditor evaluates the proposed action and signifies acceptance or rejection.

- If agreed, the proposed actions are implemented by the organization. If the proposed actions are not agreed, revised proposals are presented until agreed.

- Implementation of the agreed actions are checked by the auditor – either through correspondence or a repeat site audit – to verify that the original nonconformity has been resolved effectively.

Completing audit records

- Completion of corrective actions is tracked by the auditor and liaison with the organization maintained.

- When all actions have been satisfactorily completed the audit is closed and the report updated and filed.

- Where appropriate the relevant certificates are then issued.

- Dates are established for further audits based on the results of the previous audit and the organization's response.

2 Planning internal audits

Audit strategy

The audit strategy is your overall approach to internal quality audits and influences:

- What you audit
- Who you select as auditors
- How you audit

What you audit

- Internal quality audits are not simply an examination of practice to verify that people are doing what they say they are doing.

- At the upper levels, you are auditing strategy to verify that adequate policies cause the business strategy to be implemented.

- At the middle level, you are auditing policy to verify that procedures implement policy.

- At the lower levels you are auditing procedures to verify that procedures and being implemented and decisions comply with policy.

- An internal audit can be planned like an external audit whereby the system is checked against ISO 9000.

- It should not be necessary, other than for a preliminary assessment prior to an initial external audit, to perform internal audits to ISO 9000 because the system should have been designed to comply with ISO 9000.

- Finding that practice is noncompliant with the standard indicates that the system was not proven before release or that the documented policies and procedures are not under adequate control.

Who should audit

- It is vital that you choose auditors who are appropriate for the level at which the audit will be performed.

- Choosing 'worker bees' as auditors of corporate strategy will probably not be effective and choosing corporate chiefs to audit practice against procedure will likewise not be effective.

How to audit

- The system consists of the organization, resources and processes required to implement policy and achieve objectives.

- You therefore need to ensure that the organizational and resource policies and practices are addressed in addition to the processes.

- You can audit by site, function, procedure, process, project, contract or product.

Audit planning task list

Audit programme (Audit Programme Manager)

1 Decide audit strategy – whether to audit by function, process, procedure or site.

2 Prepare an audit programme that covers the entire quality system in all areas of the organization to which it applies.

3 Assign auditors to each audit.

4 Review past performance and allocate a week/month in which the audit is to take place.

5 Define the objectives of each audit.

6 Prepare an audit brief and submit to nominated auditors.

Planning tasks (Auditor)

1 Accept audit brief and clarify any ambiguities.

2 Obtain copies of previous audit reports, if appropriate.

3 Identify which documents define the processes, functions, tasks or activities to be audited.

4 Select those documents that need to be examined.

5 Contact the auditee and agree audit date.

6 Examine quality system documentation.

7 Determine audit duration.

8 Determine audit team size.

9 Select auditors.

10 Brief auditors.

11 Prepare audit schedule.

12 Prepare check lists.

Confirm with auditee as necessary

1 Acceptability of audit team members.

2 Appointments with key managers.

3 Meeting rooms for Opening/Closing Meetings.

4 Meeting rooms for auditors.

5 Attendees at Opening and Closing Meetings.

6 Protective clothing.

7 Health and safety procedures and declarations required.

8 Selection, availability and role of guides.

Prior to departing

1 Copy of relevant standards.

2 Copies of report forms.

3 Copies of nonconformity reports.

4 Clipboards.

5 Audit schedule.

6 Audit check lists.

Audit schedule

- The audit schedule will vary in content depending on the strategy adopted.

- A procedure audit schedule has very little content: the objective (which identifies the title of the procedure) and the date.

- A function audit schedule would have more content: the objective, the titles of the procedures to be checked and the date.

- The schedule for process, project, product, contract or requirement audits would not only identify the procedures but the functions and therefore may need to indicate a timetable.

- The content of each schedule will be different if functional, procedure, process and site boundaries are to be crossed.

Check lists

Purpose of check lists

- Aids memory by indicating what has to be checked next

- Aids time management by indicating what has to be covered in a process

- Aids coverage of subject by causing a response to each requirement

- Aids the discovery of evidence by pointing the auditor in certain directions

- Aids collection of evidence by indicating what the auditor is looking for

- Aids investigation process by ordering the auditor's thought processes

Constructing the check list

Check lists should be topic-based rather than a list of questions as the form the question will take will depend on the situation at the time. There is a simple acronym to help you remember what to check – it is PDMRP^2.

P for Process	Tasks carried out in a process in the sequence that they are performed from input to output in the form of an audit trail.
D for Documents	Questions to test whether the documents used and generated in the process meet the requirements of the standard, policy or procedure and are under control.
M for Measurement	Questions to test that the measurements required by the standard, policy or procedure are carried out to verify product, service and process conformity and that the sensors are in place at the appropriate stage in the process.
R for Resources	Questions to test whether adequate resources have been provided to enable the organization's objectives to be achieved for a particular group of processes.
P for People	Questions to test whether the people managing, operating and verifying the process and its products are competent, capable, authorized etc.
P for Product	Factors affecting the product or service being processed.
D for Data	Questions to test whether the data used and generated in the process meet the requirements of the standard, policy or procedure and are under control. (Documents have been separated from data as the type of controls are often different.)
M for Material	Questions to test whether the materials used or generated by the process are under control.

| **R for Records** | Questions to test whether the quality records used or generated by the process meet the requirements of the standard, policy or procedure and are under control. |
| **P for Plant** | Questions to test whether the plant, tools and equipment used or generated by the process are under control. |

- In constructing check lists, you need to examine the documentation and compile a list of things to check against each of these topics.

- The list of topics should be sorted so that they follow a logical order.

- When you have committed the acronym to memory, you can examine any process and, at every point, where there is an input, an action, a decision or an output, ask the appropriate question.

3   Planning external audits

Information gathering

1   Accept audit brief and clarify any ambiguities.

2   Arrange date for pre-audit visit, if cost effective.

3   Prepare pre-audit visit check list.

4   Obtain and study books, articles and standards relating to the particular industry sector and its products and services.

5   Obtain copies of previous audit reports and supplier performance data, if available.

6   Complete pre-audit checks by visit or other means.

7   Register all documents obtained from pre-audit checks.

Planning tasks

1   Examine quality system documentation.

2   Prepare business operations chart.

3   Determine audit duration and audit team size.

4   Select and brief auditors.

5   Prepare audit schedule (for each site if necessary).

6   Prepare check lists.

Logistics

1   Security clearance if required.

2   Maps and directions.

3 Transport arrangements to audit location.

4 Overnight accommodation.

5 Local travel arrangements (hire car, host company car etc.)

6 Entry visas and work permits.

Confirm with auditee

1 Acceptability of audit team members.

2 Appointments with key managers.

3 Meeting rooms for Opening/Closing Meetings and for auditors.

4 Attendees at Opening and Closing Meetings.

5 Lunch arrangements.

6 Car parking.

7 Protective clothing.

8 Health and Safety procedures and declarations required.

9 Dress code.

10 Security.

11 Selection, availability and role of guides.

Prior to departing

1 Copy of relevant standards and report forms.

2 Copies of nonconformity reports.

3 Agenda for Opening Meeting.

4 Proforma agenda for Closing Meeting.

5 Clipboards.

6 Security clearance.

7 Confidentiality declaration.

8   Attendance list completed for audit team.

9   Audit schedule and audit check lists.

10 Auditees documents to be returned.

Pre-audit visit check list

Business

1   Type of industry sector, such as service, manufacturing, process, software.

2   Scope of business.

3   Scope of quality system.

4   Turnover.

5   Age of business and development history.

Products and services

1   What products and services are supplied.

2   Types of contracts which are executed by the organization.

3   Key quality characteristics for the products and services.

4   National standards relating to the products and services with which the company declares compliance.

5   Typical control issues of particular industry, technology, processes etc.

6   Expected norms for defect levels.

7   Processes for which capability needs to be assured.

8   Key failure modes critical to product or service performance.

Personnel

1   Identify key managers and their availability for the duration of the audit.

2   Number of guides and their availability for the duration of the audit.

3   Explain role of guides and selection criteria for guides.

   Working hours.

   Staff numbers and distribution.

6   Need for interpreters.

Facilities

1   Obtain site plan.

2   Explore site to determine complexity and accessibility.

3   Number of sites and their contribution.

4   Protective clothing requirements.

5   Meeting room availability.

6   Lunch arrangements.

7   Parking restrictions.

Documentation

1   Quality system documentation structure.

2   Obtain copies of relevant manuals.

3   Quality system procedures composition and complexity.

4   Obtain sample of procedures and instructions.

5   Organization chart.

6   Promotional literature.

Audit details

1   Scope of registration and pertinent standard.

2   Explain audit process.

3   Explain the company's responsibilities.

4   Explain the success criteria.

5   Audit dates.

6   Existing approvals.

7   Outline audit schedule.

8   Identify processes requiring specialist auditors.

9   Security.

10   Concerns.

4 Conducting audits

The Opening Meeting

The format of an Opening Meeting for an external audit is more formal than for an internal audit.

Agenda

External audit	Internal audit variations
Introduction of the audit team	Usual greetings if team is known to auditees
Introduction of company personnel	Unnecessary if auditees are known to auditors
Purpose and scope of the audit	None
Audit schedule	Rough estimate of how long it will take
Auditing process and reporting procedures	Unnecessary other than for initial audit or if auditee is new to the organization
Success criteria	Unnecessary other than for initial audit or if auditee is new to the organization
Appointment of guides	Unnecessary unless on unfamiliar territory
Agreement of findings and nonconformities	None
Health & Safety	Unnecessary unless on unfamiliar territory
Facilities needed	Unnecessary
Confidentiality	Unnecessary
Disclaimer	Unnecessary
Questions	None

Sample dialogue for Opening Meeting

This sample dialogue is written for external audits.

Introduction of team

'Good morning, my name is (A) and I will be the lead auditor for this audit. I have noted our names on this attendance sheet and would like you to add your names so that we have an accurate record.' (LA passes attendance list to CEO.)

'My team will introduce themselves. Starting on my left.'

'Good morning, my name is (B) and I will be auditing the design and development processes.'

'Good morning, my name is (C) and I will be auditing the purchasing and calibration processes.'

And so on ...

Introduction of company personnel

'Would you please introduce the members of the company present here today.'

Purpose and scope

'The purpose of this audit is to determine the extent to which the operations of (Company) meet the requirements of ISO 90001/9002 1994 for the (design, manufacture, installation and servicing*) of (types of products and services).'

> * Insert core operations of business to be covered by the registration or approval.

Audit schedule

Table the audit schedule and request comment.

Auditing process

'I/we will be seeking conformance to the requirements of the standard by interviewing members of staff responsible for work which affects product or service quality.

'I/we will examine samples of work and associated documentation to establish that the system conforms with the requirements of the standard and any findings will be recorded.

'I/we will confirm the findings with the guide before leaving the area and towards the end of the day, I/we will prepare a draft report.

'The results of the audit will be reported at the Closing Meeting scheduled for 1700hrs at which you will be informed of my conclusions and recommendations.'

Success criteria

'I/we will be seeking conformity and, in so doing, may come across nonconformity. I/we will classify nonconformities as either major or minor.

'A major nonconformity is the absence or total breakdown of the provisions required to cause product conformity, or prevent product nonconformity, with the expectations and needs of customers.

'A minor nonconformity is any failure to meet one or more requirements of the standard.'

Role of guides

Take the auditor to the person or place to conduct the audit:

- To resolve any problems encountered in the interview
- To assist in seeking information required by the auditor
- To witness and agree any findings reported by the auditor
- To assist the auditor in keeping to the schedule

Agreeing findings

'Could I/we confirm that the guides are authorized to agree findings and request that the company indicate who is authorized to agree nonconformities?'

Health and Safety

'Are there any Health and Safety issues we should be aware of?'

Facilities needed

'We will need a room in which we can prepare our report in privacy and a room for the Closing Meeting.'

Confidentiality

'Any information obtained during the audit will remain confidential and will not be disclosed to a third party without the prior agreement of the company.'

Disclaimer

'The audit is based on a limited sample of operations and, although conformance with all relevant requirements of the standard will be tested, other nonconformities than those reported may exist.'

Questions

'Are there any questions before we commence the audit?'

The audit

The documentation audit

When planning the audit you examine the documentation to determine what to check but it is also a time when you can verify whether certain requirements have been complied with.

The following checks should be made using the prepared check lists:

- That the documentation provided is under formal change control.

- That the documents provided form part of the established system.

- That (for external audits) all elements of the standard are addressed though not necessarily in the order of ISO 9001.

- That (for external audits) there is a response to each relevant requirement of the standard, either in the quality manual or in the documented procedures and standards. (There are over 300 requirements so this is by no means a simple task.)

- That adequate provision has been made to control the processes, products and services of the organization.

- That the scope and applicability of individual procedures, standards, instructions etc. are compatible with the requirements of the standard, policy or control procedures.

- That the provisions will cause conformity.

- That the provisions will prevent nonconformity.

- That the policies and practices are stated clearly and unambiguously.

- That there is consistency within documents and between related documents.

- That the policies and procedures or the quality plans address the requirements of particular contracts when contract requirements cause amendment, addition or removal of a company policy or procedure.

Do's and don'ts

- Do make further enquiries if there are any discrepancies.

- Don't record as nonconformities typographical errors and other minor errors that will not cause incorrect action or decision.

- Do bring these errors to the management representative's attention either verbally or in the report.

- In an external audit, if an element of the standard has not been addressed and it is relevant to the operations of the organization then the lead assessor should discuss the matter with the management representative.

- Do add topics to the relevant check lists where there is some doubt that provisions are adequate.

The implementation audit

Here are some factors to consider when conducting the audit:

- The primary aim of the auditor is to discover facts.

- Facts can be obtained by having a combination of observation of operations in practice, interviewing personnel responsible for carrying out such operations and examining documentary evidence (for example, procedures, plans, specifications and records).

- The auditor obtains information through interviewing people.

- Auditors should be looking for conformity not nonconformity. (If the audit objective was to find only nonconformity, their task might be over soon after the audit commences.)

- What the auditor should seek to establish is whether the nonconformity is an isolated error or is a symptom of an ineffective quality system.

- Isolated errors are often caused by human fallibility and may be inadvertent or caused by a lack of training.

- The auditor should establish the cause of isolated errors and only report those where a lack of training is evident (see Chapter 5, *Reporting audits*).

- The auditor must keep the audit objective in mind at all times.

- Auditors should work separately, not in pairs, unless one team member is a trainee or a specialist without audit skills.

Interview format

Before starting an interview the auditor should:

- Have the appropriate documentation pack available.

- Know what is to be established (that is, the subject of the inquiry).

- Have read the policies and procedures which apply to the area sufficient to be aware of the processes which apply and have added items to the check lists of things to check as a result.

During the interview the auditor should:

- Ask open questions to reveal facts.

- Ask probing questions to investigate the facts.

- Avoid emotive questions, trick questions, leading questions and multiple questions.

- Listen intently.
- Exhibit correct body language.
- Be observant and inquisitive.
- Take notes.
- Check evidence with the standard and/or auditee's documentation.
- Establish the root cause of deficiencies.
- Request sight of the objective evidence.
- Give positive feedback.
- Avoid giving advice.
- Remain calm, cool and objective.
- Ask closed questions to confirm the facts.
- Thank the auditee for his/her help and co-operation.

After the interview the auditor should:

- Confirm findings with the guide.
- Make any alterations.
- Move on to the next area.

Interview objective

When conducting an interview the auditor should keep in mind certain objectives:

That the organization has got its operations under control

- That the controls conform to the relevant standard
- That there is objective evidence of conformity and, where applicable, nonconformity

In establishing that operations are under control, the auditor should verify:

- That the auditee knows of the requirements his work has to satisfy
- That these requirements are those defined by the company's quality system

- That the auditee has access to the documentation necessary to perform the work

- That the plans and procedures are adequate to cause conformity and prevent nonconformity

- That the specified requirements are followed

- That the auditee's work is subject to verification prior to release

- That the auditee has the ability to change the process should the requirements not be met

- That provision has been made to prevent the unintended use of noncompliant work

Fact finding

To reveal facts about a process the auditor should:

- Test for conformity on one sample.

- If conforming, test two to three more samples, if more samples exist.

- If conforming, establish if samples are representative of subject. Samples taken from the same department/contract/product/project may not be representative of other departments/contracts/products/projects.

- If not representative, take other samples in other locations, processes, projects, contracts or products.

- If one sample is nonconforming, establish whether all samples would be nonconforming by virtue of the established practice or procedure.

- If all samples would not be similarly affected, take two to three more samples to establish that it is not an isolated case.

- If these are nonconforming, establish the significance with respect to its effect on quality.

- Obtain suggestions from auditee on possible root causes of nonconformity. Possible causes are inadequate procedures, plans, specifications to ensure consistency, or resources and management commitment.

- Record details of document and product identity, location and any other details to enable others to locate the incident. Both auditee and future auditors may need to locate the problem sometime later. Don't leave them with a conundrum.

Following a trail

It is better to follow a logical trail towards an objective than to shoot off in all directions aiming wide of the objective and asking questions at random without any apparent purpose. In following a trail:

- Establish where the information or the product comes from to start the process.

- Establish what they do next and so on until the final stage.

- Establish where the outputs go and with what documentation.

- Ask 'What if?' type questions to uncover whether provisions have been made to deal with changes in the flow and to prevent uncontrolled deviation.

- Explore the different pathways for routing product and information.

- Asks what happens if a revision to a document is received after work has commenced (thereby testing the change control provisions).

- Ask what happens if the instructions are incomplete, unauthorized or the input is not compliant with the input requirement (thereby testing discipline and commitment).

- Ask what a person would do if instructed by someone else who is not his/her supervisor to release product or information that was not complete (thereby testing discipline and commitment again).

What not to ask

Certain questions may appear impertinent or insensitive such as:

- 'What makes you qualified to do this job?' Instead ask: 'What qualifications are required for someone to do this job?'

- 'What training have you had to do this job?' Instead ask: 'How did you learn to do this job?'

- 'What is the quality policy?' Instead ask: 'How does the quality policy affect what you do?'

- 'Who told you to do that?' Instead ask: 'What instructions were you given to carry out this work?'

- 'May I see your procedure for handling customer supplied product?' Instead ask: 'Does your customer supply you with any product?' Then, if the answer is 'No', procedures are obviously not needed.

- 'Why is this equipment not calibrated?' Instead ask: 'What is this equipment used for?'

Being observant

Auditors need to be observant. When being shown around areas or processes or when being shown documents and products, aspects to look out for may include the following.

Documentation
- The status of the documents being used: current or obsolete, clean or dirty, complete or incomplete, with authorized or unauthorized changes.

- The validity of diagrams, forms or other extracts from documents posted on office walls or machines: current or obsolete, clean or dirty, etc.

- The availability of documentation to personnel, proximity of location to point of use, accessibility by personnel during hours of work, whether locked away, etc.

- The awareness of personnel of documentation they are required to use.

- Evidence that documentation is in use, not collecting dust on the shelf.

- Evidence that the documentation adequately reflects the operations being described.

Areas
- The general level of housekeeping: poor housekeeping may be a hazard to product or cause loss, or deterioration, of documents. An untidy office is not necessarily indicative of ineffective control.

- The layout and its relationship to the flow of product and information – displaced activities can lead to people taking short cuts to avoid delays, to avoid walking the distance, etc.

- Bottlenecks where product or information is held awaiting processing: these may indicate inadequate resource provisions, low process capabilities, etc.

- Notices: when were they posted, are they relevant, do people obey them, etc.

Product

- Condition of product: clean or dirty, undamaged or damaged, leaking, etc.

- Identity of product: part markings, modification status, inspection status, serial numbers, etc.

- Handling and segregation of product, containers, protective measures, lifting provisions, etc.

- Packaging of product: component parts, in-process and final product.

- Warning notices, when relevant, of hazards to product and personnel.

Equipment/tools

- Use: confirm what it is used for before checking other aspects as it may not affect quality of deliverable product or service.

- Condition of equipment/tools: clean or dirty, undamaged or damaged, etc.

- Identity: type numbers, serial numbers, version, etc.

- Status: calibration, verification, modification status, etc.

- Operating instructions, where necessary, either on equipment or close by.

- Warning notices, when relevant, of hazards to product and personnel.

Data

- Use: confirm what data is used for before checking other aspects as it may not affect quality of deliverable product or service.

- Validity: approval, status.

- Integrity: restricted access for changing data.

- Duplication: duplicated data increases the chance of error.

- Recency: when was the accuracy last confirmed.

Materials

- Use: confirm what they are used for before checking other aspects as they may not affect quality of deliverable product or service.

- Condition: clean or dirty, undamaged or damaged, etc.

- Identity: type numbers, batch numbers, etc.

- Warning notices, when relevant, of hazards to product and personnel.

Establishing the root cause

Don't confuse symptoms with causes.

- A *symptom* is an observable phenomenon arising from a nonconformity.

- A *cause* is proven reason for the existence of the nonconformity.

When a potential problem is discovered the auditor should establish the cause by asking the auditee to explain why the particular situation has arisen. The answer may prompt a further 'Why?' question and so on until the root cause is established.

The interview location

- Find a suitable place for the interview away from noisy machines.

- Don't conduct the interview in a conference room as there will be nothing there that you wish to examine.

- If barriers such as desks and tables cannot be avoided, as in small offices, sit alongside the auditee, not opposite.

- Try and keep at the same physical level as the auditee when interviewing. If they stand you stand, if they sit you sit (within reason). Standing alongside an auditee sitting at a desk to examine some evidence is more friendly than standing with the desk between the auditor and auditee.

The style of behaviour

- Use a friendly tone, not an aggressive one.

- Always be polite and request information or request to examine something. Do not demand. Although the auditor should seek objective evidence don't say 'show me' without being polite.

- Be assertive but be sensitive to the culture and the position of the person in the hierarchy.

- Control the interview by asking pertinent questions. Remember that the one asking the questions is in control, not the one answering.

- Don't be passive and let the auditee control the interview.

- Don't be persuaded to accept evidence that is not conclusive.

- Select your own samples and the people you wish to interview.

Oral communication techniques

- Oral communication should convey the intended meaning clearly.

- Be careful of the tone of speech. The same words spoken in a different tone can imply different meaning.

- Enter into a dialogue with the auditee in which awareness and understanding is created.

- Form your questions from what the auditee says. Do not read from your check list and ignore their responses.

- Be careful with sounds of acknowledgement. A 'hmm', or 'ah, ah!' in the wrong tone can signal that you have found an error.

- Sound appreciative and positive. Give praise where praise is due. Compliment people on their work if it impresses you.

- Don't criticize work, behaviour of others or the looks of product or documents as it can alienate you from the auditee. Whilst not being up to your standards, it may well be adequate for the particular circumstances.

Non-verbal communication

- The facial expression used when asking questions can change the intended meaning.

- The facial expression used when listening to answers can give the wrong impression.

- Look people in the eye when talking to them but do not stare. Sometimes in the culture it is impolite to look people in the eye.

- Give the impression that you are listening, don't stare around and look out of the window or at what someone else is doing.

- Be aware of cultural differences and customs, such as hand gestures and body movements.

Explaining your needs

- Give the reasons for asking questions such as:

    'I am seeking to establish what design proving is conducted before production commences. Could you outline the methods you use?'

- Don't demand information, request it politely. For example, say:

    'May I see examples of some recent design review records?'

    not:

    'Show me your design review records.'

- Don't use deception to obtain information such as waiting until the auditee has left the office before examining the files.

Steering the auditee

- Lead the auditee to the information you want.

- They may not understand your question so don't get irritated, try an alternative way of saying the same thing. Give suggestions by way of illustrating what you want to see. For example:

    You may have said: *'How do you handle nonconforming material?'*

    Rephrase this as: *'How do you deal with items that have failed to meet requirements?'*

    You can also add: *'Let's start with products that you find unacceptable on receipt from your suppliers.'*

Open questions

Ask open questions: questions which require the auditee to explain something. For example:

- What is the ... ?

- Where do you ... ?

- Why does ... ?

- When is the ... ?

- Who is responsible for ... ?

- How are ... ?

Here is some sample dialogue:

> *'What is the company policy on design reviews?'*
>
> *'Why do you only perform one design review?'*
>
> *'When is the review carried out?'*
>
> *'How is the review process controlled?'*
>
> *'Who attends the design review?'*
>
> *'Where are the records of these reviews stored?'*
>
> *'Could you please show me some examples of recent design review records?'*

Closed questions

In general, don't ask closed questions. For example:

- Could I see ... ?

- Have you got ... ?

- Are you responsible for ... ?

- Does this ... ?

- Is the ... ?

- Can you show me ... ?

- Do you have ... ?

Sample dialogue:

> *'Do you have a procedure for controlling nonconforming product?'* Auditee answers: *'Yes.'*
>
> *'Is the procedure approved?'* Auditee answers: *'Yes.'*

'Does the procedure cover software?' Auditee answers: *'No.'*

'Is the software procedure listed in the quality manual?' Auditee answers: *'No.'*

'Can I see a copy of the software procedure?' Auditee answers: *'No.'*

'Why not?' Auditee answers: *'Because we don't use any software.'*

Closed questions are useful, however, to confirm understanding.

Emotive questions

Don't ask emotive questions as you might be displaying a prejudice for certain methods. For example:

'Don't you use red reject labels?'

'Why don't you stamp these documents UNCONTROLLED?'

Trick questions

Trick questions are those designed to trick the auditee into giving an answer that they would not have given if the question had been more open, for example:

'When did you stop releasing nonconforming product?' – incorrectly implying that they make a habit of releasing nonconforming product.

'I notice you have a clock on the wall in the test laboratory; where is the calibration status label?' – incorrectly implying that the clock is a measuring instrument used in testing product.

Leading questions

Don't ask leading questions which contain an assumption since the auditee is unlikely to refute your claim. For example:

'I expect you check the documents before they are released?'

'Presumably all purchase orders contain provision for adding prequalification requirements?'

The auditee's answer to all of these questions will be *'Yes.'*

If you find yourself asking leading questions then after an answer in the affirmative, you can recover the situation by asking: *'Could you show me some examples please?'*

Hypothetical questions

Often the information examined may not show evidence that operations would remain under control when unusual circumstances arise and so the auditor may have to get the auditee to imagine hypothetical situations. For example:

'What if the results of the design review indicate that the design needs to be changed; how would these changes be handled?'

'What if the customer phones through a change to the contract and requests you implement it immediately?'

However, be wary of the answer *'It never happens.'* The standard requires a procedure for handling customer complaints.

Systematic questions

These are the most common questions to ask when following an audit trail. They are simply in the form: *'What happens next?'*

Multiple questions

Avoid asking multiple questions as they tend to confuse the auditee. For example:

'Which of these products was reworked, where is the inspection record and what happened to the others which passed inspection?'

'Could you explain the meaning of these qualifications and let me see a copy of this person's training records and his job description and competency requirement?'

Requests

In addition to asking questions, auditors need to examine objective evidence. To obtain sight of objective evidence auditors need to request that the auditee carry out an action rather than provide an answer. To avoid receiving a 'Yes' or a 'No' auditors need to express their request as an instruction. For example:

'I would like to see some results of the verification activities you performed on Project Nexus.'

'Having examined your audit procedures and found them satisfactory, I would now like to examine the file of audit reports.'

'I would like to look at the training records of your auditors if you have them available.'

The lead auditor's role during the audit

Depending on the size of the team, the time which the lead auditor spends auditing and managing the team will vary. During the audit, the lead auditor should:

- Periodically check on progress with each of the auditors.

- Determine if the auditors are having problems with the guides.

- Determine if any major nonconformities have been detected.

- Take up with the management representative any issues that may need to be resolved.

Giving feedback

When gathering information, the auditor should give feedback:

- When something is found that is in your opinion good, give praise.

- When problems are uncovered, don't jump to conclusions.

- Don't indicate that there is a nonconformity with the standard as there may not be. Other facts yet to be revealed may negate a nonconformity.

- Point out potential problems, inadvertent errors and mistakes and suggest that the auditee might like to initiate their removal. Do this verbally and politely – being sensitive to the feelings of others in the vicinity.

- If there is evidence of a nonconformity in the system then say that there is a weakness not a nonconformity, as the very term 'nonconformity' is a demotivator.

Giving advice

Internal auditors are free to give advice but don't stray outside your area of competence. Second-party auditors may give advice if permitted by their company policy. Again, don't stray outside your competency. If you do and the supplier follows your advice and it doesn't solve the problem, you may be held accountable for the cost! Third-party auditors do not give advice as to how a nonconformity may be corrected as it may result in a conflict of interest. The rules are as follows:

- Don't provide specific solutions to nonconformities.

- If asked, either refuse or indicate a range of possible solutions that would be acceptable from which the auditee can decide which would be appropriate in their circumstances.

- Don't refer to any particular company that employs any methods suggested.

- Don't indicate that a particular solution they propose would not work. Refer always to the requirements of the standard.

- Don't say that the company should do various things; phrase suggestions as opportunities for improvement. For example:

  'The frequency of errors may be reduced by providing staff with the reasons for some of the more important instructions.'

Auditee conduct

The conduct of the auditee is crucial to the effectiveness of the audit and if the auditor is not assertive it can significantly reduce the value of the audit results. Some auditees may attempt to sabotage the audit either by painting a rosy picture when in fact the opposite is true, or by delaying tactics. Here are some which auditors should know how to detect and deal with effectively.

Wasting time

The way to combat time wasting is to firstly establish that the behaviour is devious and not inadvertent and, if devious, take action and suggest that unless progress is made more quickly, the audit will have to be extended.

Provocation

The only way to combat provocation is to be sure of your facts before they are declared and use disarming techniques, such as acknowledging the person's experience and respecting their position and experience rather than entering into a contest about who is right.

Insincerity

The way to combat insincerity is to ignore it. Be polite, express sympathy but, as your job is to reveal facts which were already present in the organization, you have a duty to report as you find.

Language

The way to combat a language problem is to take along an interpreter of your choice.

Bribes

The way to combat bribes is to establish first if the offer is intended as a bribe and if so decline it.

Dealing with challenges

Often an auditor will ask a perfectly sensible question and be challenged by the auditee. Sometimes this is a defensive attitude or it could be that the auditee wishes to learn from the auditor. In response to your question the auditee may say, for example:

Do we have to do that?
If you get this response, never say 'No' but restate the question. If this gets the same response, then rephrase the question. If this gets the same response, then explain why you are seeking the information.

Where does it say that in the standard?
If you get this response, either point to the requirement or, instead of showing your ignorance by attempting to find the requirement in the standard, rephrase the question.

Why do we need to do that?
If you get this response, explain the reason for your question by relating it to the requirements.

We don't believe the (document) requires us to do that

If you get this response, your auditee has obviously read the standard, policy or procedure. Don't make assumptions or show your ignorance by consulting the standard in front of the auditee. Rephrase the question or refer the auditee to another requirement which will produce the result you desire.

That was checked on the internal audit

On an external audit this response is likely if you have asked to see evidence of an operation, or decision, that appears to be no longer available. Ask to see the records of the internal audit and check the accuracy of the statement.

Recording results

The results of the audit need to be recorded as the audit progresses so as to provide the data which will be used later to compile the audit report. As facts are established, the auditor should record:

- The facts that indicate conformance

- The facts that indicate a possible nonconformance

- Observations on effective practices

- Observations on ineffective practices

- Examples of impressive performance, products, documentation, practices, conditions, attitudes etc.

Agreeing the facts

The resultant findings from an interview, or series of interviews, in an area should be discussed with the guide or manager before moving onto the next area. In this way, the opportunity to remove any misunderstanding can be taken whilst on the scene of the action, thereby avoiding the need to return later. When the auditor enters an area, or commences an interview, he/she should have identified their objective (that is, what they want to establish). Before leaving the area, the auditor should establish that they have gathered sufficient data to draw the conclusion that their objective has been achieved.

The auditors' review meeting

During the audit, each auditor will collect objective evidence on the performance of the organization's quality system. At the discretion of the lead auditor, team review meetings may be held prior to reporting the results to the company at the end of each day. In internal or external audits, this will only be necessary when the audit is of a greater duration than one day. These meetings should be a forum where:

- Problems can be discussed with other team members.

- The audit plan can be revised if areas not in the original plan are uncovered.

- The lead auditor can direct team members to look for certain evidence or focus on particular aspects which need closer attention.

- Check lists can be reviewed and modified if necessary.

- It can be established that the audit is probing the quality system sufficiently to verify conformity with the requirements of the standard.

- Team members can exchange information for others to follow in securing objective evidence.

- Interpretations of the standard can be harmonized.

- Audit findings can be discussed and the views of other auditors considered in determining if there are nonconformities.

- Audit findings can be analysed to determine if they are common to more than one area.

- Corrective action reports can be prepared.

- The lead auditor can determine if the management representative needs to be informed of issues that require his/her attention.

5   Reporting audits

What to report

- Good points
- Degree of conformity and nonconformity
- Improvements
- System effectiveness
- Conclusions

When to request corrective action

Remember, corrective action is action to prevent a recurrence of a non-conformity. Therefore it should be requested:

- When evidence of frequent errors has been found.
- When there is evidence that the quality of all products or services of a particular type will be, is being or has been adversely affected.
- When there is objective evidence that the quality system will not cause conforming product to be delivered.
- When there is evidence that the quality system will not prevent delivery of nonconforming product or service.
- When there is evidence that the quality system will not cause objective evidence to be generated to demonstrate that operations affecting quality are under control and where all this evidence can be traced to a requirement of the standard.

When not to request corrective action

- When an isolated error can be corrected on the spot.

- When errors are attributable to the maturity of the quality system.

- When errors are attributable to new staff being on a learning curve.

- When an individual knows of inadvertent errors and accepts remedial action.

- When known problems are being resolved through an approved corrective action plan.

- When practice cannot be proven to be at variance with the requirements of the standard.

Feedback meetings

When an audit is planned to take more than one day, feedback meetings should be held to:

- Report progress against plan.

- Request extension to the programme if delays beyond the audit team's control have occurred.

- Request changes to the plan to include areas not identified in the original plan.

- Seek clarification of the company's quality system, its products and services, and the means by which it ensures their quality.

- Report problems that require action by the company.

- Request information needed to complete investigations.

- Report nonconformities and observations.

Writing the nonconformity statements

Each nonconformity statement should consist of four characteristics:

- The subject of the nonconformity defined in precise terms

- The location where the nonconformity was detected, if appropriate

- The incident which signifies the subject is nonconforming where relevant

- The requirement from the standard which has not been met

Words and phrases to avoid

'In violation of ...' or *'In contravention of ...'*

'Whilst auditing xyz *I found ...'*

'Several items of ...' or *'None of the ...'* or *'Little evidence ...'* or *'Few records ...'*

'Mr X said that ...' or *'I observed that ...'*

Observation statements

The difference between nonconformities and observations is that observations are objective evidence which do not prove a failure to meet a requirement of the standard but which impair or may impair the effectiveness of the quality system. Such observations may be situations where:

- There is insufficient evidence of a nonconformity; however, system effectiveness is impaired.

- There is a potential nonconformity.

- Prevailing occupational Health and Safety or environmental conditions may impact upon product/service quality.

The Closing Meeting

The format of a Closing Meeting for an external audit is more formal than for an internal audit.

Agenda

External Audit	Internal Audit variations
Introduction of those not present at the Opening Meeting	Usually not necessary
Expression of thanks to the company	None
Confirm purpose and scope	None
Good points	None
Summary of findings including disclaimer statement	Disclaimer is not usually necessary.
Conclusions and recommendations	A recommendation is not appropriate as no certificate or approval is being granted. It may also be inappropriate to classify the findings if major/minor classification is not policy.
Detailed findings (optional)	Necessary
Questions on the audit findings	None
Remedial and corrective action proposals	These may be provided later.
Follow-up action	None
Confirm confidentiality	Unnecessary
Approval of audit report	The report can be issued after the audit and approval obtained.
Endorsement of the manual	Unnecessary
Appeals	Unnecessary

Sample dialogue for Closing Meeting

This sample dialogue is written for external audits.

Introductions

'Before we start, I notice that there are some people present who were not in attendance at the Opening Meeting. May I request that they be introduced?'

Expression of thanks

'Thank you for attending this Closing Meeting which has been convened to present to you the results of the audit and to give you the opportunity to discuss the findings.

'I will summarize the findings, give you our conclusions and recommendations and then will report the results from the areas audited. May I therefore request that all questions be held until we have delivered the report.'

Confirmation of purpose and scope

'I would like to confirm the purpose and scope of the audit.

'The purpose of this audit is to determine the extent to which the operations of (Company) meet the requirements of ISO 9000I/9002 1994 for the (design, manufacture, installation and servicing*) of (types of products and services).'

> * Insert core operations of business to be covered by the registration or approval.

Good points

'During the audit we observed the company to have many strengths and would like to summarize these now.'

Summary of findings

'I/we covered all areas identified in our audit plan which included (identify areas covered) and found (X) major nonconformities, (Y) minor nonconformities and several observations.

'The audit was based on a limited sample of operations and although conformance with all relevant requirements of the standard has been tested, other nonconformities to those reported may exist.'

Conclusions and recommendations for external audits

A. *'Sufficient objective evidence has been found to demonstrate that the quality system meets all the requirements of ISO 9001/9002 for the (identify scope). We are therefore delighted to be able to recommend the company for certification.'*

B. *'Sufficient objective evidence has been found to demonstrate that the quality system meets most of the requirements of ISO 9001/9002 for the (identify scope). However, as the nonconformities discovered are all of a minor nature, the effectiveness of the quality system is not significantly impaired. We are therefore able to recommend the company for certification, conditional on the minor nonconformities being corrected to our satisfaction.'*

C. *'Insufficient objective evidence has been found to demonstrate that the quality system meets the requirements of ISO 9001/9002 for the (identify scope). As some of the nonconformities discovered are of a major nature, the quality system has therefore been proven to be ineffective in enabling the company to achieve the defined objectives. We are therefore unable at this time to recommend the company for certification.'*

Conclusions for internal audits

Conclusions of an internal audit should be reached as to the effectiveness of a quality system, the process, the procedure, the plan or whatever is being measured. Effectiveness is a measure of how well the system/process/procedure/plan accomplishes its objectives. The effectiveness of the quality system could therefore be a measure of how well it causes achievement of the defined policies and objectives and prevents failure to meet such policies and achieve such objectives. Nonconformities with the standard/procedure/policy may not indicate the system is ineffective; it depends on what they are. Also, the system may not be effective even if no nonconformities with the standard are detected; it depends on what the policies and objectives are. Determining system effectiveness therefore depends on the purpose of the audit.

Here are some indicators of a system being ineffective:

- Policy omissions indicating that the policies cannot be relied upon to cause the right things to be carried out.

- Procedural omissions indicating that the procedure cannot be relied upon to cause conformity.

- Informal practices indicating that the system cannot be relied upon to prevent nonconformity or cause conformity.

- Implementation inadequacies indicating ineffective training, supervision, clarification of job responsibilities and discipline.

- Probability of a recurring nonconformity indicating corrective action is ineffective.

- Failure to achieve objectives indicating ineffective planning.

Detailed findings

- What areas were audited

- Any good points worthy of note

- Number of nonconformities and observations found

- The major nonconformities followed by the minor nonconformities and the observations

Questions

'Before we move on to corrective action proposals, I would now like to invite questions on the findings of the audit.'

Corrective action proposals

'Action on the observations is not required for certification purposes but certification does depend upon action being taken on the nonconformities. I would now like to invite the company to propose the action they

intend to take to resolve these nonconformities. Proposals may be submitted now or by a date upon which we can agree.'

Corrective action proposals should:

- Correct the specific nonconforming item (that is, the subject of the audit finding).

- Seek out and correct any other similar instances of nonconformity.

- Correct that which caused the nonconformity.

Follow-up action

- An unconditional recommendation requires no follow-up action.

- A conditional recommendation requires follow-up action which may vary from resolution, through correspondence, to closure of the nonconformity during the first surveillance visit.

- A refusal to grant certification requires a repeat visit to either examine that part of the system which is nonconforming or to repeat the complete assessment where there are several major nonconformities that warrant system re-design.

Confirm confidentiality

'Any information obtained during the audit will remain confidential and not be disclosed to a third party without the prior agreement of the company.'

Approval of report

'May I request the company representative approve the report, take a copy and return the original to me.'

Endorsement of manual

If the recommendation is for certification, the lead auditor may endorse the manual with the approved stamp indicating the date and approval authority.

Appeals

A. *'The company can appeal to the certification body against the decision of the lead auditor. If the company gets no satisfaction from this avenue, an appeal to the accreditation board is the next stage.'*

B. *'The company can appeal to the customer against the decision of the lead auditor.'*

Final remarks

'We hope that you have been satisfied with the manner in which the audit has been conducted. If you do have any suggestions for improvement may we recommend you send them to (XYZ). We realize that you have a choice of certification bodies and thank you for choosing (ABC).'

Hints and tips

1   In reporting the findings the key objective is to establish the effectiveness of the quality system, not to reveal everything that occurred during the audit.

2   The best time to obtain agreement on nonconformities is at feedback meetings and these should be held at the beginning of the next day of auditing or at the Closing Meeting.

3   The difference between a major and an minor nonconformity is that a major nonconformity is a failure to cause product conformity or prevent product nonconformity.

4   Corrective action is requested when failures can be prevented from recurring, not when mistakes are found.

5   Nonconformity statements should disclose the subject, the location, the incident and the requirement not met, and avoid emotive language.

6   If there is insufficient evidence of nonconformity but system effectiveness is impaired then report as an observation.

7   System effectiveness is a measure of how well the system accomplishes its stated objectives, not how many nonconformities were found.

8 Audit reports should only contain the facts – not emotive language and conversations.

9 The main reason for a closing meeting is to obtain commitment from the company to corrective action on the findings.

10 The conclusions of the audit should relate to the effectiveness of the quality system and should be supported with objective evidence.

11 It is better to read from the report than to ad lib and elaborate, as this will only cause doubt and conflict.

12 Reporting good points and the degree of conformity provides a balanced report.

13 Team members should report their findings, as it avoids embarrassment.

14 Corrective actions should prevent the recurrence of nonconformities, not just resolve the specific incident.

15 An expression of gratitude for the facilities and help received creates a cordial note before leaving the site.

Part 5

Quality system graphics

Contents

Figures

1 Quality system graphics

This chapter contains flowcharts and others illustrations that depict some aspect of quality management.

Quality concepts

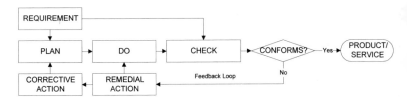

Figure 1 *Generic control process*

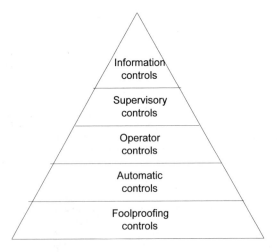

Figure 2 *The control pyramid*

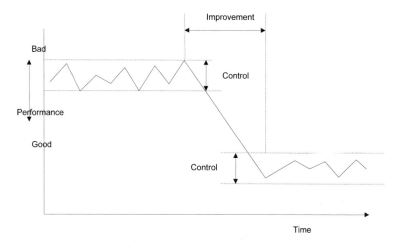

Figure 3 *Improvement and control relationships*

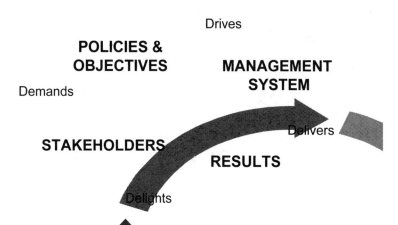

Figure 4 *Business continuity*

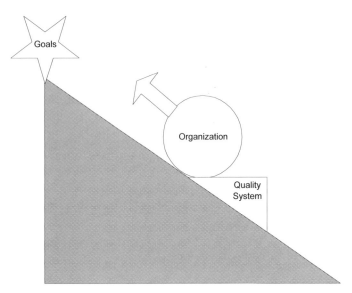

Figure 5 *Role of quality system*

Figure 6 *The chain of quality*

Figure 7 *The quality trilogy*

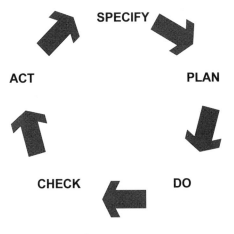

Figure 8 *The improvement cycle*

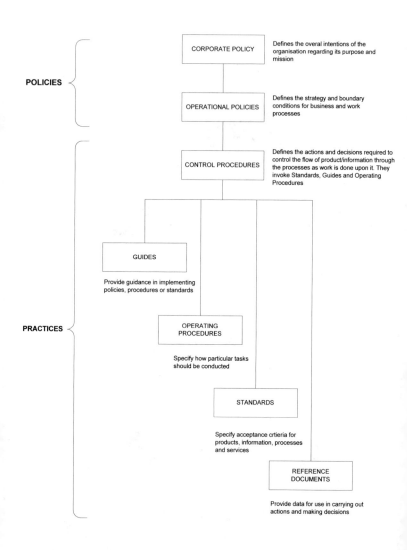

Figure 9 *Relationship between policies and practices*

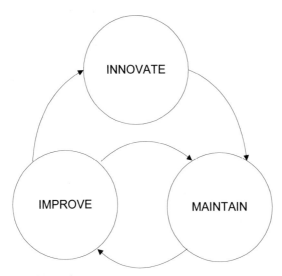

Figure 10 *The MII cycle*

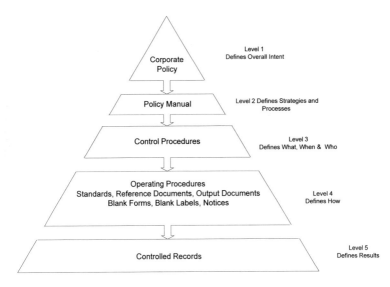

Figure 11 *Quality system documentation hierarchy*

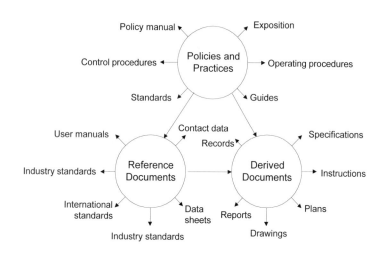

Figure 12 *Relationship between quality documents*

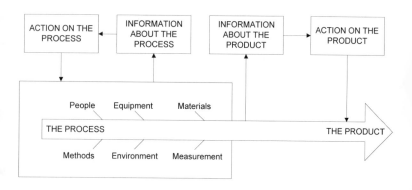

Figure 13 *Process control model*

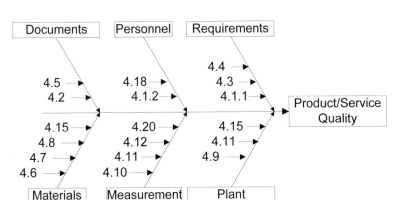

Figure 14 *Cause and effect elements*

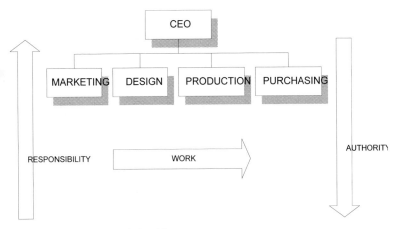

Figure 15 *Organization relationships*

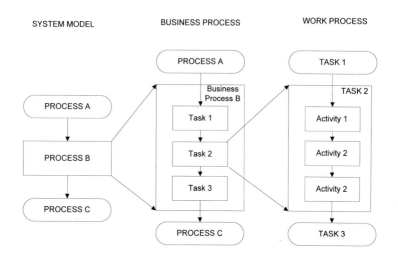

Figure 16 *Process decomposition*

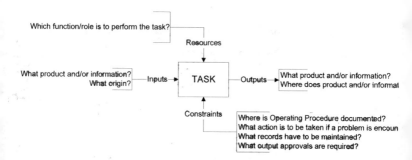

Figure 17 *Task analysis*

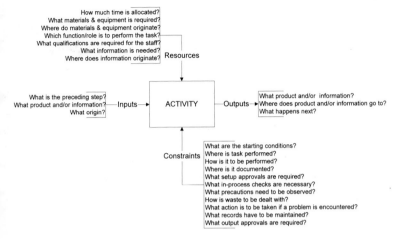

Figure 18 *Activity analysis*

Process flowcharts

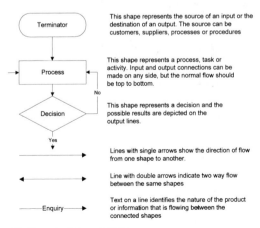

Figure 19 *Flowchart conventions*

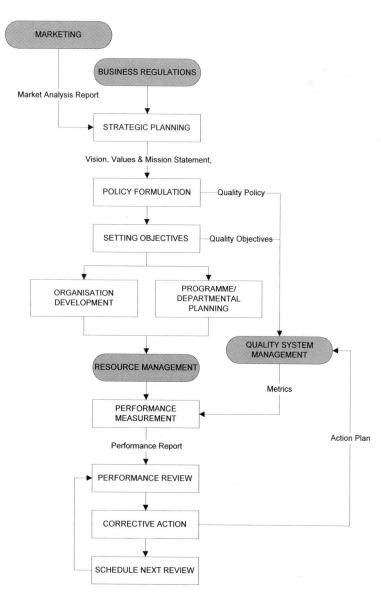

Figure 20 *Business management process*

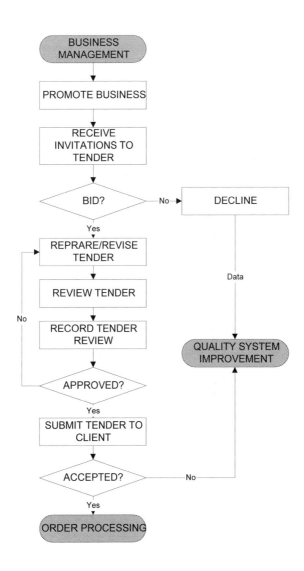

Figure 21 *Marketing process*

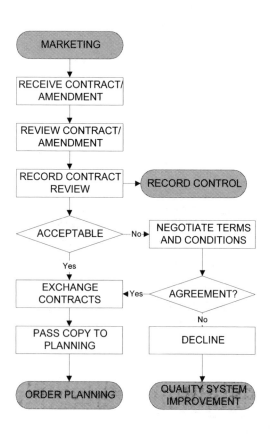

Figure 22 *Order processing proces*

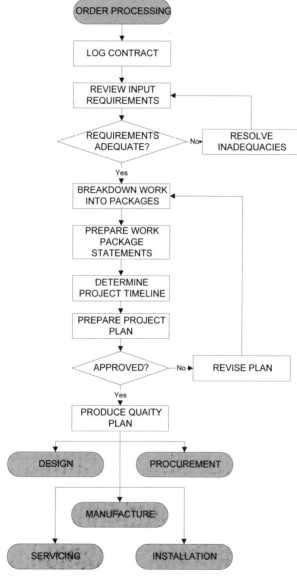

Figure 23 *Order planning process*

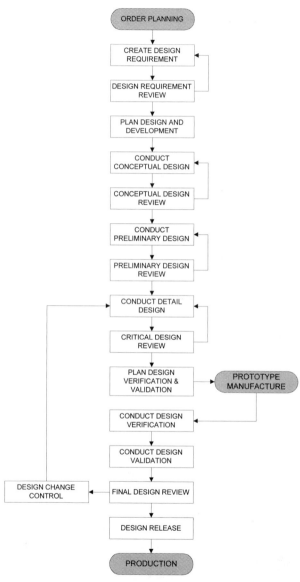

Figure 24 *Design and development process*

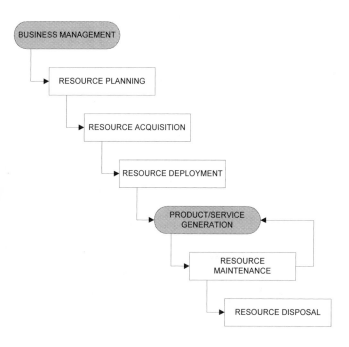

Figure 25 *Resource management subsystem*

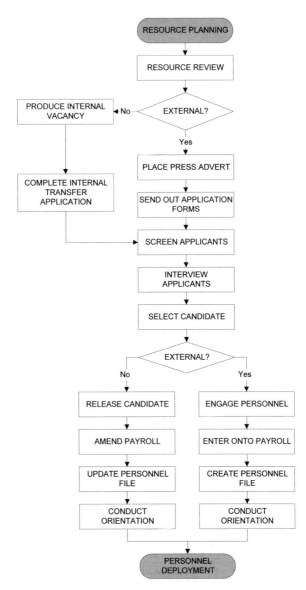

Figure 26 *Personnel acquisition process*

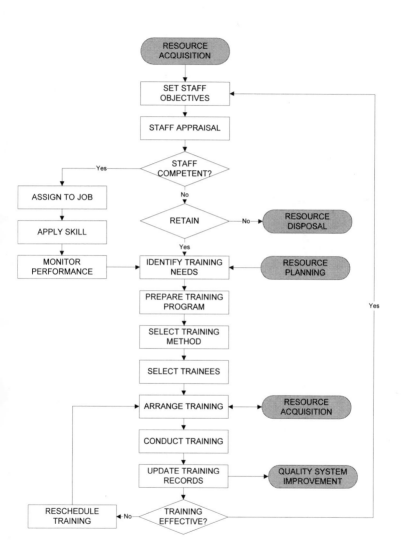

Figure 27 *Personnel development process*

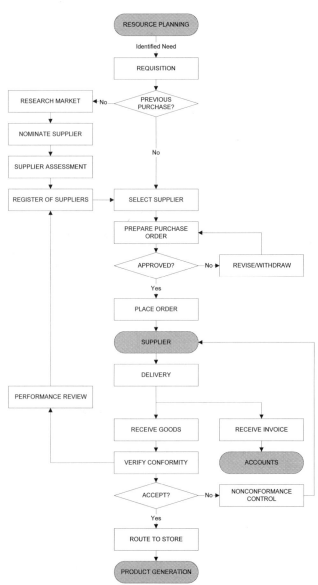

Figure 28 *Purchasing process*

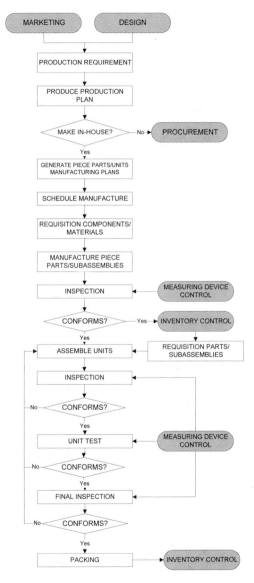

Figure 29 *Production process*

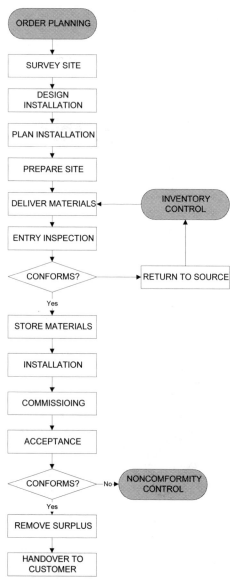

Figure 30 *Installation process*

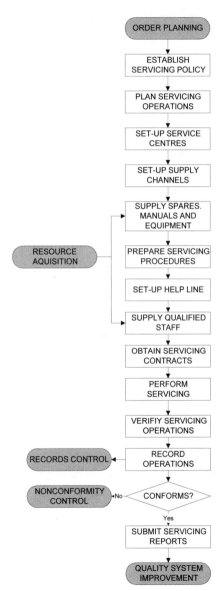

Figure 31 *Servicing process*

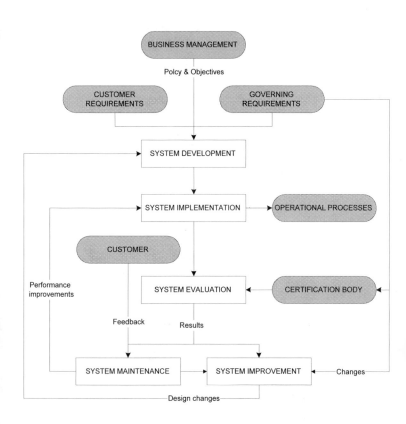

Figure 32 *Quality system management subsystem*

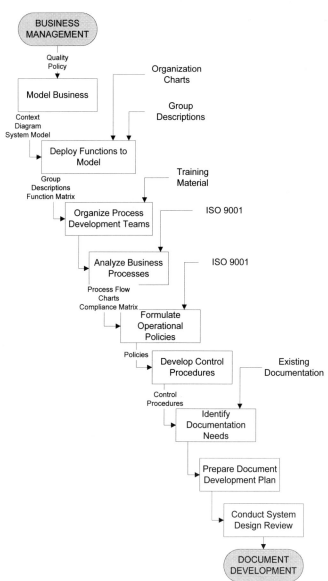

Figure 33 *Quality system development process*

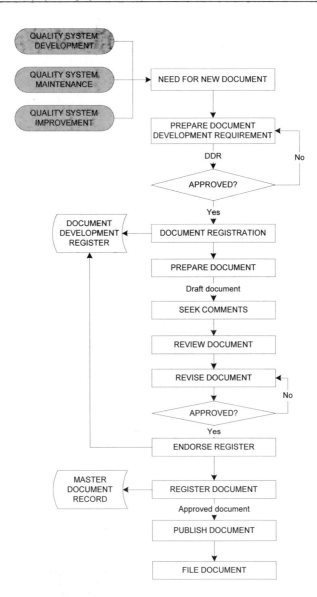

Figure 34 *Document development process*

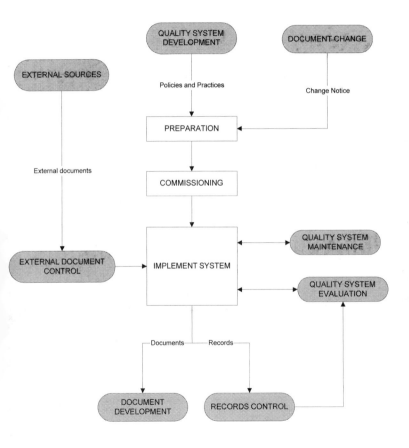

Figure 35 *Quality system implementation process*

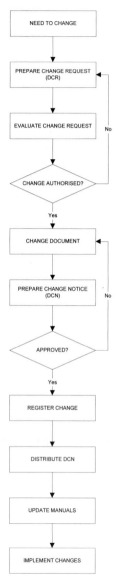

Figure 36 *Document change process*

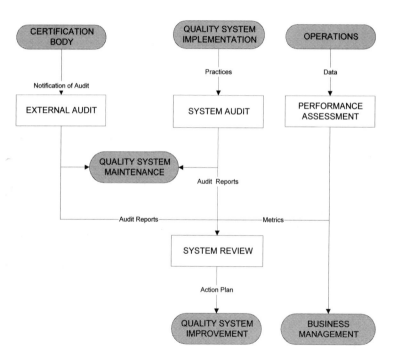

Figure 37 *Quality system evaluation process*

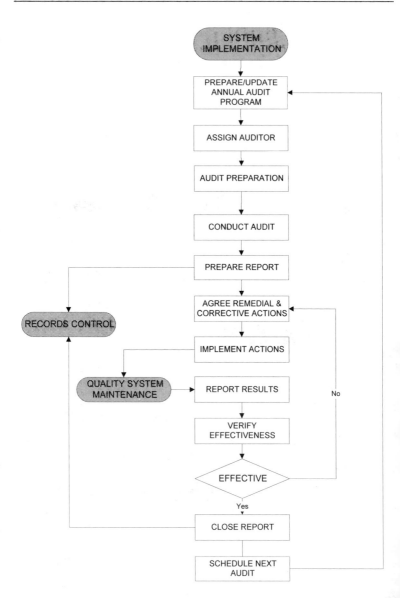

Figure 38 *Quality system audit process*

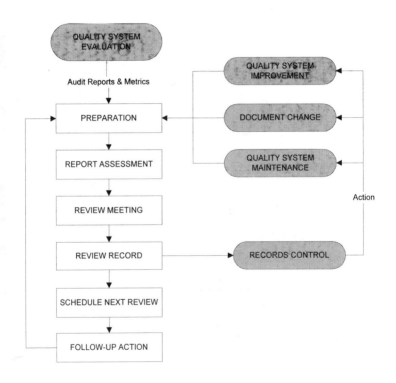

Figure 39 *Quality system review process*

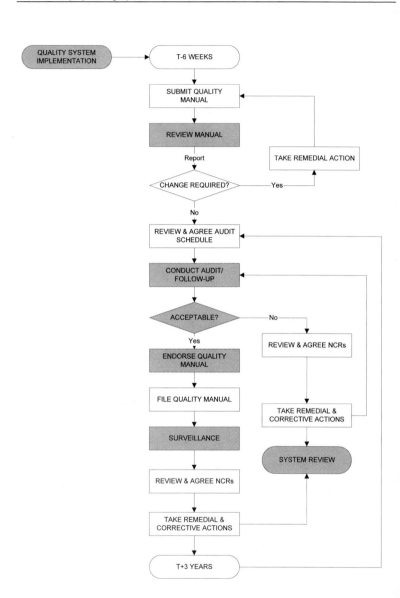

Figure 40 *External audit process*

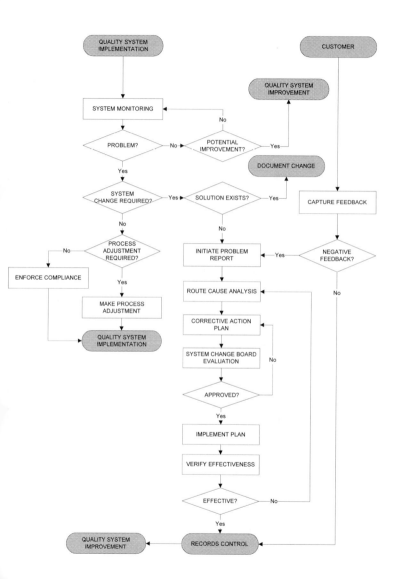

igure 41 *Quality system maintenance process*

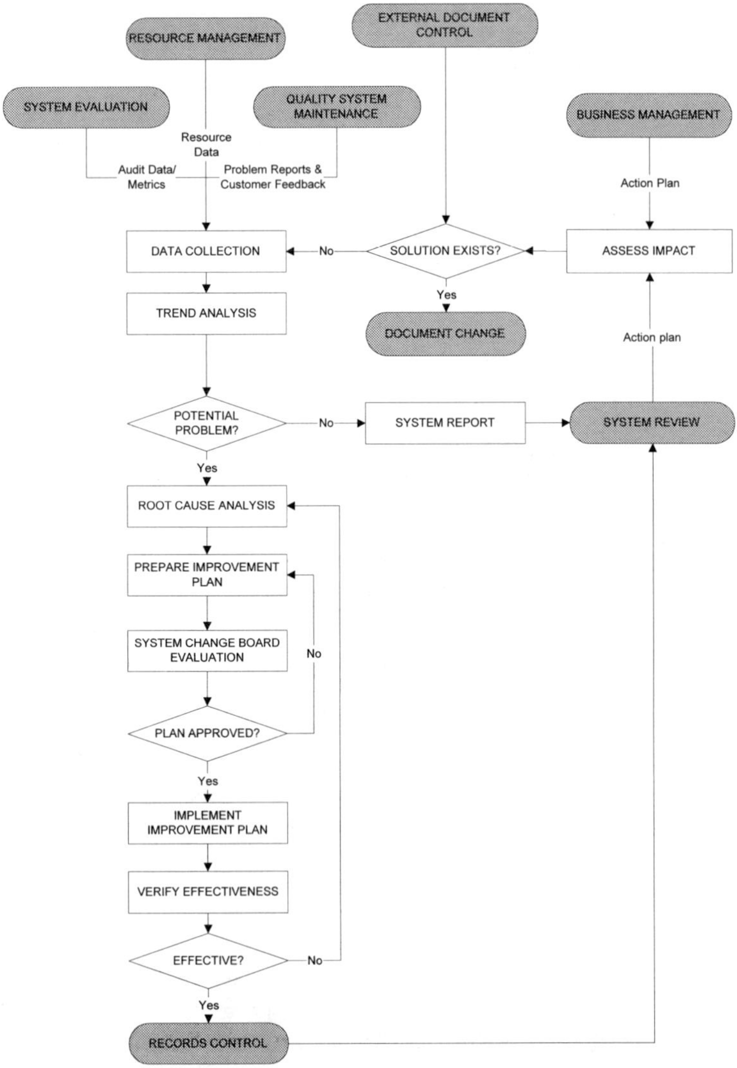

Figure 42 *Quality system improvement process*

Glossary

This glossary contains common and uncommon terms and phrases used in the ISO 9000 series of standards but does not repeat the definitions given in ISO 8402. It contains many terms and phrases not defined in these standards. (Note that BS 4778 Part 1 is identical to ISO 8402.) The explanations are given for the context in which the terms are used.

Acceptance criteria The standard against which a comparison is made to judge conformance.

Accreditation A process by which organizations are authorized to conduct certification of conformity to prescribed standards. See *Certification body* or *registrar*.

Activities affecting quality Any activity which affects the determination of product or service characteristics, their specification, achievement or verification or means to plan, organize, control, assure or improve them.

Adequacy audit An audit carried out to establish that the quality system documentation adequately addresses the requirements of a prescribed standard. Note that the adequacy audit is also referred to as a *Documentation audit*.

Adequate Adequate means suitable for the purpose. The term 'adequate' appears several times in the standard allowing the auditor to vary the criteria for adequacy and hence not use a finite process to verify that the requirements have been met.

Aggressive behaviour Behaviour likely to intimidate the auditee and reduce their co-operation. A person who forces his/her opinions or demands upon others and offers no co-operation.

Appropriate Appropriate means appropriate to the circumstances and requires knowledge of these circumstances. Without criteria, an auditor is left to decide what is or is not appropriate.

Approved Approved means that it has been confirmed as meeting the requirements.

Assertive behaviour Behaviour likely to cause positive results without intimidating the auditee. A person who offers resistance when attempts are made to distract him/her from their objective.

Assessment The act of determining the extent of compliance with requirements.

Assessment period The time, usually in months, between full assessments.

Assurance Evidence (verbal or written) that gives confidence that something will or will not happen or has or has not happened.

Audit An examination of records or activities to verify their accuracy, usually by someone other that the person responsible for them. A modifying adjective is usually used for specific types of audit e.g. Certification audit, Quality system audit.

Audit brief A statement defining the boundary conditions and requirements for an audit. Specifically, details of the organization to be audited, the audit objective and its scope.

Audit objectives The result which is to be achieved by the audit and usually one or more of the following:

- Whether certain agreed provisions, if implemented will yield the required results.
- Whether only the agreed provisions are being implemented.
- Whether the provisions have yielded results that are fit for their purpose and meet the needs of those who require them.
- Whether a certificate of conformance can be issued.
- Whether some improvement is necessary before awarding a certificate.

Audit plan A chart showing the areas to be audited during a specific audit of an organization, including the timing and names of the auditors involved.

Audit purpose To establish, by an unbiased means, factual information on some aspect of performance.

Audit report A factual account of the results of the audit including the good points, extent of compliance, nonconformities, conclusions, recommendations and corrective actions.

Audit scope The range or extent of the audit including the standard or contract against which the audit is to be conducted, the products and services and the processes to be included e.g. design, development, production, installation or servicing.

Audit trail A path of enquiry and discovery that an auditor follows in search of objective evidence.

Auditee The person whose operations are being audited.

Auditor A person who has the qualifications and is authorized to conduct an audit.

Auditors review meeting A meeting convened by the lead auditor to review progress, discuss nonconformities, resolve problems and compile the audit report.

Authorized A permit to do something, use something which may not necessarily be approved.

Authority The right to take actions and make decisions.

Authorized A permit to do something, use something which may not necessarily be approved.

Benchmarking A technique for measuring an organization's products, services and operations against those of its competitors, resulting in a search for best practice that will lead to superior performance.

Bias (in measurement systems) The difference between the observed average of the measurements and the reference value.

Business process A series of operations which are an essential part of a business.

Business process model A diagram of the key processes that convert external inputs into outputs, showing their interrelationships and channels along which product or information flows.

Business processes The composite of all processes that define how an organization conducts its business.

Calibrate To standardize the quantities of a measuring instrument.

Capability audit An audit performed to verify that a process has the capability to consistently yield product that meets agreed requirements.

Capability index P_{pk} The performance index which account for process centering and defined as the minimum of the upper or lower specification limit minus the average value divided by 3σ.

Capability index C_p The capability index for a stable process, defined as the quotient of tolerance width and process capability where process capability is the 6σ range of a process's inherent variation.

Capability index C_{pk} The capability index which account for process centering for a stable process using the minimum upper or lower capability index.

Certification A process by which a product, process, person or organization is deemed to meet specified requirements

Certification audit An audit performed for the purpose of certifying a product, process, person or organization.

Certification body An organization that is authorized to certify organizations. The body may be accredited or non-accredited.

Check list (audit) A list of topics or questions that guide an auditor conducting an audit. An aid to memory rather than a list of all questions to be asked.

Clause of the standard A numbered paragraph or subsection of the standard containing one or more related requirements such as 4.10.3. Note that each item in a list is also a clause. See also *Quality system element*.

Client feedback meeting A meeting convened by the lead auditor to report progress, resolve problems and obtain agreement to any nonconformities declared.

Closing meeting A meeting between the auditor(s) and representatives of the organization audited convened to report and agree the results of the audit and to agree follow-up action.

Code of conduct A set of rules that govern the behaviour of an auditor when conducting an audit.

Codes A systematically arranged and comprehensive collection of rules, regulations or principles.

Commitment An obligation a person or organization undertakes to fulfil: i.e. doing what you say will do.

Comparative reference A standard used to determine differences between it and another entity.

Compliance audit An audit performed to determine compliance with specified requirements. The term is sometimes limited to that part of an audit that verifies whether documented practices are being followed.

Concession Permission granted by an acceptance authority to supply product or service which does not meet the prescribed requirements.

Concurrent engineering See *Simultaneous engineering*.

Conformance audit An audit performed to determine conformance or conformity with specified requirements. See also *Compliance audit*.

Conforms to specified requirements Meets the requirements which have been specified by the customer or the market.

Continual assessment An assessment in which selected parts of the quality system are assessed on each visit and which over a given period subject the whole quality system to re-assessment.

Contract An agreement formally executed by both customer and supplier (enforceable by law) which requires performance of services or delivery of products at a cost to the customer in accordance with the terms and conditions stated therein.

Contractual requirements Requirements specified in a contract.

Control The act of preventing or regulating change in parameters, situations or conditions.

Control charts A graphical comparison of process performance data to computed control limits drawn as limit lines on the chart.

Control methods Particular ways of providing control which do not constrain the sequence of steps in which the methods are carried out.

Control procedure A procedure that controls product or information as it passes through a process.

Controlled conditions Arrangements which provide control over all factors which influence the result.

Corrective action Action planned or taken to stop something from recurring.

Criteria for workmanship Acceptance standards based on qualitative measures of performance.

Cross-functional team See *Multidisciplinary team*.

Customer complaints Any adverse report (verbal or written) received by a supplier from a customer.

Customer feedback Positive or negative information received by a supplier from a customer.

Customer supplied product Hardware, software, documentation or information owned by the customer which is provided to a supplier for use in connection with a contract and which is returned to the customer either incorporated in the supplies or at the end of the contract.

Data Information which is organized in a form suitable for manual or computer analysis.

Define and document To state in written form, the precise meaning, nature or characteristics of something.

Demonstrate To prove by reasoning, objective evidence, experiment or practical application.

Design A process of originating a conceptual solution to a requirement and expressing it in a form from which a product may be produced or a service delivered.

Design and development Design creates the conceptual solution and development transforms the solution into a fully working model.

Design of experiments A technique for improving the quality of both processes and products by effectively investigating several sources of variation at the same time, using statistically-planned experiments.

Design review A formal documented and systematic critical study of a design by people other than the designer.

Desk-top audit A documentation audit performed at a desk with the organization's quality system documentation.

Disposition The act or manner of disposing of something.

Documentation audit An audit carried out to determine whether an organization's documented quality system makes adequate provision for meeting the requirements of a given standard. See also *Adequacy audit* or *Desk-top audit*.

Documented procedures Procedures that are formally laid down in a reproducible medium such as paper or magnetic disk.

Effectiveness of the system The extent to which the (quality) system fulfils its purpose.

Employee empowerment An environment in which employees are free (within defined limits) to take action to operate, maintain and improve the processes for which they are responsible using their own expertise and judgement.

Ensure To make certain that something will happen.

Establish and maintain   To set up an entity on a permanent basis and retain or restore it in a state in which it can fulfil its purpose or required function.

Evaluation   To ascertain the relative goodness, quality or usefulness of an entity with respect to a specific purpose.

Evidence of conformance   Documents which testify that an entity conforms with certain prescribed requirements.

Executive responsibility   Responsibility vested in those personnel who are responsible for the whole organization's performance. Often referred to as top management.

Extended assessment   An assessment in which those parts of an organization excluded from the full assessment sample are subject to audit on each visit together with system maintenance monitoring and a complete re-assessment at the end of each period.

External audits   Audits carried out by an organization independent of the organization audited. Independence has to be such that there is no financial association other than a contract.

Failure mode effects analysis   A technique for identifying potential failure modes and assessing existing and planned provisions to detect, contain or eliminate the occurrence of failure.

Final inspection and testing   The last inspection or test carried out by the supplier before ownership passes to the customer.

Finding   Information revealed from an examination of documentation, items or activities.

Finite element analysis   A technique for modeling a complex structure.

First-party audits   Audits of a company or parts thereof by personnel employed by the company. These audits are also called *Internal audits*.

Follow-up audit   An audit carried out following and as a direct consequence of a previous audit to determine whether agreed actions have been taken and are effective.

Functions   In the organizational sense, a function is a special or major activity (often unique in the organization) which is needed in order for the organization to fulfil its purpose and mission. Examples of functions are design, procurement, personnel, manufacture, marketing, maintenance etc. Departments may perform one or more functions but a department is a component of the organization not a function.

Geometric dimensioning and tolerancing   A method of dimensioning the shape of parts that provides appropriate limits and fits for their application and facilitates manufacturability and interchangeability.

Guide   A person who escorts the auditor during the audit.

Hearsay evidence   Oral statements concerning a situation that has not been observed directly.

Identification   The act of identifying an entity, i.e. giving it a set of characteristics by which it is recognizable as a member of a group.

Implement   To carry out a directive.

Implementation audit   An audit carried out to establish whether actual practices conform to the documented quality system. Note that an implementation audit is also referred to as a *Conformance audit* or *Compliance audit*.

Importance of activities in auditing   The relative importance of the contribution an activity makes to the fulfilment of an organization's objectives.

Indexing   A means of enabling information to be located.

In-process   Between the beginning and the end of a process.

Inspection   The examination of an entity to determine whether it conforms to prescribed requirements.

Inspection authority   The person or organization who has been given the right to perform inspections.

Inspection, measuring and test equipment   Devices used to perform inspections, measurements and tests.

Installation   The process by which an entity is fitted into a larger entity.

Internal audits   See *First-party audits*.

Issues of documents   The revision state of a document.

Lead auditor   A person qualified and authorized to lead an audit team.

Linearity (in measurement systems)   The difference in the bias values through the expected operating range of the measuring device.

Major nonconformity (General)   The absence or total breakdown of the provisions required to cause product conformity or prevent product nonconformity with the expectations and needs of customers. Absence means a lack of adequate provisions in theory and in practice. A total breakdown means that adequate provisions are in place but they are currently not being implemented.

Major nonconformity (QS-9000)   The absence or total breakdown of a system to meet a requirement of QS-9000. Any noncompliance that would result in the probable shipment of a nonconforming product. A noncompliance that judgement and experience indicate is likely either to result in the failure of the quality system or to materially reduce its ability to assure controlled processes and products.

Manage work   To manage work means to plan, organize and control the resources (personnel, financial and material) and tasks required to achieve the objective for which the work is needed.

Management representative   The person management appoints to act on their behalf to manage the quality system. Their actual title is irrelevant.

Master list An original list from which copies can be made.

Measurement capability The ability of a measuring system (device, person and environment) to measure true values to the accuracy and precision required.

Measurement uncertainty The variation observed when repeated measurements of the same parameter on the same specimen are taken with the same device.

Minor nonconformity A failure to meet one requirement of a clause of the standard that cannot be classified as a major nonconformity, or a single observed lapse in meeting the requirements of a clause of the standard. See also under *Requirement of the standard*.

Minor nonconformity (QS-9000) A failure in some part of the supplier's documented quality system relative to a QS-9000 requirement. A single observed lapse in following one item of a company's quality system.

Modifications Entities altered or reworked to incorporate design changes.

Monitoring To check periodically and systematically. It does not imply that any action will be taken.

Multidisciplinary team A team comprising representatives from various functions or departments in an organization, formed to execute a project on behalf of that organization.

Nationally recognized standards Standards of measure which have been authenticated by a national body.

Nature of change The intrinsic characteristics of the change (what has changed and why).

Nonconformity A failure to meet a specified requirement.

Objective The result which is to be achieved, usually by a given time.

Objective evidence Findings that can be substantiated by information which is factual and which can be verified.

Obsolete documents Documents that are no longer required for operational use. They may be useful as historic documents.

On-site audit An audit performed on the auditee's premises.

Opening meeting A meeting between the auditor(s) and representatives of the organization to be audited convened to confirm the arrangements prior to commencing the on-site audit.

Operating procedure A procedure that describes how specific tasks are to be performed.

Organization audit An audit performed to verify that the organization is structured and resourced to implement its stated policies and will achieve the stated objectives efficiently and effectively.

Organizational goals Where the organization desires to be, in markets, in innovation, in social and environmental matters, in competition and in financial health.

Organizational interfaces The boundary at which organizations meet and affect each other, expressed by the passage of information, people, equipment, materials and the agreement to operational conditions.

Passive behaviour Behaviour of someone who offers no resistance and is likely to be lead by a more assertive person.

Passive-aggressive behaviour Someone who offers neither resistance nor co-operation.

Periodic assessment An assessment in which the quality system is subject to system maintenance monitoring between periods and complete re-assessment at the end of each period.

Plan Provisions made to achieve an objective.

Planned arrangements All the arrangements made by the supplier to achieve the customer's requirements. They include the documented policies and procedures and the documents derived from such policies and procedures.

Planning audit An audit performed to verify that the organization's plans or proposals for supplying a product or service will, if properly implemented, result in product or service that complies with specified requirements.

Policy A guide to thinking, action and decision. Policies can exist at any level in an organization from corporate level to the lowest level where activities are performed.

Policy audit An audit performed to verify that the documented policies of an organization promulgate the requirements of the market and the objectives of the business.

Positive recall A means of recovering an entity by giving it a unique identity.

Positively identified An identification given to an entity for a specific purpose which is both unique and readily visible.

Potential nonconformity A situation which if left alone will in time result in a nonconformity.

Predictive maintenance Work scheduled to monitor machine condition, predict pending failure and make repairs on an as-needed basis.

Pre-launch A phase in the development of a product between design validation and full production (sometimes called *pre-production*) during which the production processes are validated.

Prevent To stop something from occurring by a deliberate planned action.

Preventive action Action proposed or taken to stop something from occurring.

Procedure A sequence of steps to execute a routine activity. Procedures can address interdepartmental, departmental, process, group, section or individual activities.

Process A sequence of tasks which combine the use of people, machines, methods, tools, environment, instrumentation and materials to convert given inputs into outputs of added value.

Process capability The ability of a process to maintain product characteristics within preset limits.

Process parameters Those variables, boundaries or constants of a process which restrict or determine the results.

Product Anything produced by human effort, natural or man-made processes.

Production The creation of products.

Proprietary designs Designs exclusively owned by the supplier and not sponsored by an external customer.

Prototype A model of a design that is both physically and functionally representative of the design standard for production and used to verify and validate the design.

Purchaser One who buys from another.

Purchasing documents Documents which contain the supplier's purchasing requirements.

Qualification Determination by a series of tests and examinations of a product, related documents and processes that the product meets all the specified performance capability requirements.

Qualification approval The status given to a supplier whose product has been shown to meet all the specified requirements.

Qualified personnel Personnel who have been judged as having the necessary ability to carry out particular tasks.

Qualified personnel Personnel who have been judged as having the necessary ability to carry out particular tasks.

Quality activities Any activity that affects the ability of a product or service to satisfy stated or implied needs or the organization's ability to satisfy those needs. If the quality system defines the activities which need to be executed to achieve quality then any activity specified in the documented quality system is also a quality activity.

Quality conformance The extent to which the product or service conforms with the specified requirements.

Quality costs Costs incurred because failure is possible. The actual cost of producing an entity is the no-failure cost plus the quality cost. The no-failure cost is the cost of doing the right things right first time. The quality costs are the prevention, appraisal and failure costs.

Quality function deployment A technique to deploy customer requirements (the true quality characteristics) into design characteristics (the substitute characteristics) and deploy them into subsystems, components, materials and production processes. The result is a grid or matrix that shows how and where customer requirements are met.

Quality objectives Those results which the organization needs to achieve in order to improve its ability to meet current and future customer needs and expectations.

Quality planning Provisions made to prevent failure to satisfy customer needs and expectations and organizational goals.

Quality plans Plans produced to define how specified quality requirements will be achieved, controlled, assured and managed for specific contracts or projects.

Quality problems The difference between the achieved quality and the required quality.

Quality records Objective evidence of the achieved features and characteristics of a product or service and the processes applied to its development, design, production, installation, maintenance and disposal as well as records of assessments, audits and other examinations of an organization to determine its capability to achieve given quality requirements.

Quality requirements Those requirements that pertain to the features and characteristics of a product or service which are required to be fulfilled in order to satisfy a given need.

Quality system A tool for achieving, sustaining and improving quality. Such a system should integrate interconnected business processes that collectively cause the supply of conforming product/service and prevent the supply of nonconforming product/service.

Quality system assessments External audits carried out by second or third parties. They include a documentation audit, implementation audit and the determination of the effectiveness of the system.

Quality system element A distinct part of the system which is governed by a set of requirements. A subsection of the standard identified by a two-digit number such as 4.1, 4.2 and 4.3.

Quality system requirements Requirements pertaining to the design, development, implementation and maintenance of quality systems.

Quarantine area A secure space provided for containing product pending a decision on its disposal.

Random failure A failure which has a low probability of recurrence and which requires only remedial action to eliminate.

Registrar See *Certification body*.

Registration A process of recording details of organizations of assessed capability which have satisfied prescribed standards.

Regulatory requirements Requirements established by law pertaining to products or services.

Related results Results which arise out of performing an activity or making a decision. In the context of quality activities they may be documents, records, approval and acceptance decisions, disapproval and reject decisions, products, processes.

Remedial action Action proposed or taken to remove a nonconformity. See also *Corrective action* and *Preventive action*. The action applies to the affected item, process or activity.

Repeatability (in measurement systems) The variation in measurements obtained by one appraiser using one measuring device to measure an identical characteristic on the same part.

Representative sample A sample of product or service which possesses all the characteristics of the batch from which it was taken.

Reproducibility (in measurement systems) The variation in the average of the measurements made by different appraisers using the same measuring instrument when measuring an identical characteristic on the same part.

Requirement of the standard A sentence containing the word 'shall'. Note that some sentences contain multiple requirements, such as 'to establish, document and maintain ...'; this is in fact three requirements.

Responsibility An area in which one is entitled to act on one's own accord.

Review Another look at something.

Second-party audits Audits carried out by customers upon their suppliers.

Self audit An audit carried out by a person responsible for the activities audited.

Service Results which do not depend on the provision of products.

Service reports Reports of servicing activities.

Servicing Action to restore or maintain an item in an operational condition.

Shall A provision that is binding.

Should A provision that is optional.

Simultaneous engineering A method of reducing the time taken to achieve objectives by developing the resources needed to support and sustain the production of a product in parallel with the development of the product itself. It involves customers, suppliers and each of the organization's functions working together to achieve common objectives.

Specified requirements Requirements prescribed by the purchaser in a contract or requirements prescribed by the supplier in a market requirement or design brief as a result of an analysis of the market need.

Stability (in measurement systems) The total variation in the measurements obtained with a measurement system on the same part when measuring a single characteristic over a period of time.

Status The relative condition, maturity or quality of something.

Status of an activity in auditing The maturity or relative level of performance of an activity to be audited.

Strategic quality audit An audit performed to verify that the strategic plans of the organization address current and future legal, environmental, safety and market quality requirements.

Subcontract requirements Requirements placed on a subcontractor which are derived from requirements of the main contract.

Subcontractor A person or company that enters into a subcontract and assumes some of the obligations of the prime contractor.

Subcontractor development A technique for promoting continuous improvement of subcontractors by encouraging customer-supplier relationships and communication across all levels of the involved organizations.

Supplier A person or company who supplies products or services to a purchaser.

Supplier approval audits See *Vendor audits*.

Surveillance (quality system) An activity performed to verify that the organization has maintained its quality system and it continues to be suitable for achieving its stated objectives and effective in providing an adequate degree of control over the organization's operations.

System audit An audit carried out to establish whether the quality system conforms to a prescribed standard in both its design and its implementation.

System effectiveness The ability of a system to achieve its stated purpose and objectives.

Systematic failure A failure which has a high probability of recurrence due to an inadequacy in the system and for which corrective action can be specified to eliminate the cause and prevent recurrence.

Technical interfaces The physical and functional boundary between products or services.

Tender A written offer to supply products or services at a stated cost.

Theory of constraints A thinking process optimizing system performance. It examines the system and focuses on the constraints that limit overall system performance. It looks for the weakest link in the chain of processes that produce organizational performance and seeks to eliminate it and optimize system performance.

Third-party audits External audits carried out by personnel who are neither employees of the customer nor the supplier and are usually employees of certification bodies or registrars.

Traceability The ability to trace the history, application, use and location of an individual article or its characteristics through recorded identification numbers.

Unique identification An identification which has no equal.

Validation A process for establishing whether an entity will fulfil the purpose for which it has been selected or designed.

Value engineering A technique for assessing the functions of a product and determining whether the same functions can be achieved with fewer types of components and materials and the product produced with less resources. Variety reduction is an element of value engineering.

Vendor audits An external audit of a supplier by its customers.

Verification The act of establishing the truth or correctness of a fact, theory, statement or condition.

Verification activities A special investigation, test, inspection, demonstration, analysis or comparison of data to verify that a product or service or process complies with prescribed requirements.

Verification requirements Requirements for establishing conformance of a product or service with specified requirements by certain methods and techniques.

Work instructions Instructions which prescribe work to be executed, who is to do it, when it is to start and be complete and how, if necessary, it is to be carried out.

Workmanship criteria Standards on which to base the acceptability of characteristics created by human manipulation of materials by hand or with the aid of hand tools.

Zero defects The performance standard achieved when every task is performed right first time with no errors being detected downstream.

Index